Q&A

Routledge•Cavendish Questions & Answers Series

Company Law
2007–2008

MICHAEL OTTLEY

Routledge·Cavendish
Taylor & Francis Group

Fifth edition first published 2007
by Routledge-Cavendish
2 Park Square, Milton Park, Abingdon, Oxon OX14 4RN

Simultaneously published in the USA and Canada
by Routledge-Cavendish
270 Madison Ave, New York, NY 10016

*Routledge-Cavendish is an imprint of the Taylor & Francis Group,
an informa business*

© 1993, 2003 Jennifer James

© 2007 Routledge-Cavendish

Previous editions published by Cavendish Publishing Limited
First edition   1993
Second edition   1996
Third edition   2001
Fourth edition   2003

Typeset in Garamond by
Newgen Imaging Systems (P) Ltd, Chennai, India
Printed and bound in Great Britain by
TJ International Ltd, Padstow, Cornwall

British Library Cataloguing in Publication Data
A catalogue record for this book is available from the British Library

Library of Congress Cataloging in Publication Data
Ottley, Michael.
Q&A company law : 2007–2008 / Mike Ottley.—5th ed.
p. cm.
1. Corporation law—Great Britian—Examinations, questions, etc.
I. Title. II. Title: Q and A company law. III. Title: Questions and
answers company law. IV. Title: Company law.
KD2079.4.O85 2007
346.41'066076—dc22   2006100821

ISBN10: 1–85941–959–3
ISBN13: 978–1–85941–959–5

PREFACE

Company law is less open to judicious question spotting than many others. If you are preparing for examinations, at least if you are sensible, you will ensure that you have an overview of the whole subject, even if you choose to concentrate revision in a limited number of areas. With this combined overview and specialised knowledge, you will be able to answer a question which is principally on topic X while pointing out that you realise that minor points Y and Z also arise—even if there is little that you can say on those points. An overview of company law also enables you to tackle general questions which cut across a major part of the syllabus, for example, questions on disclosure or the distinctions between public and private (particularly 'quasi-partnership') companies. When selecting specific areas for detailed revision, it is obviously sound practice to ensure that, where topics are linked, you study both; there is little point in knowing all about the rules relating to the fiduciary duties of directors without being equally at home with the procedures for the enforcement of those duties.

Since no two syllabuses are identical and individual lecturers will have laid stress on particular topics, which they will have approached in differing ways, there can be no definitive list of typical examination questions. However, in this fifth edition I have tried to produce questions which would be at home on an examination paper of any university or equivalent body and, I hope, the Legal Practice Course. Some of the questions may demand a consideration of the recent proposals and suggestions for reform of company law in key areas. To this extent, reference to the work of the Law Commissions and the Company Law Review Steering Group may need to be made, as well as reference to provisions to the Companies Act 2006 (www.dti.gov.uk/companiesact), which at the time of writing, has been passed (November 2006) but with very few provisions in force. The Act is not expected to be fully implemented until 2008.

The answers featured in this book are not meant to be model answers that could be used to write an assessment; rather, they are the type of answer which a good student could hope to achieve in the course of a written examination. Answers are around 2,000 words, which you should be able to write in about 40–45 minutes if you are well prepared. If you find that you cannot write this quickly, try to speed up, perhaps by using recognised abbreviations of standard terms.

In suggesting answers to questions, I have assumed that a student is permitted to take statutes into his/her examination. Consequently, I have not cited anything other than section numbers as authority for propositions unless the wording of a statute is of particular significance. If you do not have access to the legislation, you can legitimately expect to receive some credit for remembering the content of relevant sections.

All references to Table A are to Table A of the Companies (Tables A–F) Regulations 1985 unless otherwise stated (for example, Table A of the First Sched to the Companies Act 1948). This is in common with the procedure adopted by most examiners.

This edition is an update of previous editions, authored by Jennifer James.

Michael Ottley

February 2006

CONTENTS

TABLE OF CASES

TABLE OF STATUTES

CHAPTER 1

FORMATION OF COMPANIES AND CONSEQUENCES OF INCORPORATION

■ INTRODUCTION

Questions are rarely set solely upon the rules relating to the formation of companies. However, in tackling questions on the consequences of incorporation, some appreciation of the rules of formation (and the differing types of company) is appropriate. Factors which might influence the decision to incorporate, the effects of incorporation and 'lifting the veil' are common areas for questions. Questions involving 'lifting the veil' generally require some form of critical analysis rather than a mere recitation of decisions. Another, broader type of question regularly encountered involves advice about incorporation and running of companies and possible types of investment in a company either in general or for specified persons (generally a brilliant but unbusinesslike inventor, his aware brother-in-law and a doddery relative of means). Material relating to formation should also be incorporated in questions relating to the different legal regime applicable to public and private (particularly quasi-partnership) companies and general questions about disclosure.

The law relating to promoters and pre-incorporation contracts can be regarded as part of the formation of a company. Questions on promoters may be linked with the liability of directors and a question could combine a pre-incorporation contract with a post-incorporation contract. However, the increasing use of 'off-the-shelf' companies for small private companies renders promoters and pre-incorporation contracts of diminishing importance. Some courses may require students to be familiar with methods of raising capital—such material is likely to form a small part of a problem or be examined by means of a simple essay which merely demands a competent recitation of facts; but, obviously, every question setter has their own hobbyhorse(s).

Checklist

Students should be familiar with:

- how a company can be formed and the differing types of company;
- advantages and disadvantages of incorporation;
- effects of incorporation;
- circumstances in which the separate legal personality of a company can be disregarded, both at common law and by statute (particularly fraudulent and wrongful trading);
- promoters, particularly their duties and rights;
- liability for pre-incorporation contracts.

Students should be aware that related issues which could be linked to questions based on this area include:

- the distribution of power within a company;
- enforcement of the articles of association;
- liability and/or protection of directors/investors, including disqualification of directors;
- restructuring of share capital.

Question 1

Do the advantages of incorporation compensate for the bureaucracy involved in running a company?

Answer plan

A question such as this—a variant on the very well-worked theme of the advantages and disadvantages of incorporation—can only be tackled by someone who knows the material. It is very difficult to score high marks on such a question, since there is little scope for anything but a neat summary of the advantages of incorporation and a further summary of the bureaucratic requirements alluded to—a rare question where a list might be beneficial. It should be noted, however, that the wise student does not comment on the dullness of the question.

Answer

Incorporation of an existing or projected enterprise (not necessarily a business) can be achieved either by forming a company in compliance with the procedures laid down in the Companies Act (CA) 1985 or by buying a pre-existing company 'off-the-shelf' (the latter procedure accounts for about 60% of 'formations'). In either case, the company will require a memorandum of association (s 1 CA 1985), which must contain certain information (s 2) and articles of association, although the CA 1985 has proposed that the memorandum and articles should be replaced by a single registration form and constitution. The content of the articles, which are the company's internal rules, can be determined by the founders of the company, but, if none is registered, the appropriate form of Table A will automatically apply (s 8 CA 1985) if the company is limited by shares. The advantage of purchasing an off-the-shelf company is that the company already exists and there is no delay between deciding to form a company and the company coming into existence through the registration process; there is merely a transfer of shareholding. This obviates the problem of pre-incorporation contracts and the possibility of having stationery printed bearing a name which, by the time the company is registered, has been taken by another company. However, an off-the-shelf company would not have been formed with the specific requirements of the promoters in mind and alterations of the memorandum or articles might be required. Indeed, problems can arise when the new shareholders of the company fail to make the necessary amendments. For example, in *Re A Company (No 005287 of 1985) (1986)*, a 'shareholder' who wished to use s 459 CA 1985 to bring an action against his fellow 'shareholders' was denied *locus standi* when it was discovered that the shares in the company, which had been purchased off-the-shelf, had never been transferred to the purchasers. For most people interested in forming (or buying) a company, the appropriate form of company will be a private company limited by shares (s 1 CA 1985).

The UK has traditionally had more companies than other European countries of comparable size (there are almost one and a half million at present). What are the attractions of incorporation? The principal advantage of incorporation, from which a variety of benefits flow, is that a company is a distinct legal entity with rights and duties independent of those possessed by its shareholders, directors and employees—it is a legal person. In consequence, for example, business conducted in the name of a registered company is separate from the personal affairs of the human beings who act for the company, and separate also from the affairs of any other business that those human beings may conduct on behalf of another registered company. Corporate personality was created by statute in the first half of the nineteenth century, but the full significance of this provision was not appreciated until the famous case of *Salomon v Salomon & Co* in *1897*.

In *Salomon*, S converted his existing, successful business into a limited company, of which he was the managing director. S valued his business at £39,000 (an honest but optimistic valuation) and received from the company, in discharge of this sum, cash, a debenture (an acknowledgment of debt) and 20,001 £1 shares out of the issued share capital of £20,007. S's wife and five children each held one of the remaining issued shares (seven being the minimum number of shareholders at that date), probably as his nominee. The company went into insolvent liquidation within a year with no assets to pay off the unsecured creditors. The issue for the courts was whether S was liable for the company's unpaid debts. The House of Lords, reversing the Court of Appeal, held that the company had been properly formed and was a legal person in its own right, separate from S, notwithstanding his dominant position within the company. The company was not S's agent and, consequently, S's liability was to be determined solely by reference to the Companies Act 1862. The Act required a shareholder to contribute to the debts of a company only where he held shares in respect of which the full nominal value had not been paid. S had paid for his shares in full by transferring the business to the company, so he had no liability to the creditors of the company. Thus, the *Salomon* case established that legal personality would be recognised even when one shareholder effectively controlled the company and had fixed the value of the assets used to pay for his shares.

The effects of separate legal personality are many and include the following:

• a company can sue and be sued in its own name;

• a company has perpetual succession. A company cannot die simply because all its shareholders are dead, although it can be wound up or struck off the Register by the Registrar of Companies if it appears to be moribund. Because a company exists unless and until it is wound up or deregistered, property, once transferred to the company, remains the property of the company, to do with as it pleases. There are no death duties to pay on the property because the company does not die and no costs are incurred in transferring the legal title to the property on a change of shareholder or director;

• the shareholders, directors and employees are not liable for criminal or tortious acts committed by the company, although they may incur personal liability concurrent with that of the company. For example, a company might, through the combined acts or omissions of several employees, establish and operate an unsafe system of work which caused the death of an employee. The company would be liable but an individual director or employee would not be liable unless he was personally negligent or the company was acting as an agent or employee of that individual;

• the shareholders, directors and employees are not liable on (nor can they enforce) contracts entered into by the company. As with criminal and tortious liability, an individual may incur personal liability concurrent with that of the company if he also enters into the contract. Furthermore, when the company acts as the agent of a shareholder or director (or an employee, but this is a rare event), the individual is liable under the normal rules of agency;

- a company may be formed with limited liability (s 2(3) CA 1985). Limited liability allows the members of a company to limit their responsibility for a company's debts. Liability may be limited to a predetermined sum, payable on winding up (a company limited by guarantee—s 2(4) CA 1985), or to the nominal value of the shares held, unless this sum has been paid by the current or a former shareholder (a company limited by shares—s 2(5) CA 1985). Since most shares are issued fully paid, shareholders have, effectively, no liability for the company's debts;

- where a company has transferable shares, ownership of the company can be split or transferred without affecting the company itself;

- formation of a company may bring financial benefits. For example, a company can raise money to create floating charges and, perhaps, to minimise the tax liability of shareholders.

There are drawbacks to separate legal personality, in that the property of the company, not being that of the members, cannot be insured by a member and the company cannot claim on an insurance effected by a person on property which he then owned but subsequently transferred to the company (see *Macaura v Northern Assurance (1925)*). Moreover, the assets of the company are the property of the company and a shareholder, even a controlling shareholder, cannot simply help himself to the company's cash. In addition, there is a limited number of situations where Parliament or the courts have decreed that corporate personality should be ignored. For example, where the directors have engaged in fraudulent or wrongful trading, they incur liability to creditors (ss 213 and 214 of the Insolvency Act (IA) 1986). Section 349(4) CA 1985 imposes liability upon an officer of the company who has signed company cheques, etc, on which the name of the company does not appear in full.

But what bureaucratic drawbacks are there to incorporation? In return for the advantages of incorporation, Parliament requires the observation of mandatory rules on the operation of a company. These rules are lengthy and complex and there can be no doubt that, in most companies, many administrative rules, for example on the conduct of meetings, are largely ignored. Perhaps in recognition of the widespread lack of use of some of the rules, the government has sought to reduce the administrative burden on companies, especially smaller companies, by the insertion of new sections into the CA 1985 Act. Sections 381A–81C CA 1985 permit a private company to dispense with meetings and pass resolutions by unanimous written agreement. Section 379 CA 1985 permits a private company to elect to disregard certain requirements of the CA 1985 if all the shareholders agree either in person or by proxy.

Such reforms are small measures and even when the provision, of the Companies Act 2006 on certain administrative aspects of the formation and running of companies are implemented, there is still an immense amount of law imposing obligations upon companies, shareholders and directors which would not apply to a sole trader or to a partnership. These obligations fall into five broad groups:

(a) Much of company administration is subject to statute (ss 348–62 CA 1985) and there are rules as to the qualification of directors and the company secretary (ss 282–310 CA 1985). The conduct of meetings of shareholders or directors is subject to statutory control (ss 366–84 CA 1985), although many of these rules are ignored in small companies.

(b) The power of the directors, who in smaller companies will almost certainly be majority shareholders, are limited, in that certain things cannot be done while others can be done only with the agreement of the shareholders. Many of these constraints on directorial power relate to the ability of the directors to benefit themselves (ss 311–48 CA 1985). For example, s 330 CA 1985 provides that the directors cannot lend the company's money to a director (there are innumerable exceptions) and s 320 CA 1985 restricts the ability of a director to engage in 'substantial property transactions' with his company. The power of the directors to raise capital by the allotment of shares is restricted (ss 80–116 CA 1985).

(c) The ability of the directors or shareholders to do as they wish with the shares of the company is restricted, so that, for instance, the share capital of the company cannot be reduced without the approval of the court (s 135 CA 1985) and a company cannot buy its own shares (s 143 CA 1985, but there are exceptions). The wishes of minority shareholders may have to be taken into account (ss 125–28 and 459 CA 1985) despite the wishes of the majority.

(d) The major statutory requirement which imposes a continuing burden relates to company accounts. The financial results of the company must be presented to the shareholders in a balance sheet and profit and loss account (ss 221–62A CA 1985). The length and technicality of the accounting rules mean that company accounts must, in effect, be prepared by a qualified accountant and a company must have its accounts checked (audited) by a qualified accountant (ss 384–94A CA 1985). All companies must send their accounts to the registrar of companies, where they are open to public inspection, although small and medium sized companies, as defined by the CA 1985, can elect to send an abridged version instead. The obligation of a company to produce audited accounts in compliance with the CA 1985 imposes an annual financial burden on a company, although, 'small companies' (defined in s 249A CA 1985) have been either wholly (for those with a turnover of less than £90,000) or partially exempted from the statutory audit unless members holding at least 10% by value of a class of shares require the company to obtain an audit.

However, there can be little doubt that a number of business people think that the bureaucratic drawbacks are more than outweighed by the benefits of incorporation.

NOTE

When the Companies Act 2006 is in force, reference should be made to the lifting of the burdens associated with the formation and administration of companies, as identified by the Company Law Review Steering Group.

Question 2

In forming a company, its shareholders may seek to minimise the liability of the company and themselves to creditors. To what extent, if at all, do the courts endorse this practice?

Answer plan

This question requires:

- discussion of whether shareholders and companies can minimise their liability to creditors; and
- a discussion of the case law in this area.

While questions on lifting the veil are fairly common, such questions (including this one) are not well answered by saying that there are a large number of cases where the courts will lift the veil and then listing them. A question such as this calls for effective deployment of the relevant cases and a critique of those cases.

Answer

The fundamental attribute of corporate personality is that the company is a legal entity distinct from its members—a company is a legal person. Corporate personality was created by statute in the first half of the nineteenth century, but the full significance of this provision was not appreciated until the famous case of *Salomon v Salomon & Co* in *1897*.

In *Salomon*, S converted his existing, successful business into a limited company of which he was the managing director. S valued his business at £39,000 (an honest but wholly inaccurate valuation) and received from the company in discharge of this sum, cash, a debenture and 20,001 £1 shares out of the issued share capital of £20,007. S's wife and five children each held one of the remaining issued shares (seven being the minimum number of shareholders at that date), probably as his nominee. The company went into insolvent liquidation within a year, with no assets to pay off the unsecured creditors. The issue for the courts was whether S was liable for the company's unpaid debts. The House of Lords, reversing the Court of Appeal, held that the company had been properly formed and was a legal person in its own right notwithstanding the dominant position of S within the company. The company was not S's agent, and consequently, S's liability was to be determined solely by reference to the Companies Act (CA) 1985. S had paid for his shares in full (by transferring the business to the company) and so his liability to creditors was exhausted—the full nominal value had been paid. Prior to *Salomon* it had been suggested that the owner-managed type of company could not be treated as a separate legal person from its owner(s), but *Salomon's* case established that, in the absence of fraud, legal personality would be recognised even when one shareholder effectively controlled the company and had fixed the value of the assets used to pay for his shares (note now the valuation requirements for non-cash consideration for shares in public companies: s 103 CA 1985).

While not mandatory, the majority of companies are formed with limited liability. This does not mean that the liability of the company is limited—it is liable for all its debts. However, if a company is insolvent it has no money to satisfy creditors, and the creditors will look elsewhere for satisfaction of their debts. If a company is formed as a limited company, it means that the shareholders (even controlling shareholders and others engaged in the management of the company) can restrict their liability for the debts of the company which the company cannot pay. Most companies are limited by shares so that a shareholder who owns shares is liable only to the extent that he or a previous owner of those shares has not paid the nominal value of those shares to the company. Since, in practice, most shares have a low nominal value (generally 10 pence or £1) and it is paid when the shares are first issued, the amount which a shareholder has to contribute on the insolvency of the company is nothing. Of course, if a company is required to have a large share capital, then the company will at least have received a large sum during its lifetime, which may mean that it has fewer unsatisfied debts. Unfortunately, company law does not require private companies to have more than one share, so a private company might have as little as 1 p share capital. Even public companies are not required to have a large share capital (since s 118 CA 1985 provides that public companies must have a share capital of at least £50,000, of which at least a quarter must have been subscribed for in cash). In addition, the rules relating to the payment for shares (ss 99–115 CA 1985) allow private companies to sell their shares for non-cash consideration, which may be (as in *Salomon*) worth less than the nominal value of the shares allotted provided the consideration is not 'wholly illusory'. The rules are slightly stricter for public companies so that, for example, they must have non-cash consideration professionally valued. If a company is in financial difficulty it may be able to restructure itself (with court approval), which has the effect of discarding debts; but could it move all its assets to a new subsidiary knowing that it is about to be found liable for large amount of compensation for some disease to which it has exposed its workforce? Certainly, Parliament has not prohibited companies from setting up subsidiaries (probably wholly owned) which undertake risky enterprises on behalf of the parent company. If the risky enterprise fails, the holding company is unaffected and can ignore any debts of the subsidiary, while if it succeeds, the profits can be transferred to the holding company. Thus, in *Adams v Cape Industries plc (1990)*, a UK-based company was not liable to pay damages to employees employed by a subsidiary company operating in South Africa who had been negligently exposed to asbestos and were now suffering from asbestosis. Indeed, it is sound business practice to ring-fence risk in this way. Parliament has determined that the benefits of encouraging entrepreneurial activity outweigh the disadvantages of permitting undercapitalised companies to operate.

Parliament has, in a very limited number of cases, restricted the effect of incorporation. Is there any theme behind these exceptions which might indicate areas in which the courts should lift the veil of incorporation? And, perhaps more importantly, do these exceptions indicate that the courts ought to be more willing to lift the veil to protect creditors? There are a number of minor provisions. For example, s 24 CA 1985 makes a person who is the remaining shareholder after a six month period in which a company has had less than two shareholders, jointly and severally liable for the company's debts. The provision does not apply to single-member private companies (s 24A CA 1985), and the Companies Act proposes to allow for the formation of single-member public companies. Another example can be found in s 349(4) CA 1985, which imposes liability upon an officer of the company who has signed company cheques, etc on which the name of the company does not appear in full (minor variation is permitted by the Companies Act 2006, when in force). However, the most important provisions are those relating to fraudulent or wrongful trading and the special rules for groups. Sections 213–15 of the Insolvency Act (IA) 1986 impose liability for the debts of a company where a person has engaged in fraudulent or wrongful trading (wrongful trading is limited to directors). The rules on group accounts are immensely complicated, but broadly they are designed to ensure that the accounts of associated companies are looked at as a whole to provide a 'true and fair view'. What can we discern as the concern of Parliament in providing exceptions to *Salomon*'s case? Is it clear, for example, that an element of wrongdoing or impropriety should disqualify a person from the manifold benefits of corporate personality (particularly that of limited liability)?

The courts have been willing to lift the veil of incorporation where a company has been used to avoid the existing liability of an individual. Such cases may be called cases where the corporate form is 'a mere façade' or a 'sham' but the description changes with the years. For example, in *Jones v Lipman (1962)*, the owner of land contracted to sell it to the claimant but then transferred the land to a company which he controlled. When the claimant sought completion of the sale, the vendor said that he could not complete because he no longer owned the property; the court allowed the claimant to bring a claim against the company which had been set up simply to avoid the vendor's existing legal obligation. Similarly, in *Gilford Motor Co Ltd v Horne (1933)* H had worked for the claimant company and was contractually bound not to compete with it after leaving the company. H's wife set up a company which competed with Gilford and this company employed H. Gilford successfully sought an injunction against H and the new company. In both of these cases the courts imposed liability on the companies and so can hardly be said to have ignored corporate personality. A more common situation is where a company's controlling shareholders remove corporate assets from the company, leaving the company unable to satisfy its debts—in such a case should the shareholders be ordered to return the assets or be personally liable for the unsatisfied claims of creditors? The courts have continued to adhere to the decision in *Salomon* and have been reluctant to disregard corporate statutes and treat the shareholders as directly responsible for the debts of the company or require them to return assets.

Both *Adams v Cape Industries plc (1990)* (mentioned above) and *Yukong Line Ltd of Korea v Rendsburg Investment Corp (No 2) (1998)* are clear authority for the proposition that where a company and its shareholders arrange its affairs in order to avoid potential liability (that is, liability that could arise) and in so doing transfer assets out of the hands of the company, there can be no claim upon those assets and no liability imposed on the shareholders. This appears to be the case even where the liability is imminent and will arise. For example, in *Yukong*, the company had entered into a chartering agreement with R which it broke, leaving it liable to pay damages for breach of contract. On the day of breach and shortly thereafter, but before R had commenced proceedings against the company, its assets were transferred to another company. The court refused to allow R to claim that sum of money from the transferee or bring a claim against the director-shareholder who had authorised the transfer (he might have been liable to Yukong for breach of fiduciary duty owed to Y or under the IA 1986). A similar approach can be seen in *Ord v Belhaven Pubs Ltd (1998)*, in which the claimant, O, had entered into a 20-year lease of a public house owned by the defendant (B). O was now alleging breach of contract and misrepresentation on the part of B. B was part of a group of companies which owned hotels and public houses, and subsequent to O's claim the group was restructured and ownership of the property leased by O was transferred from B to another company in the group, leaving B with no assets to satisfy any judgment which O might obtain. O sought to extend his claim to B's parent company and the other company which had taken over B's activities and assets. The court rejected O's claim, finding that the restructuring was a genuine commercial decision and not one designed to defeat O's claim (even if its effect was to make any judgment against B valueless). In the absence of some impropriety, the court would not lift the veil and allow O to bring a claim against the shareholder which had removed the asset from B or the new owner of that asset. Both *Yukong* and *Ord* rejected the earlier case of *Creasey v Breachwood Motors Ltd (1993)*, in which the director-shareholders transferred all the assets of the company to another company which they controlled in order to ensure that if C's legal claim against the company succeeded it would have no funds to meet the judgment. Perhaps it is possible to reconcile these cases by treating *Creasey* as a case where there was no legitimate commercial reason for the transfer of assets, unlike the situation in *Ord*. However, this explanation does not apply to *Yukong*, where the sole reason for the transfer seemed to be to ensure that the company would not have to meet R's legal claim if it was successful. Subsequently, in *Trustor AB v Smallbone (2001)*, the court took the view that the veil of incorporation will not be lifted simply because 'justice' would suggest that it should be done (see also *Adams v Cape Industries plc (1990)*). If the courts are to lift the veil, whether to protect creditors or others, there must, in the absence of statutory grounds, be such impropriety in the use of the company to justify the court disregarding an action which is otherwise legally effective. A recent example can be found in *Kensington International Ltd v Republic of Congo (2005)*, where Cooke J held that it was appropriate to pierce the corporate veil where a series of transactions within a structure of companies lacked legal substance and which was designed with a view to defeating the claimant's claim against the entity responsible for setting up the transactions and the structure of companies. The court was prepared to hold that the claimant was entitled to recover from one of the defendant companies a debt which was originally owed by the Republic of Congo.

The attitude of the courts can be summarised thus:

- where a defendant has used a company to evade his obligations (to a creditor or another), the company can be ordered to comply with the obligation;

- if the company has at the behest of its controlling shareholders organised its affairs to avoid potential liabilities (or even, arguably, existing liabilities), then neither the directors nor the shareholders are liable in the absence of impropriety. Simply avoiding one's debts is not sufficient to constitute impropriety, it seems.

NOTE

A student could expand upon the policy reasons underpinning 'corporate personality' and limited liability and might comment on the economic entity theory, even though this is now largely discredited.

Question 3

Laura, a talented designer, and her husband, Bernard, are running a small business engaged in the printing and selling of silk scarves and ties. They are seeking to expand the business and have persuaded Laura's parents to provide funds for expansion. Laura's parents do not wish to participate in the day to day running of the business, nor do they need an income from their investment, but they would like to be consulted on major matters of policy and to be able to recover their capital in the future. Laura and Bernard wish to retain control of the business but want to give Laura's brother, Mark, who works for them, greater involvement in the business. Laura and Bernard have decided to form a company in which they will own the majority of shares and be directors. They seek your advice about how to structure the company and to accommodate the wishes of Laura's parents, Mark and themselves.

Answer plan

Again, a fairly typical question which might apply to many small family businesses. The answer should address the specific concerns of those involved, rather than be a general description of company formation. Since the decision to incorporate has been taken, there is no need to consider the advantages and disadvantages of incorporation.

Answer

Laura (L) and Bernard (B) wish to incorporate their existing business. The appropriate form of company will be a private company limited by shares (s 1 of the Companies Act (CA) 1985). L and B may choose to establish a new company; the company will require a memorandum of association, which must contain certain information (s 2 CA 1985) and articles of association, before it can be registered by the Registrar of Companies. The content of the articles, which can be called the company's internal rules, can be fixed by the founders of the company, but, if none is registered, the appropriate form of Table A will apply (s 8 CA 1985). Alternatively, they may choose to buy a pre-existing company 'off-the-shelf'. The advantages of an off-the-shelf company are that the company becomes theirs immediately, without going through the registration process; all that is required is a transfer of shareholding, but such a company would not have been formed with their specific requirements in mind and alterations of the memorandum or articles might be required. Perhaps the most important things for L and B to grasp are that a company is a separate legal person and that, by establishing it, they can no longer treat the business as entirely their own affair. To take an extreme example, they must, as directors, formally approve any contracts they enter into with the company (see *Re Neptune (Vehicle Washing Equipment) Ltd (1995)*, in which the only director was required, formally, to inform himself of his interest in a contract entered into by the company).

Turning to the mechanics of formation, the memorandum must give the name of the company, which must appear on the company's seal, business letters, cheques, etc, and be affixed outside all places of business—brevity reduces printing costs. The final word of the company's name must be 'Limited' (which can be abbreviated to 'Ltd'). There are restrictions upon the names which can be used (ss 25–34 CA 1985). The principal restriction is that their company cannot have the same name as an existing company. Consequently, if their name is Smith, Smith Ltd is unlikely to be acceptable. Indeed, a name which has been registered may, within 12 months of registration, be directed to be changed by the Secretary of State if it is too similar to the name of an existing company or is misleading (see *Association of Certified Public Accountants v Secretary of State for Trade and Industry (1997)*, where the court held that the name suggested company's members possessed a level of qualification which was not in fact required). Other names are banned if the name would be a criminal offence or be 'offensive'. Yet further names can be used only if the Secretary of State gives permission, for example, names suggesting a connection with Her Majesty's Government or a local authority. It is possible to change the name of the company at a later date, if need be. Further provisions dealing with names and the use of particular words, letters or symbols are contained in the Companies Act 2006.

The memorandum requires the company to state whether its registered office is in England and Wales or in Scotland. Finally, s 2(1)(c) CA 1985 requires the company to state the objects of the company. This provision, whereby the company sets out what it intends to do, is of diminishing importance. L and B would probably adopt s 3A CA 1985 and register the objects of the company as being to carry on any trade or business whatsoever. L's parents might wish to restrict the company's business to the existing trade, rather than see their money being expended on new schemes; limiting the memorandum would provide some protection for their investment (if they became shareholders), in that they could seek to restrain activities not sanctioned by the objects clause (s 35 CA 1985). The effect of s 35 CA 1985 is that a shareholder can only restrain contemplated acts, and not those already legally binding on the company. It might be better for L's parents to have a contract with L and B which determines what the money can be used for. If parents do become shareholders and the directors (likely to be L and B) who overstep the objects clause in their dealings on behalf of the company, the company could sue them for breach of directors' duty, although an issue of who has the power to bring legal proceedings on the company's behalf would likely arise. The objects of the company can, in any case, be changed (ss 4 and 5 CA 1985) but a shareholder with a 15% shareholding in any class of share has *locus* to object to the change, although the change may still be sanctioned by the court.

Section 2(5) CA 1985 requires a statement of the amount of the company's share capital, how the share capital is divided up and the 'value' of each share. This value—the nominal value—is an arbitrary figure which does not necessarily bear any relation to the asset value of the company or its earning potential. The minimum nominal value of a share is one penny and, at present, a company must have at the outset at least two shareholders (other than a private company limited by shares or guarantee, which can be formed by one person (s 1(3A) CA 1985). Thus, the company could have two one penny shares and L could buy one and B the other. These two shares have to be paid for in cash. Two shares create a rather inflexible share structure and most private companies have a share capital of £100 or £1,000 divided into £1 or 10 p shares. L and B could give M a stake in the business by allotting shares to him. If L and B wish to retain control of the company, they need to ensure that their shareholding is at least 50% plus one vote (sufficient to pass an ordinary resolution) or, preferably, 75% (sufficient to pass a special resolution), although M might not regard less than 25% as a very worthwhile shareholding in the company. L's parents could also be given shares in the company but, unless they had a majority, which would not suit L and B, they would have no effective control over their investment. As shareholders, L's parents would have to be notified of meetings and would have *locus* under s 459 CA 1985 to raise the issue of unfair prejudice, etc.

Assuming that L and B are the principal shareholders, they may choose to pay for the shares by transferring the business to the company or by agreeing to work for the company—this is perfectly acceptable (s 99 CA 1985). Assuming that the value of the business is to exceed the modest nominal value currently encountered, L and B may be owed money for the business by the company. This debt could be secured by debenture, giving, in theory, L and B priority over other creditors on winding up. Indeed, by incorporating, L and B appear to have removed their personal assets from the perils of the company's insolvency. In practice, the benefits of limited liability do not exist for founders of small private companies—the banks which form the major creditor for most businesses require personal guarantees (often secured on homes) from directors, etc, before extending the company credit. The share structure of a company can be changed: see, for example, ss 121 (alterations) and 135 (reduction) CA 1985. Since L and B are the promoters of the company, the articles should reveal any profits which they have made on incorporation.

Turning to the articles of association, the main issue is the extent to which Table A of the Companies (Tables A–F) Regulations 1985 should be adopted. Most private companies amend Table A and in such cases it is safest to draft a self-contained set of articles for the company, lest there be any doubt about what rules have been adopted. Common amendments are to insert a restriction upon the transferability of the company's shares—in this case, L and B will not want M or any other shareholder transferring shares to outsiders, to vary the rules on quorums at meetings and the maximum number (and age) of directors. It is in the articles that L and B might choose to insert a provision permitting L's parents to block changes of policy. This could be achieved in one of two ways. L's parents could be given weighted voting rights (approved by the House of Lords in *Bushell v Faith (1970)*) in respect of certain transactions. For example, Art 70 of Table A, which most companies adopt, vests the running of the company in the directors, subject to 'directions given by special resolution'. If L's parents are given weighted voting rights, they can ensure that they can always issue 'directions'. Such a clause should be protected against alteration. Alternatively, L's parents could be given a right to veto in the articles (protected against alteration), which, by virtue of s 14 CA 1985, gives them a contractual right of veto if they are shareholders.

The difficulty with the latter approach is that the ability of shareholders to enforce the contract which is contained in the articles is uncertain. The traditional view is that a shareholder can enforce the articles only insofar as the relevant article creates a 'membership' right, that is, a right attaching to each and every share which relates to the holding of shares. This view derives from the first instance decision of Astbury J in *Hickman v Kent or Romney Marsh Sheepbreeders' Association (1915)* and would appear to preclude the enforcement of a right vested only in L's parents. However, powerful arguments have been raised against this interpretation of the s 14 contract. Lord Wedderburn in particular relies heavily upon the House of Lords' decision in *Quin and Axtens v Salmon (1909)*, where a shareholder was held to be entitled to enforce an article which required his consent to the sale of company land, to advance the view that a shareholder has a personal right to require the company to act in accordance with its articles. Variations on Lord Wedderburn's argument would restrict the shareholder to having a right to ensure that the appropriate corporate body carries on the affairs of the company. The uncertainty surrounding the s 14 contract makes this route an uncertain one for L's parents. Either of these proposals would limit L and B's ability to run the company as they wished. A freestanding shareholder agreement would provide a contractual means of restraining L and B's actions even if it did not bind the company.

Since L and B are forming a private company, they should be informed of the provisions for written resolutions (s 381A CA 1985) allowing decisions to be made by written agreement without the need to call a meeting, and elective resolutions permitting a company to exempt itself from some of the formal requirements of the CA.

If L and B are to be the first directors of the company (only one is required by law—s 282 CA 1985), no further directors are required, although there is no reason why M could not be invited to be a director. The proceedings of the directors will be governed by the articles. All directors are subject to the usual rules pertaining to directors' duties. These duties which derive from equity, the common law and statute are immensely complex and the directors should be advised of the need to seek proper legal advice before entering into transactions. The company would almost certainly be classified as a quasi-partnership company (even if M becomes a shareholder-director) and any serious breakdown in the relationship of the three principals could lead to a petition for just and equitable winding up under s 122(1)(g) IA 1986—a parallel provision would operate if the business had been run as a partnership. Further, attempts to exclude M's participation in the company, or attempts to block L's parents exercising any right to consultation and/or veto, could be unfair prejudice and consequently in breach of s 459 CA 1985.

The final question to be addressed is how to protect the financial stake being provided by L's parents. Ordinary shares in a private company are not readily marketable and offer no protection against insolvency; they are not an appropriate choice. Preference shares are subject to the same handicaps, although redeemable shares would guarantee a return of capital if the company was still a going concern. The best solution would appear to be a secured loan, preferably redeemable at a fixed date, in their favour. Obviously, the company must have an asset of sufficient value to stand as security for the loan and a specified asset subject to a fixed charge is more likely to guarantee repayment than a floating charge. A charge on the assets of the company must be registered (s 395 CA 1985).

NOTE

There are provisions in the Companies Act 2006 which, when in force, will have a bearing on some of the issues raised in the question. For example, the Act provides that there should be a single document—the constitution—and that those things that would otherwise be found in the memorandum will be contained either in a number of statutory statements or the articles. The memorandum will serve as historic value only, that is, it will contain only details of founder members (the subscribers to the memorandum). Another example relates to the objects clause. Under the Act, new or existing companies will no longer be required to have an objects clause. Companies will be able to opt to have restricted objects, but the Act provides that these will need to be contained in the articles. The Act also provides that shareholders will no longer be able to restrain a company from entering in a proposed *ultra vires* transaction.

Question 4

Archie, Brian and Colin, who are all self-employed plasterers, agree to combine their businesses and to operate as a company, Cornice Ltd. A document is prepared which states: 'It is hereby agreed that all expenses incurred by Colin in the formation of Cornice Ltd shall be repaid from company funds within 12 months of the date of incorporation of the company.' It is signed: 'For and on behalf Cornice Ltd, as agents only, Archie and Brian.'

Upon advice by an accountant, Colin duly formed Cornice Ltd and its shares were divided equally among the three participants, who all became directors. The articles of the company provide that: 'Any person who has incurred expenses in connection with the formation of the company shall be entitled to reimbursement of those expenses by the company.' After formation, Brian signed a cheque, bearing the name 'Cornice', in favour of the accountant for his advice in connection with the formation; this cheque has not been paid. It has also emerged that Archie made a profit from the incorporation, which he did not reveal to Colin. Colin protested about the failure to pay the accountant and Archie's undisclosed profit. At a meeting of the board of directors, Archie and Brian resolved not to reimburse him for his expenses and to take no action to recover the profit from Archie.

Advise Colin and the accountant.

Answer plan

Three principal issues arise in this question:

(a) whether Colin can initiate proceedings to recover the profit made by Archie;

(b) whether Colin has any claim for the expenses which he incurred in forming the company, either against the company or against Archie and Brian;

(c) whether the accountant has any claim against the company or Brian for his services.

Answer

The law is a little hazy as to who is a promoter, it is a question of fact in all cases; there is no doubt that Archie (A), Brian (B) and Colin (C) are the promoters of Cornice Ltd. They are the people who decided to form the company, who set it going and who organised the registration, all of which are factors in determining whether a person is a promoter (see *Emma Silver Mining Co v Lewis (1879)* and *Whaley Bridge Printing Co v Green (1880)*). In contrast, despite any help he may have provided, the accountant is not a promoter if he merely acted in a professional capacity (*Re Great Wheal Polgooth Co (1883)*).

A promoter owes certain obligations to the company which he is forming— essentially, a duty of good faith in all dealings with the incipient corporation.

This is because promoters are in a position of total dominance over the company and there is much scope for them to profit from the promotion. The courts have had to determine whether a promoter cannot derive a profit from the promotion or whether to allow the retention of profit in certain cases. The courts have adopted the second view. In *Erlanger v New Sombrero Phosphate Co (1878)*, the House of Lords held that a promoter could keep any profit he made out of the promotion, provided that full disclosure was made to an independent board of directors.

While still valid, this test is almost impossible to satisfy. Promoters of private companies, as in this case, are likely to become the first directors and have a continuing involvement with the company; there is no independent board. Consequently, the courts have treated disclosure to the members as full disclosure (*Salomon v Salomon (1897)*), provided that the initial members do not intend to bow out once disclosure has been achieved.

A has not made full disclosure of his profit to all shareholders and, even if this is an indirect profit, he has broken the duty which he owes to the company. *Gluckstein v Barnes (1900)*, the promoters sold property (Olympia) to a company they were promoting, which profit was duly disclosed. The promoters did not reveal that, prior to their acquisition of Olympia, they had acquired certain debts (for less than face value, since it was generally thought that they would never be paid) secured on the property. Prior to transferring the property to the company, they arranged for these debts to be paid and the profit they made when the debts were discharged was not disclosed. The promoters were required to repay this profit to the company.

While there may be no doubt that A has broken his duty to the company, can C do anything about it? The duty is owed to the company and the company appears to have resolved to do nothing about A's action. Since a company is an abstraction, a person acting on behalf of the company must initiate litigation. By virtue of Art 70 of Table A, this power is vested in the board, who, in this case, have decided not to sue. C, as a shareholder, cannot force the company to sue A, nor has he the power to sack the board; but he may be able to bring a derivative action on behalf of the company alleging fraud by the controlling shareholders. However, given the inauspicious start to the joint venture, he might be better advised to seek a just and equitable winding up under s 122(1)(g) of the Companies Act (CA) 1985 of the IA 1986 or bring an action for unfair prejudice (s 459 CA 1985) on his own account and seek to be bought out of the company.

C's next cause for complaint is the failure to obtain reimbursement for the expenses which he incurred in the course of promotion. A promoter is not entitled to reimbursement from the company unless he can establish a valid contract to pay. Is there such a contract? The document signed by A and B purports to bind the company to reimburse C, but the case of *Kelner v Baxter (1866)* has long established that a company cannot be bound by a contract entered into prior to its incorporation—the company did not exist at the relevant time, so it cannot contract. In *Kelner*, the promoters ordered wines and spirits on behalf of a hotel company they were forming. The goods were not paid for by the company; nor could they be recovered, since they had been consumed. The company was not liable on the contract, although the promoters were. Nor can the articles be said to ratify the pre-incorporation contract: *Kelner v Baxter* also held that a principal which did not exist at the time that its agent purported to act on its behalf cannot ratify the acts of the 'agent'. If the company was to enter into a new contract with C post-incorporation, he could sue on the new contract, but he would have to show that he had provided consideration which was not past.

C may seek to rely on the provision in the articles authorising the reimbursement of promotion expenses. This article plainly authorises the directors to pay these expenses if they choose, but it almost certainly does not entitle C to demand payment. Section 14 CA 1985 provides that the articles of the company bind the company and its members. The wording of the section seems tolerably clear—the articles create a contract between the company and its members. Since a contract exists—even if a rather odd one, in that it can be altered by one party (s 9 CA 1985)—it would seem that C could sue on the articles and obtain his due. Unfortunately, the courts have interpreted the s 14 contract rather oddly. The traditional view is that a shareholder can enforce the articles only insofar as the relevant article creates a 'membership' right, that is, a right attaching to each and every share and which relates to the holding of shares. This view derives from the first instance decision of Astbury J in *Hickman v Kent or Romney Marsh Sheepbreeders' Association (1915)* and would appear to preclude the enforcement of a right which, while vested in all shareholders (and others), does not relate to the ownership of shares. What constitutes a membership right is far from clear, but it seems clear that a reimbursement of promotion expenses does not fall into this category (*Melhado v Porto Allegre Rly Co (1874)*). However, powerful arguments have been raised against Astbury's interpretation of the s 14 contract. Lord Wedderburn in particular relies heavily upon the House of Lords' decision in *Quin and Axtens v Salmon (1909)*, where a shareholder was held entitled to enforce an article which required his consent to the sale of company land, to advance the view that a shareholder has a personal right to require the company to act in accordance with its articles. Variations on Lord Wedderburn's argument would restrict the shareholder to having a right to ensure that the appropriate corporate body carries on the affairs of the company. The conventional view seems likely to be applied to a case such as this and C would not be reimbursed.

C would, however, be able to bring an action against A and B personally for the reimbursement of his expenses. Section 36C CA 1985 provides that a contract 'which purports to be made by or on behalf of a company at a time when the company has not been formed has the effect...as one made with the person purporting to act for the company as agent for it, and he is personally liable on the contract accordingly'. The courts have interpreted this section (and its forebears) purposively and there seems little doubt that A and B will be liable. *Phonogram Ltd v Lane (1982)* illustrates the operation of the section. L had entered into a contract with the claimant on behalf of a company he was forming to manage a rock group (Cheap, Mean and Nasty) and had received approximately £12,000 on behalf of the intended company to aid his endeavours. The company was never formed and, even though it was accepted that the money had not necessarily benefited L personally, he was liable to reimburse the claimant.

The final issue concerns the accountant who has not been paid. Obviously, the accountant must establish some legal right if he wishes to bring an action to recover the sum due. First, he could seek to sue the company on the pre-incorporation contract, but this will not succeed, because:

- it is not clear that he was contracting with the company rather than with C personally;
- even if he was contracting with the company, the company, as we have seen, is not liable on a pre-incorporation contract.

Second, he could sue the company as the drawer of the cheque and, if the company fails to pay, he might be able to seek a winding up order, although it is unlikely that the sums would justify this. He could not sue the company on the provision in the articles which seems to authorise the payment of incorporation expenses, because he is not a shareholder and is not a party to the s 14 contract. Indeed, even if he was a shareholder, he would face the same difficulties as C in enforcing what appears to be a non-membership right. If a court was prepared to disregard the conventional view on the s 14 contract and hold that all the articles constituted contractual rights (or that a member had a right to have the articles complied with), he would still have to depend upon C suing on his behalf (unless he was a shareholder). If C sued on behalf of the accountant, the rules of privity would seem to provide that any damages payable to C would reflect C's loss and not that of the accountant (if C has to reimburse the accountant, his losses might be recoverable).

Third, he could sue Brian as the signatory of a company cheque which does not bear the full name of the company. Section 349(4) CA 1985 states that any person who signs a cheque on behalf of a company on which the name of the company does not appear in full—B signed on behalf of Cornice and not Cornice Ltd—is personally liable on the cheque. While the omission of 'Ltd' seems minor and there is no question of the accountant being misled as to the status of the body with which he was dealing, the law is strict. The omission of '&' in the name of a company has triggered the section and, while the courts feel that claims under this provision may be wholly unmeritorious, they have left it to Parliament to amend the law. Indeed, the Companies Act 2006, when in force, does permit a minor variance so long as it does not cause confusion. If the accountant sues B under this provision, B is entitled to an indemnity from the company, provided that it is solvent.

Both C and the accountant should be able to recover their money, provided that A and B are solvent. One cannot see much future for Cornice Ltd, however.

Question 5

Rendell Ltd has a number of wholly owned subsidiaries, including Barbara Ltd and Vine Ltd. The directors of Rendell Ltd are also directors of these two subsidiaries.

Land belonging to Barbara Ltd is being compulsorily purchased by the government for a road widening scheme; the amount of compensation has not yet been agreed.

Vine Ltd, while originally engaged in house building, has incurred huge losses in speculative property dealings which were entered into by the managing director of the company without the knowledge of the other directors, who took no active part in its management. The creditors of Vine are pressing Rendell to pay its subsidiary's debts. Without further support from Rendell Ltd, Vine Ltd will go into insolvent liquidation.

Advise Rendell Ltd and its directors.

Answer plan

A number of issues arise. They can be split into those affecting the holding company and those affecting its directors.
Rendell Ltd are seeking:

- to obtain the best possible compensation for the land acquisition;
- to escape liability for the debts of Vine Ltd;
- to avoid the speculative building contracts;
- to pursue all or some of the directors of Vine in respect of the losses already incurred.

The directors of Rendell are trying to escape any liability for their actions and inactions as directors of Vine Ltd.

Answer

Rendell wishes to maximise the compensation payable in respect of the road widening scheme which affects Barbara Ltd, and to minimise its losses in respect of its subsidiary, Vine Ltd.

(a) Barbara Ltd

Barbara Ltd is a wholly owned subsidiary of Rendell Ltd but, as a registered company, it is a separate legal person from its shareholder. Traditionally, a shareholder has no legal interest in the property of the company. Thus, in *Macaura v Northern Assurance (1925)*, a shareholder was unable to claim on a policy of insurance which he had effected on certain of the company's assets and which had been destroyed by fire; one cannot insure another's property and the assets belonged to another—the company. Thus, the amount payable for the road widening scheme would seem to be limited to an appropriate sum under the legislation necessary to compensate Barbara Ltd for its loss. However, the forfeiture of the land may also have an adverse affect upon other companies within the Rendell Ltd group, resulting in greater loss than that which is payable to Barbara Ltd.

Can Rendell Ltd claim that the veil of incorporation cloaking Barbara Ltd can be torn aside, so that Rendell and Barbara are treated as one company for the purposes of compensation? There are some circumstances in which a court will ignore the separate legal personality of a company. This disregard of corporate legal status may be required by statute or, in exceptional cases, be decreed by the courts. One statutory situation is pertinent. The statutes which permit compensation for persons whose real property is subject to a compulsory purchase order allow a court to disregard the separate legal personality of individual companies within a group and consider the effect of the order on the business of the group as a whole. An example, with facts very similar to those of this case, arose in *DHN Food Distributors v Tower Hamlets LBC (1976)*.

(b) Vine Ltd

The situation in respect of this subsidiary is more complex:

Turning to the first issue, is Rendell liable for the debts of its subsidiary? Once again, the existence of the corporate veil shields the shareholder, Rendell, from the attentions of the disgruntled creditors of Vine Ltd. The situation is similar to that in *Salomon v Salomon & Co (1897)*, in which S, who had converted his existing, successful business into a limited company of which he was the managing director and principal shareholder, was found not to be liable for the company's unpaid debts. This strict adherence to the separation of company (Vine) and its shareholders (Rendell) causes loss to creditors but, as yet, this position has not been ameliorated by the courts (see the somewhat caustic comment on this by Templeman LJ in *Re Southard & Co Ltd (1979)*). Hence, unless there is some reason to disregard the corporate personality of Vine, the creditors have no call upon Rendell. Grounds for lifting the veil include where a company is being used to conceal some fraudulent purpose, as, for example, in *Jones v Lipman (1962)*, where the defendant sought to evade a binding contract of sale between himself and the claimant by conveying the subject matter of the contract to a company he controlled—the corporate status of the transferee was disregarded by the court.

However, where the claimant's right of action is against a company in the first place, the veil cannot be lifted so as to enable the claimant to bring proceedings against a person who controlled the company but who is not otherwise liable to the claimant (*Yukong Line Ltd of Korea v Rendsburg Investment Corp (No 2) (1997); Ord v Belhaven Pubs Ltd (1998)*). There seems to be no evidence of fraud by the shareholder in *Vine* in this case. An alternative approach might be to claim that the company had engaged in wrongful trading and should contribute to the assets of Vine Ltd. However, wrongful trading becomes relevant only if Vine Ltd goes into insolvent liquidation. If such liability arose (see below for a fuller discussion of this point), Rendell might also be liable if it could be regarded as a shadow director, that is, a person in accordance with whose directions the directors of a company are accustomed to act (s 741 of the Companies Act (CA) 1985). It seems probable that Rendell exercised this degree of control over at least some of the directors and the section might apply.

The contracts entered into by the reckless director are binding on the subsidiary, even if not authorised by the objects clause of Vine Ltd, because the validity of a company's contracts cannot be called into question simply because it lacked the capacity to enter into it (s 35 CA 1985). However, the directors of Vine can be held liable to the company if they permitted the company to overstep its legal capacity, unless the default by them is ratified by special resolution (s 35(3) CA 1985). Clearly, Rendell has a claim against the directors (it cannot be enforced by the creditors) but may not wish to exercise it or could choose to ratify the wrongdoing. While the contracts bind Vine, they are not enforceable against Rendell, since to attempt to do so would disregard Vine's legal personality.

Liability may sometimes be imposed upon the directors in respect of corporate activities. A director can incur liability for the company's debts where he was knowingly a party to a company's fraudulent trading. Fraudulent trading occurs when a director allows his company to continue trading in the knowledge that it cannot pay its debts at present and that there is no reasonable prospect that it will be able to pay them. Since fraud must be proved beyond reasonable doubt, actions for fraudulent trading are rarely successful (s 213 of the Insolvency Act (IA) 1986). It does not seem very likely here. It is wrongful trading, as contained in s 214 IA 1986, which appears more likely to be the basis for the imposition of personal liability upon the directors of Vine Ltd and Rendell, if it is a shadow director. However, wrongful trading is applicable only where a company has gone into insolvent liquidation, which is not the case here. It might be worth Rendell propping up Vine Ltd to avoid insolvency and the possible imposition of personal liability, which would mean that the creditors of Vine would be paid. The sums must be done carefully to see which is most beneficial. Where, in the course of the winding up of a company, it appears that a director is guilty of 'wrongful trading', the courts, on the application of the liquidator, may declare him liable to make a contribution to the company's assets of such an amount as it thinks proper.

The power to make a declaration under s 214(1) IA 1986 applies in relation to a director if:

- the company has gone into insolvent liquidation;
- at some time before the winding up of the company, that person knew, or ought to have concluded, that there was no reasonable prospect of the company avoiding insolvent liquidation; and
- he was a director at that time.

However, the court must not make a declaration if, after the person concerned first knew or ought to have concluded that there was no reasonable prospect of the company avoiding insolvent liquidation, he took every step to minimise the potential loss to the company's creditors as he ought to have taken. Section 214(4) IA 1986 provides that, for the above purposes, the facts which a person ought to have known, the conclusions he ought to reach and the steps which he ought to take, are those which would be known, reached or taken by a reasonably diligent person with the general knowledge, skill and experience that may reasonably be expected of a person carrying out the same functions as are carried out by that director (that is, the director who is potentially subject to an order). This somewhat obscure provision seems to mean that what a director should have known or done is to be judged by reference to a theoretical director who possesses those skills that may 'reasonably be expected' of a director, unless the director is better qualified than this theoretical director, when he is to be judged by reference to his own qualifications.

The question is whether the directors of Vine Ltd have exercised sufficient skill—certainly, the inactive directors might be at fault if some degree of activity or active supervision could be expected from them. In *Re Produce Marketing Consortium Ltd (No 2) (1989)*, it was found that, once the directors should have concluded from the falling profitability and increasing debts of the company that liquidation was inevitable, and they had failed to take all steps to minimise loss, since the directors had not limited their dealings to running down the company's stocks (which action might have been justified as an attempt to minimise liability to creditors), they were required to contribute £75,000 to the assets of the company, this being the loss which could have been averted by speedy liquidation.

Could the directors of Vine Ltd be liable to that company or Rendell Ltd, or the creditors in some other way? Directors owe a duty to the company of which they are directors but not to any holding company. Consequently, the directors of Vine Ltd are not directly liable to Rendell for any default (*Lindgren v L & P Estates Ltd (1967)*), although any failure on their part as directors of Rendell may be actionable and it is hardly good policy for a director to upset the sole shareholder. Nor can they be liable to the creditors of Vine, since no duty is owed to creditors of a company, except, perhaps, when the company is already insolvent or on the point of collapse. Indeed, in *Kuwait Asia Bank EC v National Mutual Life Nominees Ltd (1991)*, the Privy Council seemed unwilling to countenance even this possibility. However, as directors of Vine, they do owe duties to that company. The enforcement of those duties is vested in the company itself but the company is controlled by its directors (by virtue of Art 70 of Table A), so that directors appear to be able to decide whether to pursue themselves in respect of any alleged wrongdoing on their part. However, the shareholders in a company can instruct the directors how to act (that is, sue themselves), provided that they do so by special resolution and, since Rendell can command such a resolution, there is no difficulty in bringing an action against the directors. Alternatively, Rendell could commence an action itself. In addition, whether or not the directors are in default, they can be sacked by ordinary resolution (s 303 CA 1985), although this may constitute breach of a service contract and prove to be expensive (see s 303(5) CA 1985).

Merely because there is a claimant who could bring an action, it does not mean that the directors are in breach of duty. Apart from the director who engaged in speculative property dealings, which might be *ultra vires*, the directors who took no active part in management might be in breach of their duty of care and skill. The common law duty of care and skill borne by directors is traditionally very modest, in that directors are merely expected to carry out their duties with an appropriate degree of care and skill. The traditional formulation of the nature and extent of this duty is that given by Romer J in *Re City Equitable Fire Insurance Co Ltd (1925)*, in which he held that a director:

• need display only such skill as may reasonably be expected from a person of his knowledge and experience;

• need not give the affairs of the company continuous attention; and

• is entitled to leave the day to day running of the company to the officials of the company and is entitled to assume, in the absence of suspicious circumstances, that such officials are performing their duties honestly.

These propositions remain good law with regard to non-executive directors, but executive directors will generally be constrained by their service contracts to devote a set percentage of their time to the affairs of the company. However, in *Dorchester Finance Co Ltd v Stebbing (1989)*, two directors were qualified accountants. They left the running of the company to S, doing little more than calling in periodically and signing blank cheques for S to use, which S converted for his own use. They were held to be negligent. The judge found that their complete failure to do anything in respect of the running of the company was, even for non-executive directors, negligent, as well as in breach of several sections of the Companies Act. On this basis, the directors might incur liability for failure to restrain actions by the active director.

▌NOTE

Some greater discussion of *Yukong Line Ltd of Korea v Rendsburg Investment Corp (No 2) (1997)* and *Ord v Belhaven Pubs Ltd (1998)* might be useful. Other cases on s 214 IA 1986 could be considered.

Question 6

In May 2002, the shares of Large plc, a quoted international company, stood at £3. That month, the company issued listing particulars, in which the directors announced that the company was seeking finance to embark on gold mining in Siberia. The listing particulars contained a report by Bering Associates, stating that the area over which Large had the mining concession was rich in easily mined gold and that enormous profits could be expected.

Midas read the listing particulars and subscribed for 5,000 £3 shares at a total cost of £15,000. On the last day of June, Midas sold half his shares at £3.80 each to Croesus, who had also read the company's listing particulars. In early July, it was announced that a further survey revealed that, while there was gold in the area, it was extremely difficult to mine, making the project barely profitable, and the price of Large plc's shares tumbled to £1.80.

Advise Midas and Croesus as to any remedies which may be available to them.

Answer plan

An answer to this question should differentiate between Midas, who will seek a remedy from the company and/or the directors and/or Bering Associates, and Croesus, who might seek to pursue a claim against Midas. In respect of each complainant, the statutory and any common law remedies should be considered, noting that the Financial Services and Markets Act (FSMA) 2000 came into force in 2001.

Answer

(a) Midas

FSMA 2000

When a company applies for listing of its shares which are to be offered to the public before admission to the Stock Exchange, a prospectus must be issued (s 84 FSMA 2000). Where a company applies for listing of its shares in other circumstances, listing particulars or a prospectus is issued (s 79 FSMA 2000). Here, listing particulars have been issued.

The remedy most easily available to Midas (M) is that provided by the FSMA 2000, which is based upon certain EU directives (although criticism could be made of the adequacy of the implementation, thus leaving open the question of whether an individual could rely on a directive in preference to the Act). The FSMA 2000 provides for both civil and criminal sanctions against those who fail to comply with its provisions, or who induce subscription by false representations or engage in other improper practices. The first issue is whether there has been a false representation.

Section 80(1) FSMA 2000 imposes a general duty of disclosure in respect of listing particulars (and prospectuses) and provides that the listing particulars must contain

> all such information as investors and their professional advisers would reasonably require, and reasonably expect to find there, for the purpose of making an informed assessment of (a) the assets and liabilities, financial position, profits and losses, and prospects of the issuer of the security.

Further guidance is given on the information which might reasonably be expected in s 80(4) FSMA. Is the information given to M about the mining operation, etc, information falling within sub-s (1)? It would seem so.

The second issue is, who incurs liability in respect of this false statement? Section 80 FSMA 2000 states that the information to be included in the particulars is such information as is mentioned in s 80(1) 'which is within the knowledge of any person responsible for the listing particulars or which it would be reasonable for him to obtain by making enquiries'. Liability is imposed upon the person(s) responsible for the listing particulars by s 90 FSMA, subject to certain defences contained in Sched 10 (s 82, which allows the non-disclosure of certain information, does not apply here).

The persons responsible are set out in the **Public Offer of Securities Regulations 1995** (POSR). They are:

- the company (reg 13(1)(a));
- the directors (reg 13(1)(b));
- each and every person who accepts (and is stated as accepting) responsibility for all or part of the particulars (reg 13(1)(c)); and
- each other person who has authorised the contents of the particulars or any part of it (reg 13(1)(d)).

Subject to Sched 10 FSMA 2000 or reg 15 POSR 1995, there is little doubt that Large plc and its directors incur liability. Bering Associates would also appear to incur liability, that is, for the parts of the particulars for which they were responsible, if they have accepted responsibility for or authorised the contents. However, Bering will not be liable unless the misleading material included in the particulars appeared in substantially the form and context to which Bering had agreed. Are any of the parties, who would appear to be liable, exempt?

The FSMA 2000 and POSR 1995 exempt any person 'if he satisfies the court that at the time when the particulars were submitted…he reasonably believed, having made such enquiries (if any) as were reasonable, that the statement was true and not misleading…', provided that he continued in his belief until the time that the securities were acquired, or he continued in his belief until after dealings in the shares had begun and they were acquired after such a lapse of time that he ought reasonably to be excused. This can be called the 'reasonable belief exemption' and it might apply here to Large and its directors—it seems unlikely to apply to Bering.

Of greater relevance for Large and its directors are Sched 10, para 2 FMSA 2000 and reg 15(2) POSR 1995. This provision exempts from liability those who relied upon a statement made by an expert (in this case, Bering), provided that they can establish that they had reasonable grounds to rely upon the expertise of the provider of the misleading information (and the expert had agreed to its inclusion) and they continued to believe that Bering was an expert until after the shares had been bought, or they continued in that belief until after dealings in the shares had begun and they were acquired after such a lapse of time that they ought reasonably to be excused. Note that the mere fact that Bering gave misleading advice does not necessarily mean that they are not competent. Even experts make mistakes.

There are special rules where misleading information is corrected, but these do not apply in the case of M. It should be noted that the onus of exempting themselves from liability falls upon those responsible for the particulars.

The third issue is the nature of any liability incurred. Section 90 FSMA 2000 provides that those responsible for misleading listing particulars are liable to pay compensation to M for the loss he has suffered; the measure of damages is thought to be that applicable in tort, that is, restoration to his original position. Originally, M had £15,000 and no shares; he now has 2,500, worth £1.80 each (£4,500) and has received (it is assumed) £3.80 for each share sold to Croesus (C) (£9,500), so that he needs £1,000 to restore him to his original position (plus any incidental expenses). If a contractual measure of damages was applicable, greater damages could be recovered (on the loss of expectation basis). It should be noted that M will not be able to claim compensation if he knew that the relevant statement was untrue.

Other sources of liability

M should have no need to look beyond the FSMA 2000, but other possible sources of compensation are the tort of deceit (where there is conduct akin to fraud) or negligent misstatement either in tort or by virtue of s 2(1) of the Misrepresentation Act 1967 (the last of these would only be available against the company). M could not rescind the contract, it seems, because he has sold half the shares. The fact that he could not rescind would not debar M from monetary compensation (s 111 A of the Companies Act (CA) 1985, reversing *Houldsworth v City of Glasgow Bank (1880)*).

(b) Croesus

The position of C is not dissimilar to that of M, in that he, too, may have a remedy under the FSMA 2000. The right to sue those responsible for the misleading listing particulars is not restricted to those who purchased the shares from the company. Now, anyone who has acquired shares and who can show that he has suffered loss as a result of the misstatement has a *prima facie* case for compensation. C will have to prove that there is a causal connection between the misstatement and the loss. Factors which will tend to negate such a connection are purchase after the true facts became known, which does not apply here, or such a lapse of time that the particulars can no longer be said to have any influence on the market. The gap between the publication of the misstatement and the purchase in this case does not seem so long as to debar C from seeking compensation.

Do any of those liable to M have a defence in the case of C? The only possibility would seem to be that the company or directors could establish that C bought the shares before it was reasonably practicable for them to bring a correction or inform people of the incompetence of the expert. The common law remedies seem unlikely to apply in this case, except, perhaps, with regard to M.

Whatever the outcome of any claim under the FSMA 2000, C has the usual common law remedies against M. Thus, if he can show that M knew the truth when he sold the shares, he may have a remedy for misrepresentation, but only if he relied upon an untrue statement made by M. If M knew the truth but kept quiet and made no statements, there can be no liability on the part of M—he is obliged to refrain from lies but has no obligation to disabuse C, unless he is in a fiduciary relationship with him.

CHAPTER 2

THE COMPANY AND INSIDERS

INTRODUCTION

In this chapter, students are directed specifically to the internal relationships within a company. This involves the rights and duties of the members in their dealings with each other and with the company (see, also, below, Chapter 5). The articles of association are the primary source of the provisions determining these internal relationships. The status of the articles and their enforceability (which touches on the rule in *Foss v Harbottle (1843)*) is a standard area for questions, both problem and essay. Specific regard will also be paid to the appointment, payment and dismissal of officers of the company and the division of power between the shareholders and the directors. Such material can form the basis of a question or be combined with aspects of directors' duties, variation of class rights and s 459 of the Companies Act (CA) 1985 or the external relationships of the company. Students should have at least background knowledge of the types of resolution and the majorities required, and of the conduct of meetings and votes. Arguably, the duties of the directors could form part of this chapter, but it is such a large topic that they are dealt with separately (see below, Chapter 4). Employees of the company are also insiders, but company law syllabuses rarely address issues relating to employees other than directors as they have no *locus standi* to enforce the company's constitution or the duty owed to them by the directors under s 309 CA 1985.

Checklist

Students must be familiar with the following areas:

- the nature of the articles and their legal effect;
- alteration of the articles;
- the appointment, payment and dismissal of directors; and
- the division of power in a company.

Students should be aware that related issues which could be linked to questions based on this area include:

- variation of class rights, reduction of capital and s 459 CA 1985;
- directors' duties and their enforcement; and
- the ability of officers of a company to bind the company.

Question 7

To what extent, if at all, does s 14 of the Companies Act 1985 give a shareholder enforceable contractual rights against a company?

Answer plan

Outline the contents of the memorandum and articles. Assess the efficacy of the s 14 contract and the ability of the company to alter the contractual rights of a shareholder, and tie up the law by reference to the question. You should also consider the proposals for reform in this area.

Answer

The memorandum and articles of association are the key constitutional documents of a company. The minimum contents of the memorandum, which all companies must register, are set out in ss 1 and 2 of the of the Companies Act (CA) 1985. A company cannot decline to comply with these sections; for example, a company cannot have no-par value shares, although extra provisions can be inserted. The memorandum, broadly speaking, defines the position of a company vis à vis the outside world, although its contents are subject to s 14 CA 1985, which, *prima facie*, also renders them enforceable internally. While all companies must have articles of association, a company limited by shares may use the statutory form of articles—Table A—and, unless and to the extent that articles to the contrary are registered, Table A will apply automatically (s 8 CA 1985). The articles, again broadly speaking, define the internal relationships within a company—the division of power and the allocation of risk.

Section 14 CA 1985 provides that the memorandum and articles

bind the company and its members to the same extent as if they ... had been signed and sealed by each member, and contained covenants on the part of each member to observe all the provisions of the memorandum and of the articles.

What does this rather peculiar provision mean? The first instance decision of Astbury J in *Hickman v Kent or Romney Marsh Sheepbreeders' Association (1915)* established that the memorandum and articles constitute a contract between the company and the members. Consequently, in *Hickman*, a provision requiring a member to refer any dispute with the company to arbitration was held binding on the member. The contract, despite the wording of s 14 CA 1985, is bilateral and binds both the company and the members; it is also binding between the members (*Rayfield v Hands (1960)*).

It is a contract with a number of unusual features. First, it is subject to the provisions of the CA 1985, which include s 9 CA 1985. Section 9 CA 1985 provides that a company may alter its memorandum by special resolution. Thus, one party to the contract (the company) can alter that contract contrary to the wishes of another contracting party—a shareholder—provided that an appropriate majority of shareholders agree. Are shareholders, in voting to amend the articles by special resolution, entitled to vote with regard only to their own interests? Certainly, there are *dicta* in the cases which suggest that, on a vote to change the articles, the shareholders must vote '*bona fide* for the benefit of the company' (*Allen v Gold Reefs of West Africa Ltd (1900)*), but this is probably overstating the position. It seems clear that, where the proposed change of articles is designed to appropriate the shares of the minority, the court will strike down the amendment unless it is objectively in the best interests of the company. In *Sidebottom v Kershaw Leese (1920)*, the Court of Appeal upheld an amendment which permitted the company to require a shareholder who had an interest in a competing business (as S, who was a director of the company, did) to transfer his shares to nominees of the directors for a fair price. The court held that this was beneficial to the company, thus indicating that, had they not reached this view, the judges would have struck the amendment down. In *Dafen Tinplate Ltd v Llanelly Steel Co (1920)*, an amendment allowing any shareholder to be required to sell his shares was rejected by the court as going beyond that which was necessary to benefit the company.

Whether there is a general requirement that shareholders vote on proposals to alter the articles in a manner which is objectively in the best interests of the company is uncertain. In *Greenhalgh v Arderne Cinemas Ltd (1950)*, the majority shareholders in the company passed a special resolution which in effect required any shareholder so directed to transfer his shares to a nominee of the majority shareholders at a fair price. G, who was the only shareholder likely to be affected by this scheme, objected and the Court of Appeal, while rejecting G's case, seemed to suggest that all shareholder resolutions were subject to the *bona fide*, etc, test. The test requires a voting shareholder to 'proceed on what, in his honest opinion, is for the benefit of the company as a whole'. The Master of the Rolls, Lord Evershed, sought to explain what 'the company as a whole' meant by reference to whether the proposal was in the interest of a hypothetical member of the company not directly concerned in the contentious proposal. Given the uncertainty surrounding the nature of this test, and the fact that G was unsuccessful in his action, it is difficult to find much support for a general duty cast upon shareholders to act *bona fide*, etc. However, limited support for such a duty can be found in two first instance decisions—*Re Holders Investment Trust (1971)* (the majority must consider the interests of the minority in deciding whether to vary class rights) and *Clemens v Clemens Brothers Ltd (1976)* (the majority is not able to issue further shares to deprive the minority of negative voting control). The statutory remedy for disadvantaged shareholders, s 459 CA 1985, seems likely to provide a more effective remedy than the somewhat elusive general principle relied upon in the *Greenhalgh* case to limit the power of the majority to use their statutory power to amend the articles.

Despite the use of the word 'may' in s 9 CA 1985, it is well established that the company is not bound by a provision in the articles or a shareholder agreement which purports to abolish the right to change the articles; that is, 'may' means 'can' (subject to the appropriate number agreeing). The ability to alter a contract without the agreement of all other parties is unusual but not unique; clubs and societies are often empowered to amend their rules without the unanimous agreement of the membership. While it is not possible for a company to abrogate its right to change its articles, it is acceptable for the articles to provide that on a vote to alter the articles the shares of a particular member shall carry extra votes (*Bushell v Faith (1970)*). A weighted voting clause of this type could ensure that certain articles are entrenched. While a weighted voting clause in the articles is capable of change by special resolution, it could itself be entrenched by providing that class rights (which it would be) can only be amended with the concurrence of the relevant class. Alternatively, a weighted voting clause could be placed in the memorandum and class rights placed in the memorandum cannot be altered other than as provided for in the memorandum. Class rights placed in the memorandum are not subject to s 17 CA 1985, which, in other cases, provides that provisions placed in the memorandum, but not required to be so located by statute, can be changed by special resolution. In addition to the use of weighted voting clauses, a shareholder who wishes to protect himself from the effect of s 9 CA 1985 could enter into a shareholder agreement with his fellow members. Such an agreement would not bind the company and could not be used to prevent a change of the articles. It would, however, allow an action for breach of contract against fellow members who voted to change the articles.

It is the second feature of the s 14 contract which is more controversial. The ability of a shareholder (or the company) to enforce the contract which is contained in the articles is uncertain. The traditional view is that a shareholder can enforce the articles only insofar as the relevant article creates a 'membership' right, that is, a right attaching to each and every share, which relates to the holding of shares. This view also derives from the decision of Astbury J in *Hickman v Kent or Romney Marsh*

Sheepbreeders' Association (1915) and would appear to preclude the enforcement of a right which does not fall into this obscure category. There are two difficulties with this decision. First, the precise nature of a 'membership right' is indistinct. It would seem that a right vested in only some of the membership (*Eley v Positive Life Assurance Co (1876)*, where articles providing that E was to be company solicitor for life did not give E any contractual right of employment) or a right conferred, potentially, on all shareholders but relating to a shareholder in a non-member capacity is not such a right. For example, where the articles permit the reimbursement of promotion expenses, a member who, while acting as a promoter of the company, incurred such expenses could not rely on the articles to establish a contractual right to reimbursement (*Melhado v Porto Allegre Rly Co (1874)*) and, in *Beattie v E & F Beattie Ltd (1938)*, a provision requiring members to submit disputes to arbitration did not apply to a dispute between the company and a shareholder in respect of his directorship. However, membership rights (or individual rights) are contractual rights and any attempt to ignore such a right is a breach of contract subject to legal action by the shareholder; in other words, membership rights are an example of a situation where the rule in *Foss v Harbottle (1843)*, which restricts the right of a member to sue the company, does not apply. Examples of membership rights are the right to receive dividends when duly declared and payable, the right to attend general meetings and the right to participate on winding up.

The second, and more fundamental, objection to Astbury's view is that the section does not differentiate between membership and non-membership rights and powerful arguments have been raised against this interpretation of the s 14 contract. Lord Wedderburn in particular relies heavily upon the House of Lords' decision in *Quin & Axtens v Salmon (1909)*, where a director-shareholder was held entitled to enforce an article which required his consent to the sale of company land, to advance the view that a shareholder has a personal right to require the company to act in accordance with its articles (subject to those matters of internal management, breach of which is ratifiable by ordinary resolution). Lord Wedderburn would even argue that a shareholder can enforce an article which benefits an outsider or himself in a non-membership capacity. If a court was prepared to disregard the conventional view on the s 14 contract and hold that all the articles constituted contractual rights (or that a member had a right to have the articles complied with), an outsider would still have to depend upon a member suing on his behalf. This would cause no difficulty where an injunction was sought, but, where a member sued for damages on behalf of a third party, the rules of privity would seem to provide that any damages payable would reflect the member's loss and not that of the third party.

Variations on Lord Wedderburn's argument would restrict the shareholder to having a right to ensure that the appropriate corporate body carries on the affairs of the company—on this analysis, S succeeded in the *Quin & Axtens* case because the general meeting purported to take a decision which could only be taken by the board.

Other unusual features of the s 14 contract are that the 'contract' does not provide each party with a list of contractual duties, it is potentially infinite and it is not subject to rescission for misrepresentation.

The precise scope of the s 14 contract is still far from clear; these difficulties may be explained by the fact that the wording of s 14 CA 1985 (and its predecessors) derive from provisions relating to unincorporated joint-stock companies which are legally an entirely different type of being. It is certainly possible to conclude that the combination of Astbury J's interpretation of ss 14 and 9 CA 1985 significantly diminish the rights of an individual shareholder. However, it could be argued that, at least in larger companies, it is entirely appropriate that the minority tail should not wag the majority dog. This is particularly true when an individual shareholder may be able to rely on s 459 CA 1985 to ensure that he is bought out of a company with which he is at loggerheads.

The Company Law Review Steering Group expressed the view that 'section 14 is so misleading that it would be desirable to lay down a statutory provision explaining the extent to which individual shareholders and members are entitled to enforce the constitution against the company and that the contractual character of the rights should be abolished' (*Modern Company Law for a Competitive Economy: Developing the Framework* (London: DTI, 2000)). The Companies Act 2006 does contain a 'single constitution' for all companies, but the interpretation by the courts of s 14 CA 1985 remains unaffected.

▌NOTE

Discussion of other ways in which the s 14 contract differs from 'normal' contracts could be made.

Question 8

It is a basic principle of company law that all the corporators, acting together, can do anything which is *intra vires* the company (*Cane v Jones (1980)*, *per* Michael Wheeler QC).

Consider the efficacy of, and the problems caused by, 'shareholder agreements'.

Answer plan

This is a question concerning the control of companies by reference to non-statutory documents—shareholder agreements. It simply requires a relatively factual description of the nature and function of such agreements in the context of company control. Some discussion of why shareholder agreements are used is also appropriate.

Answer

A company is an association of persons in pursuance of some common object, generally, but not necessarily, for profit. Despite the immense complexity and size of the Companies Acts, forming a company is easy and relatively straightforward. All that the law prescribes by way of a corporate constitution is two documents—the memorandum of association and the articles of association. But the Companies Act proposes that there should, in future, be one document—the constitution. The contents of these documents are partly decreed by statute but derive principally from the choice of the founders of the company. Sections 1 and 2 of the Companies Act (CA) 1985 provide that the memorandum must state: the name of the company; the situation of its registered office; the objects of the company; the amount of share capital and how it is divided up; and whether the company is public or private. The CA 1985 does not specify the contents of the articles, although draft forms for different types of company are set out in Tables A–F of the Companies (Tables A–F) Regulations 1985. Tables A–F can be accepted or rejected as the founders of the company see fit, although the format of the Tables, that is, numbered paragraphs, is compulsory (*Gaiman v National Association for Mental Health (1971)*). As can be seen, there is considerable freedom in the drafting of the basic constitutional framework of a company. This freedom is reduced when it is sought to change the memorandum or articles. After all, it is argued, a shareholder has acquired shares in a company on the basis that his rights and liabilities are as set out in the memorandum and articles and, while he knows from the outset that these rights and liabilities may be changed if a majority of shareholders so wish, the courts should be empowered to intervene to restrain the wish of the majority in certain cases. Others argue that, where an appropriate majority has sanctioned a change in the memorandum and/or articles, the courts should not intervene to restrain such changes, however detrimental to the wishes of a shareholder, because Parliament has decreed that the shareholders can amend their mutual rights and duties as they see fit.

There are some statutory restraints placed upon the powers of the majority to alter the constitution of the company and consequently to run the company as they wish. For example, ss 4 and 5 CA 1985 (alteration of objects) and ss 125–27 CA 1985 (variation of class rights) provide examples of specific restrictions or procedures on amendment of the company's constitution. The requirement that changes generally require a special resolution (75% majority of the votes cast) to implement them restrains the freedom of shareholders to amend the rights and liabilities of other shareholders. There are also rare examples of the courts requiring shareholders to exercise their right to vote in a manner which takes into account interests other than their own. For example, the courts have determined that they can reject an alteration of the articles, which complies with all statutory requirements, if the alteration is not *'bona fide* for the benefit of the company' (*Allen v Gold Reefs of West Africa Ltd (1900)*), although this seems to operate only where an expropriation of shares is involved (*Dafen Tinplate Ltd v Llanelly Steel Co (1920)*). However, any imposition of a fiduciary obligation on the majority contrasts with the normal position, which is that shareholders, as owners of property, are permitted to do what they like with their property (shares) regardless of the wishes of others (*Welton v Saffery (1897)*). The ability of shareholders to do as they wish with their property may leave minority shareholders in a vulnerable position, in that they may see their rights amended by the majority to their disadvantage, with little they can do about it.

Where it is all the shareholders who wish to vary their mutual rights and duties, can there be any objection to them doing so? Obviously, the shareholders may choose to amend their respective interests by revision of the articles or the memorandum but, as indicated above, this may attract judicial intervention— although this is hardly likely if all shareholders agree. However, it is not uncommon for shareholders to supplement, suspend or amend the memorandum or articles with 'shareholder agreements'. The majority may also use shareholder agreements to, for example, provide a 'voting block' to retain control of the company or evade provisions in the articles designed to protect the minority. It is the shareholder agreement between all shareholders which the case of *Cane v Jones* (1980) addresses.

In *Cane v Jones*, two brothers, P and H, formed a company, of which they were the 'life directors'; they were the only directors. All the shares were owned by close family members or on trust for such members. The articles provided that the chairman of directors had a casting vote at directors' and general meetings of the company. In 1967, all of the then shareholders agreed that the chairman would not use his casting vote and that, where the director-brothers could not agree, an independent chairman (with a casting vote) would be appointed. The two sides of the family fell out and P's side claimed that P, as chairman, had a casting vote. H's daughter, the claimant, who was not a party to the 1967 agreement (although trustees acting for her were), sought to rely on that agreement and petitioned for a declaration that P's casting vote had been abrogated. Michael Wheeler QC determined that P's casting vote had disappeared and held that the 1967 agreement was, in essence, a general meeting, which was effective to override the articles. The judge seemed to say that, where all the shareholders agreed to amend the articles, this could take effect as an alteration of the articles, despite the failure to comply with s 9 (meeting and special resolution required), because s 9 CA 1985 was merely a way, but not the only way, of altering the articles.

Whether this case should really be seen as an alteration of the articles can be doubted—if it was an alteration, it would now be subject to the official notification procedure (s 42 CA 1985) so that the 'alteration' would only operate internally and would not bind third parties. Further, if it was an alteration of the articles, new shareholders would also be bound. This case should be treated as a shareholder agreement rather than an alteration of articles. What, then, is a shareholder agreement, and can such agreements outflank the statutory requirements?

Shareholder agreements fall into two broad groups:

(a) agreements between all or some of the shareholders and the company; and

(b) agreements between all or some (a majority) of the shareholders which do not involve the company.

Shareholder agreements will generally constitute contracts, the consideration being the agreement of the other parties to be bound by the agreement. Such agreements may be positive, for example, providing a method for the resolution of disputes between member and member or member and company; or negative, for example, an agreement that the articles shall not apply or that non-compliance with the articles will not be actionable. In some cases, a shareholder agreement may be regarded as an informal equivalent to a resolution of the members in general meeting—if it is unanimous and in writing, and Art 53 of Table A expressly recognises the practice and treats such agreements as equivalent to formal resolutions. Where there is unanimous agreement to a proposal, there can be little objection to treating the agreement as binding between those who have agreed and as equivalent to a 'statutory' resolution, although official notification (s 42 CA 1985), when required, would be necessary to bind third parties. Is this also the case when the informal agreement conflicts with substantive statutory rules (as opposed to procedural rules) designed to protect members? This issue is unresolved. It could be argued that a shareholder agreement should not be treated as an informal resolution where company legislation provides a substantive rule to protect shareholders (even though they have all agreed). Many shareholder agreements cannot be treated as informal resolutions of the company, either because that was not the intention of the parties or, it seems, because the Acts may specify that the formal route is the *only* method of doing certain things. However, it should be noted that, in *Re Barry Artist Ltd (1985)*, the court approved a reduction of capital to which all members had merely given informal approval, despite s 135 CA 1985, which provides that a company may 'by special resolution reduce its share capital'. Where a shareholder agreement constitutes an informal resolution, it may, it seems, bind subsequent transferees of shares (unlike a pure shareholder agreement), subject to the official notification rules.

An agreement between all shareholders (and perhaps the company), as predicated in the question, can be compared with the articles of a company. The agreement can be said to govern the internal workings of the company. However, unlike the articles, all aspects of such an agreement are, presumably, mutually enforceable, and not merely those which create membership rights (provided the agreement is a contract), and the agreement cannot be changed without the agreement of all the parties to it unless the agreement so provides. A further contrast with the articles is that the agreement creates personal rights which bind parties to the contract as such, rather than as shareholders. Consequently, successors in title can neither enforce nor be bound by a shareholder agreement. However, it seems that a shareholder agreement, even if entered into by all of the shareholders, cannot fetter the directorial discretion of a director-member (*Boulting v ACTAT (1963)*) or the ability of a company to change its articles (*Allen v Gold Reefs of West Africa Ltd (1900)*); such rights and/or duties are incapable of abrogation. In the case of the directors, it is thought that their fiduciary duty outweighs any contractual right to bind their future conduct. In respect of alteration of the articles, the courts have almost unanimously held that s 9 CA 1985, which provides that 'a company may by special resolution alter its articles', means that a company cannot be restrained from altering its articles by special resolution, even if the resultant alteration causes a breach of contract which may result in damages being payable (*Southern Foundries v Shirlaw (1940)*). What is uncertain is which provisions of company law cannot be abrogated by unanimous agreement of the shareholders. Where an agreement is held incapable of rendering a statutory provision inoperative, the agreement still binds the members—so that a shareholder could sue his fellow members for exercising their statutory rights even if he could not obtain an injunction to restrain them from so doing.

There is no doubt that shareholders can enter into a shareholder agreement which provides how they will vote in meetings of the company, although it has been suggested that an agreement without limit of time may be invalid (*Greenhalgh v Mallard (1943)*, but see *Russell v Northern Bank Developments Corp Ltd (1992)* for a contrary view).

The House of Lords considered the effect of shareholder agreements in *Russell v Northern Bank Developments Corp Ltd (1992)*. In this case, the bank had lent money to two companies—TP Ltd, which had incurred large losses, and TB Ltd, which had proved extremely successful. As part of a restructuring agreement devised by the bank, it was decided that the shares controlling the two companies would be brought together in a new holding company, Tyrone, which would run both companies and would be able to set TP's losses against TB's profits, thereby reducing the tax liability of TB. Four executives, including the claimant, were transferred from TB to run Tyrone and each of them was allotted 20 shares in Tyrone. The remaining issued shares (120) of Tyrone were allotted to the bank. One of Tyrone's articles (equivalent to Art 32 of Table A) allowed the company to increase its share capital but a shareholder agreement entered into by the bank, Tyrone and the four executives provided, *inter alia*, that no further share capital would be created or issued without the written consent of all parties to the agreement. Subsequently, the company sought to increase its share capital and the claimant, R, sought an injunction to restrain it from so doing, on the grounds that this was a breach of the agreement.

Despite the agreement of all the shareholders, it was not argued that this was an informal alteration of the company's articles. The majority would not have accepted that this was an informal alteration (had it been argued), saying that such a finding would be inconsistent with the company being a party to the agreement. The respondent bank argued that since the relevant statute (equivalent to s 121(2)(a) CA 1985) permitted a company to increase its share capital, provided that its articles sanctioned such an increase, which Tyrone's articles did, a shareholder agreement which fettered the statutory power must be invalid. The House of Lords decided that the shareholder agreement was separate and distinct from the company's articles and was of a purely personal nature. It was open to the shareholders to make such an agreement. Lord Jauncey approved the famous *dictum* of Lord Davey in *Welton v Saffery (1897)*:

> Of course, individual shareholders may deal with their own interests by contract in such a way as they see fit. But such contacts ... would create personal obligations against themselves only, and would not become a regulation of the company, or be binding on the transferees of the parties to it, or upon new or non-assenting shareholders.

Consequently, there was no objection to the shareholders making such an agreement as this, although it could not bind the company, because that would fetter the company's statutory right to issue shares. While the court declared the power to issue shares to be an inalienable statutory power, the effect of upholding this agreement was to render the company incapable of issuing shares. This is the first case to treat the power to issue shares as inalienable, even if the finding was nullified by the upholding of the shareholder agreement. The court did not provide any guidance upon which statutory powers are to be treated as inalienable and not subject to amendment or deletion even by unanimous agreement of the shareholders.

Russell stressed the primacy of certain statutory rights but then allowed the parties freedom to negotiate between themselves as to how to run the company, and could be seen as representing a non-interventionist approach by the court, allowing those who risk their money to outflank the intention of Parliament. The case would appear to allow a majority to decide to stymie the statutory rights of a minority by informal agreement—perhaps a case for the use of s 459 CA 1985.

Question 9

Sober Ltd was incorporated by Arnold in 1996 to import and sell non-alcoholic fruit drinks; he was the sole director of the company. Arnold held 90% of the issued shares and his wife, Helen, held 10%. The articles of the company named Helen as company secretary 'for life'. On Arnold's death, his shares were inherited equally by his three sons, who became the directors of the company.

The sons are proposing to amend the objects of the company, with consequential amendments to the articles, to permit the importation and sale of alcoholic drinks. Helen objects strongly to this proposal. Her sons tell her that they propose to employ a different company secretary and to insert a provision in the company's articles allowing the directors to require any shareholder whose statements or conduct is, in their opinion, detrimental to the company's future prosperity to transfer his or her shares to the directors at a fair price.

Advise Helen.

Answer plan

The issues that arise in this question are:

- can Helen prevent the alteration of the objects of the company?;
- can Helen prevent any consequential amendments to the articles?;
- is Helen entitled to be company secretary for life?; and
- can Helen object to the article permitting compulsory acquisition of the shares?

The latter three issues overlap.

Answer

It is not uncommon for a new generation which takes over a family company to have very different ideas about how the company should be run. The law will not intervene to restrain the directors from pursuing a different policy or business, even where it is a new venture in which the company has no expertise. For example, in *Re A Company (No 002567 of 1982) (1983)*, a minority shareholder in a company which was engaged in advertising failed in his attempt to prevent the company from using some of its surplus funds in opening a wine bar. However, where the change of policy necessitates a change of the memorandum or articles, there are appropriate statutory procedures which must be complied with and dissident shareholders may have the right to make their objections known to the court and sometimes to have the change struck down. The courts, in considering applications by disgruntled shareholders, have to balance the right of the majority of members to run the company (or have the directors run it on their behalf) as they wish and the question of whether there is any necessity, especially where statute does not give a remedy, to protect the interests of individual shareholders, even if this stymies the majority.

The first thing that the company wishes to do is to amend its objects clause, permitting the company to trade in alcoholic as well as non-alcoholic beverages. The objects are the purposes which the company is empowered to pursue and are a statement to potential shareholders of the type of business in which their money will be expended. However, Parliament has permitted the alteration of the objects of a company (s 4 CA 1985) so that a shareholder may find that he has invested in a company which he believes will pursue object X, only to find that the company is now engaged in object Y. Parliament has provided that alteration must be by special resolution (that is, passed by shareholders present or voting by proxy who command at least 75% of the votes cast). Since the CA 1985 lays down a procedure for qualified shareholders to object to the alteration, the courts have not thought it appropriate to impose further judicial barriers to alteration—if the majority of investors are happy, the court will not prevent the company from following a new line.

Helen (H) cannot block a special resolution, nor is she eligible to rely on the statutory safeguard created by s 5 CA 1985, which provides that, unless a qualified shareholder objects, the alteration automatically takes effect after 15 days. Section 5 CA 1985 gives *locus standi* to a shareholder, or shareholders, who hold not less than 15% of a class of the shares of the company, who have voted against the resolution and object within 15 days. H, with 10% of the shares, will not have *locus* to petition the court to strike down the alteration. Once the objects have been altered, the company must notify the Registrar of Companies to comply with the provisions of 'official notification' (s 42 CA 1985). Even where no alteration to the objects clause has been made, acts which are beyond the company's objects are valid and binding by virtue of the amendment introduced into the CA 1985 by the CA 1989 (s 35 CA 1985). This provision protects both the company and any third party, although a shareholder under s 35(2) CA 1985 can seek an injuction to prevent the company from carrying out a proposed *ultra vires* transaction.

Turning to any consequential amendments to the articles (the articles should not be altered first, as this could introduce a conflict with the unamended memorandum, which would potentially invalidate the new articles), s 9 CA 1985 provides that a company has the right to change its articles, provided that the change is effected by special resolution and there is no way in which this provision can be excluded. In *Southern Foundries v Shirlaw (1940)*, a director-shareholder sought an injunction to restrain a change of articles, which would have the effect of dismissing him from his directorship in breach of his service contract. The House of Lords refused to grant the injunction, holding that the right of those who own the company and whose money is hazarded thereby cannot be deprived of their right to change the internal constitution of the company. Thus, the company could change its articles but S was entitled to damages for breach of the service contract.

Again, H cannot prevent the passage of a special resolution and there is no statutory procedure for challenging the alteration of the articles. However, H is permitted to petition the court for the striking out of the alteration if it is illegal, inconsistent with the memorandum or if the amendment is not *'bona fide* for the benefit of the company as a whole'. This judicial gloss, that the alteration must be *bona fide*, etc, on the apparently unfettered right of the shareholders to amend the articles is a rare illustration of a fiduciary duty being imposed on shareholders; shareholders are normally entitled to vote without regard to any interest but their own (*Welton v Saffery (1897)*). This *dictum*, which appears to place some limit upon majority power, derives from *Allen v Gold Reefs of West Africa Ltd (1900)*. However, it should be noted that in this case a claimants' challenge to an alteration of the articles, which gave the company a lien over fully paid up shares in respect of any debt owed by a shareholder to the company, was unsuccessful. The claimant was the executor of the only shareholder with fully paid up shares. While the Court of Appeal may have expounded this limitation on the power of the majority to change the rules of the company, the operation of the limitation has proved somewhat disappointing to minority shareholders.

Apart from any general consequential amendments to the articles, H is objecting to the particular change which permits the expropriation of shares of a member who expresses views, etc, held, by the board, to be detrimental to the company. These issues can be considered together. Does *Allen v Gold Reefs* assist H? It seems clear from later cases that, where the proposed change of articles is designed to appropriate the shares of the minority, the court will strike down the amendment unless it is objectively in the best interests of the company. In *Brown v British Abrasive Wheel (1919)*, the company was in urgent need of capital which the majority of shareholders were willing to provide. However, 2% of shareholders were not willing and the majority were willing to proceed only if they could buy out the 2%. The articles were changed to permit the acquisition of the objecting shareholders but was successfully challenged by one of them. The judge held that this alteration was for the benefit of the majority rather than the company.

Even if one agrees with the idea that an alteration must benefit the company, this seems a strange application of the principle—the stymied majority, presumably, did not provide the needed capital and the company went into liquidation. *Brown* was distinguished in *Sidebottom v Kershaw Leese (1920)*, in which the Court of Appeal upheld an amendment which permitted the company to require a shareholder who had an interest in a competing business (as S, who was a director of the company, did) to transfer his shares to nominees of the directors for a fair price. The court held that this was objectively beneficial to the company.

Finally, in *Dafen Tinplate Ltd v Llanelly Steel Co (1920)*, an amendment allowing any shareholder to be required to sell his shares was rejected by the court as going beyond that which was necessary to benefit the company. Consequently, if H can convince the court that this alteration is not for the benefit of the company, she may succeed in having it struck down.

Whether there is a general requirement that shareholders vote on proposals to alter the articles in a manner which is objectively in the best interests of the company is less certain. In *Greenhalgh v Arderne Cinemas Ltd (1950)*, the majority shareholders in the company passed a special resolution which in effect required any shareholder so directed to transfer his shares to a nominee of the majority shareholders at a fair price. G, who was the only shareholder likely to be affected by this scheme, objected and the Court of Appeal, while rejecting G's case, seemed to suggest that all shareholder resolutions were subject to the *bona fide*, etc, test. The test requires a voting shareholder to 'proceed on what, in his honest opinion, is for the benefit of the company as a whole'. The Master of the Rolls, Lord Evershed, sought to explain what 'the company as a whole' meant by reference to whether the proposal was in the interest of a hypothetical member of the company not directly concerned in the contentious proposal. Given the uncertainty surrounding the nature of this test, and the fact that G was unsuccessful in his action, it is difficult to find much support for a general objective duty cast upon shareholders to act *bona fide*, etc. However, limited support for such a duty can be found in two first instance decisions—*Re Holders Investment Trust (1971)* (majority to consider interests of minority in deciding whether to vary class rights) and *Clemens v Clemens Brothers Ltd (1976)* (majority not able to issue further shares to deprive minority of negative voting control).

It seems improbable that H will be able to challenge the 'consequential amendments', which, even if the benefit of the company test applies, appear to be in the best interests of the company both subjectively and objectively. The statutory remedy for disadvantaged shareholders, s 459 CA 1985, may provide a remedy for H, but the courts have set their face against using the section to provide a remedy for shareholders who object to the board's *bona fide* actions if they do not impinge upon the 'legitimate expectations' of the shareholder; see for example, *Re A Company (No 002567 of 1982) (1983)*, the wine bar case mentioned above, and *Re Saul Harrison & Sons plc (1995)*. In the latter case, Hoffman LJ accepted, however, that there are cases where the memorandum and articles do not represent the understandings upon which the shareholders are associated and, in such cases, it may be unfair applying equitable considerations to a shareholder for those who control a company to exercise the powers set out in the memorandum and articles if to do so denies the legitimate expectations of the shareholder. He gives an example: the widow of a joint venturer might have legitimate expectations about the benefits she should receive from the company founded by her deceased husband.

The final complaint put forward by H concerns her dismissal as company secretary. H will have considerable difficulty, as we have seen, in blocking an amendment of the articles to delete this provision; but she may have an action for damages if the amendment (or dismissal without the amendment) is a breach of contract. However, H may not have an enforceable contract—there is no difficulty if she has a service contract independent of the articles (which is improbable) but, if she wishes to rely on the articles as providing the contract, she faces two difficulties. First, a contract based on the articles changes if the articles are validly altered (*Read v Astoria Garage Ltd (1952)*); and, second, even if the articles are not altered, it is unlikely that they give H an enforceable contractual right. The traditional view (which derives from the decision of Astbury J in *Hickman v Kent or Romney Marsh Sheepbreeders' Association (1915)*) is that a shareholder can enforce the articles only insofar as the relevant article creates a 'membership' right, that is, a right attaching to each and every share which relates to the holding of shares. It would seem that a right vested in only some of the membership is not such a right. For example, in *Eley v Positive Life Assurance Co (1876)*, where the articles provided that E was to be company solicitor for life, E was held to have no contractual right of employment as solicitor. There seems little comfort for Helen here.

In conclusion, one can advise H that, with the exception of the expropriation of shares, her only chance of blocking the dissipation of the traditional business of the company lies in s 459 CA 1985, but even this seems a forlorn hope.

▌NOTE

Reform of the nature of a company's constitution and a company's objects is contained in the Companies Act 2006. For example, when in force, companies will no longer be required to have an objects clause, or if it is desired for a company to have objects, they will be located in the company's articles. The provisions are aimed at both new and existing companies.

Question 10

In 1998, Robin, Swan and Turkey incorporated their existing printing business as Birdsong Ltd. They each hold 17% of the share capital and are the directors of the company. Four employees of the company each hold 5% of the share capital and the remaining shares are unissued.

The articles of the company depart from Table A in the following respects:

(a) Robin, Swan and Turkey are named as directors for life and may only be removed by special resolution.

(b) On a vote to remove a director, that director would be entitled to three votes per share.

(c) In the event of any additional shares being issued, such shares must be offered to existing shareholders in proportion to their then shareholding.

The directors have decided to restructure the business and many processes will, in future, require appreciably less staff than at present. In addition, machinery will be sold off. The employees are opposed to the restructuring and consequent reduction in the workforce and consider the price proposed for the sale of machinery to be a gross undervalue. The directors propose to allot the unissued shares at a high price, knowing that it is unlikely that the employees will have the funds to purchase them.

Advise the employees.

Answer plan

- Consider whether the shareholder-employees can in law block the restructuring either as employees or as shareholders.
- Can the shareholder-employees question the sale of assets, either as employees or shareholders?
- Look at the terms in the articles relating to the directors—can they be sacked or can pressure be put on them to abandon the restructuring?
- Finally, appraise the proposed allotment.

Answer

(a) Locus standi

The employees are seeking advice about the restructuring of their company. The first issue to consider is whether they have any *forum* for objection or *locus* to object either as employees or as shareholders in the company. While the Companies Act (CA) requires the directors to have regard to the interests of employees in performing their functions as directors (s 309 CA 1985), it does not give the employees *locus* to object to decisions of the directors and shareholders. Obviously, the employees can make their feelings known, but they have no status in company law. The employees who are also shareholders are in a different position: they are members of the company and can attend company meetings and vote on resolutions. However, a restructuring of the business by the board does not require approval by the shareholders unless it necessitates a change in the memorandum or articles for which a special resolution would be required. For example, if the restructuring needed a change in the objects of the company, a special resolution would be necessary (s 4 CA 1985). The employees have sufficient votes to block a special resolution (20 out of the 71 issued). If no shareholder approval is required, it is likely that the restructuring falls within the general power to manage the company vested in the board by Art 70 of Table A.

Can the shareholder-employees require a meeting to be held to discuss their objections? Section 368 CA 1985 permits members holding not less than 10% of the issued share capital to require the directors to call an Emergency General Meeting. On receipt of such a requisition, the directors have 21 days to call a meeting to discuss those matters specified in the requisition. Thus, the shareholder-employees can obtain a meeting. Can they do anything more?

(b) Restructuring

At the meeting, the shareholder-employees can raise their objections to the restructuring but cannot block it; nor have they the power to sack the board (a simple majority is required—s 303 CA 1985). They could argue that the proposals are unfairly prejudicial to them, but the courts have been reluctant to use s 459 CA 1985 where there is a dispute between shareholders as to the policies of the company with no allied impropriety. For example, in *Re Saul Harrison & Sons plc (1995)*, a shareholder failed to prevent the directors of a company, who had substantial assets but a revenue deficit, from continuing to operate the company, rather than, as she wished, winding up the company and distributing its assets. The Court of Appeal held that unfairness for the purposes of s 459 CA 1985 was primarily governed by the memorandum and articles of the company and, if they had been complied with, the section was unlikely to be operative. Here, the majority of shareholders (the directors) approve the new policies, so the fact that it does not suit others is unlikely to give the disgruntled individuals a remedy. If, however, the directors are exercising their powers of management for an improper purpose, an action under s 459 CA 1985 might succeed.

(c) Sale of assets

The shareholder-employees could try to argue that the sale of an asset at an undervalue, if proven, might be evidence of impropriety and thus strengthen the s 459 claim. Is the proposed sale of an asset a breach of company law or in some way improper? Since the articles of the company incorporate Table A and thus, by virtue of Art 70, the directors are the people who run the company, subject only to the direction of the general meeting by special resolution, there can be no doubt that the directors *prima facie* have the power to deal with the assets of the company. Wrongful dealing with the assets of a company by the directors is a breach of directors' duty. However, since this duty is owed to the company (*Percival v Wright (1902)*), a shareholder has no right to sue the directors for their action because it is well established by the famous case of *Foss v Harbottle (1843)* that wrongs done to a company can be litigated only by the company. Consequently, when, as here, the power to run a company is vested in the directors, it is the directors who must determine whether to initiate litigation for such wrongs, unless, as it has been argued, all the directors have committed the wrong, in which case a residual power to litigate would lie with the general meeting.

However, since the alleged wrongdoers are also the majority shareholders, there can be no question of the shareholders using their residual power to instruct the directors to sue. It is this difficulty which has led to the possibility of a minority shareholder bringing a derivative claim in the company's name where the wrong done to the company is of the requisite type and the wrongdoers control the company. However, it is not very likely that the alleged wrong is of the appropriate type to permit a minority shareholder action. If the allegation is that the directors are selling corporate assets at an undervalue, that is, an allegation of negligence, it would seem that the case of *Pavlides v Jensen (1956)* (where a mine was sold for approximately one-fifth of its value and it was held that the shareholders had no *locus* to sue in company's name) precludes a shareholder from acting in the name of the company. A different conclusion might be reached if the majority directors were benefiting from the sale, for this would constitute equitable fraud. For example, in *Daniels v Daniels (1978)*, a minority shareholder had *locus* to sue, on behalf of the company, a director who had sold an asset to herself which she later resold at a profit of £115,000. Unless there is an element of fraud, it seems that there is no remedy for the sale of the asset at an undervalue.

(d) Articles of association

We must now turn to the provisions in the articles relating to the terms of employment of the directors; first, the weighted voting clause which effectively renders a director impregnable unless all other shareholders vote to dismiss him (he has 51 votes and the rest of the issued shares could muster 54) using s 303 CA 1985. Despite powerful objections, it is well established that a weighted voting clause of this type is valid (*Bushell v Faith (1970)*), at least in companies of this type—small and private. Such a clause could be deleted using the procedure set out in s 9 CA 1985, which states that a company can change its articles by special resolution. However, this would require all the shareholders except a single director to vote in favour of the change, which may be difficult to achieve. The court is even less likely to upset the clause than in *Bushell*, since, even with the clause, s 303 CA 1985 is not nullified, as all the shareholders together could dismiss any one director. Nor will the fact that the directors' service contracts exceed five years (contrary to s 319 CA 1985) aid the shareholders. It may be that the contracts were approved in advance by the shareholders in general meeting—in which case they are unchallengeable—but, even if this is not the case, the breach of s 319 CA 1985 does not automatically avoid the contracts. The effect of a breach of s 319 CA 1985 is thought to be that the service contract remains in place but becomes terminable by reasonable notice. This notice is given by the company and it is the directors of the company who determine the company's decision to give notice.

(e) Allotment

Finally, can the shareholder-employees block the proposed allotment of shares? Whether it is the board or the general meeting which has the power to allot shares (s 80 CA 1985 vests the power in the general meeting unless and until revested in the board), the three directors between them can control the general meeting, and so they, as the general meeting or the board, have the power to allot these shares.

Section 89 CA 1985 requires shares to be offered to existing shareholders in the proportion of their current holding; this the directors seem willing todo, confident that the shareholders cannot take up the offer. Even if the pre-emption right was ignored, the allotment would be valid and the disadvantaged shareholders would be limited to an action for damages. An alternative course would be for the directors to offer the shares in return for non-cash consideration when the pre-emption right is inapplicable. However, the ability of the directors to allot shares is subject to the requirement that the directors, as fiduciaries, exercise their power *bona fide* for the benefit of the company and for a proper purpose (*Bamford v Bamford (1970)*). The so called proper purpose test has been interpreted by the courts as giving judges the power to determine the purpose for which a power has been allocated to the directors by the shareholders and to strike down any attempt to use the relevant power for other purposes. Thus, in *Bamford v Bamford*, the Court of Appeal ruled that an attempt to block a takeover bid by allotting shares to associates was an improper use of directors' powers. In a case similar to this one, *Pennell v Venida (1974)*, a rights issue which the directors knew could not be taken up by one impoverished shareholder was struck down as designed to emasculate the shareholder who objected to certain proposals by the board.

While, *prima facie*, these cases seem to stymie the directors, there is no doubt that an act which is for a collateral purpose can be ratified by the company in general meeting by ordinary resolution (*Bamford v Bamford (1970)*; *Hogg v Cramphorn (1967)*), and the majority could achieve this. While ratification of the rights issue may be possible, it would seem to be an obvious case for an application under s 459 CA 1985. While a blatant attempt to emasculate one group of shareholders appears to be a clear case of unfair prejudice which would leave a court with an unfettered discretion to devise an appropriate remedy, it might be thought that the shareholders in this case were merely trying to impose their view of the company's future on the majority and, consequently, the s 459 application could fail. If an action were to succeed, the most likely remedy would be an order for the purchase, by the majority shareholders or the company, of the dissenting member's shares.

In conclusion, the position of the employees appears less than hopeful.

Question 11

(a) 'Corporate power lies with the board of directors.' Comment on this proposition.

(b) The shares of Rail Nostalgia Ltd are owned equally by its five shareholders, A, B, C, D and E. A, B and C make up the board of the company. The company needed to purchase iron chairs and agreed to buy them from Alpha Bros, of which A is a partner. A disclosed to the board that he was a partner of Alpha Bros but did not reveal that he would receive a commission on the sale. On discovering the truth, D proposed to the board that the company should seek to rescind the purchase, but the board refuse to do so. At a subsequent general meeting, D and E vote to take legal action against A but the board have refused to act. What is the legal position?

Answer plan

Two part questions always call for effective time management. It is to be hoped that such questions allow for cross-referencing, which should ameliorate the time problem.

Part (a) is essentially a description of the division of power within a company, with a concluding paragraph to be added as comment.

Part (b) involves a possible breach of director's duty by A. As with any such question, the general issue of *locus standi* arises, while the final issue is a specific question as to the ability or inability of the general meeting to instruct the board to initiate litigation.

Answer

(a) Corporate power

The shareholders are the owners of the shares of a company and can, generally, do what they wish with their property. They are free to run the company as they see fit (subject to the rules of company law), either in person or by appointing representatives to act on their behalf. In practice, the shareholders appoint such representatives—a board of directors. The directors of a company may be co-extensive with the shareholders (for example, in small family owned and run companies), be existing shareholders on appointment (majority or minority), acquire shares on appointment, or own no shares in the company. When the shareholders in general meeting and the board are not co-extensive, even if there is an overlap in membership, there is potential for conflict. The issue that then arises is who makes the decisions for the company.

Early cases suggested that the power to run a company must be vested in its members—the shareholders—but the Court of Appeal in *Automatic Self-Cleansing Filter Syndicate Co Ltd v Cunninghame (1906)* made it clear that the division of power between the board and the shareholders in general meeting depended on the articles of the company. Where the articles had vested power in the board, it was the board, said the court, and the board alone which ran the company. This view was affirmed by later cases including the House of Lords' decision in *Quin & Axtens v Salmon (1909)*, and it is now well settled that, where the articles give the power to manage to the board (for example, Art 70 of Table A), they have an exclusive power to do so, subject only to the provisions of company law and any restrictions upon their powers contained in the articles themselves. This does not mean that the board's authority is inalienable; a power given in the articles can be amended or deleted by altering the articles. However, alteration of the articles requires a special resolution (a three-quarters majority of those present and voting—s 9 CA 1985), so that changing the articles is not easy; indeed, if the board members hold 25% or more of the votes, it is impossible without the agreement of the board.

Where the general meeting is unable to alter the articles, the drastic step of dismissing all or some of the directors and the substitution of more pliable office holders might be possible. Section 303 CA 1985 provides that the general meeting can dismiss a director by ordinary resolution (that is, at least 50% of those present and voting). While easier to achieve than amendment of the articles, dismissal of the directors, even where possible, will leave any new directors with the same powers of management as those possessed by the former board. Moreover, directors of small companies can effectively nullify s 303 CA 1985 by the use of a weighted voting clause, which gives their shares extra votes where there is a proposal to dismiss a director (*Bushell v Faith (1970)*). Such a clause could be deleted using the procedure set out in s 9 CA 1985 but this requires a special resolution.

Consequently, one can conclude that the board is not susceptible to the control of the general meeting *unless* the articles provide a method of control.

Since 1906, the majority of companies have adopted the relevant provision of Table A to determine the division of power between the general meeting and the board: the current provision is Art 70. This provides that, 'Subject to the provisions of the Act, the memorandum and the articles and to any directions given by special resolution, the business of the company shall be managed by the directors who may exercise all the powers of the company.' Thus, it can be seen that the shareholders can give the directors instructions on how to manage—but only in compliance with any particular provision in the articles or by special resolution. Where directions are given, they cannot invalidate any prior act of the directors (Art 70) but can, presumably, instruct the directors not to implement that prior act if it is still executory. The wording of Art 70 seems also to allow the shareholders to instruct the directors to undertake a course of action which the board had resolved not to pursue. It might be thought peculiar that the board can be sacked by ordinary resolution but cannot be instructed other than by special resolution, particularly where the company is small or of the quasi-partnership type, and it has been suggested that model articles for such companies might depart from Art 70 and allow more day to day control over directors by the general meeting.

From the above discussion, it can be concluded that the board always runs the company, but, where the board cannot or will not exercise the power vested in it, the general meeting regains, at least temporarily, the power to run the company. For example, in *Barron v Potter (1914)*, the two directors of the company were not on speaking terms and board meetings could not be held—the power to conduct the company's affairs vested in the shareholders until an effective board was in place. Note that the default powers of the general meeting operate only where the board is completely incapable of acting and not when a minority of directors use their powers to block a decision by the majority of the board (see, for example, *Breckland Group Holdings v London & Suffolk Properties (1989)*), for, in the latter case, the board is precluded from acting by the operation of the articles, not by an incapacity to act. Moreover, in a limited number of cases, it seems that an individual shareholder can commence legal proceedings on behalf of the company even if that is not the wish of the board or the general meeting (the fraud on the minority exception to *Foss v Harbottle (1843)*).

This is a situation where shareholders might be wise to agree to a shareholder agreement which could provide remedies against the other shareholders, even if it did not bind the company.

(b) Rail Nostalgia Ltd

Rail Nostalgia has articles in the form of Table A (s 8 CA 1985), so that the directors have the power to manage the company (Art 70). The directors of the company, A, B and C, own 60% of the shares of the company and are, while united, immune from dismissal or the giving of directions as to how the company should be run. As directors, they owe duties of care and skill commensurate with their abilities and qualifications (if any), fiduciary duties and certain statutory duties; these duties are generally owed to the company and not to the shareholders (*Percival v Wright (1902)*). In this case, D and E are seeking to initiate litigation against A, alleging that, in breach of his director's duty, he failed to make adequate disclosure of the circumstances surrounding the contract to buy iron chairs from A. Any attempt to sue a director raises two issues: first, who has the *locus* to sue; and, second, is there a breach of duty?

Since a breach of duty by a director is a wrong done to the company, the person who can sue the director is the company. The relevant body to determine whether to sue is the body with the power to run the company—in this case, the board (Art 70 of Table A). Consequently, it might be concluded that, since the board is not in favour of litigation, A is immune from suit. Certainly, D and E cannot instruct the board how to act (only 40% are shareholding, whereas 75% are required to give directions), nor could they sack A, B and C. Where the company declines to sue, the rule in *Foss v Harbottle (1843)* generally precludes litigation by a minority shareholder. However, where a wrong done by a director who exercises control over the company can be categorised as 'fraud', the courts may permit a shareholder to bring an action on behalf of the company to vindicate the company's rights (a derivative claim), since the wrongdoer is hardly likely to sue himself. If a derivative claim is permitted it cannot be blocked by the directors and the litigant may be able to claim an indemnity for his costs (*Wallersteiner v Moir (1975)*).

A derivative action can be brought only where the wrongdoer has acted fraudulently, but fraud in this context embraces a general lack of *bona fides* and an apparent lack of fair dealing, in addition to legal fraud. For example, in *Daniels v Daniels (1978)*, a shareholder was given *locus* to sue a director who had sold land to herself at an alleged undervalue. Templeman J ruled that a director who was negligent might not be the subject of a derivative action but that a director whose negligence resulted in a profit of £115,000 to herself could be so liable. In this case, the 'wrongdoers' control the company (by virtue of both Art 70 and their 60% shareholding). In *Smith v Croft (No 2) (1988)*, Knox J further refined the notion of control by ruling that the crucial issue is whether the claimant is being 'improperly prevented from bringing these proceedings on behalf of the company'. He then concluded that, where an independent organ of the company rather than a wrongdoer was blocking litigation, the shareholder had no right to drag the company into litigation—the denial of proceedings was entirely proper. This does not seem to apply here and, presumably, a derivative action could be brought. What, then, is the 'wrong' committed by A and ignored by B and C?

A, as a director, has a fiduciary duty to ensure that there is no conflict between his duty to the company and his own personal interest. One area where the possibility of such conflict arises is when a director benefits either directly or indirectly from a contract made by the company of which he is a director. In *Aberdeen Rly Co v Blaikie Bros (1854)*, the House of Lords ruled that a director cannot benefit from a contract entered into by the company, even if the contract is perfectly fair. This strict approach was extended to indirect contractual benefits, as in this case, by *Imperial Mercantile Credit Association v Coleman (1873)*. However, directors are not trustees and they are not prohibited from benefiting from their directorship, *provided that* any benefit is revealed in advance to the shareholders or, where permitted, to some other relevant body. Where there is no disclosure, the transaction is voidable at the company's option (*Hely-Hutchinson v Brayhead (1968)*). This company has adopted Art 85 of Table A, which provides that the contractual benefit to a director will be valid if disclosed to the board. Statute has limited this principle by declaring that disclosure must additionally comply with s 317 CA 1985. Here, A has declared his interest to the board in compliance with Art 85 but has failed to comply with s 317 CA 1985, in that he has not declared the nature of his interest. For failing to comply with s 317 CA 1985, A is liable to a fine and, under the general law, the relevant contract is voidable, albeit at the option of the company (that is, the board can ratify and A can vote). In addition to a possible breach of s 317 CA 1985, the transaction might be a substantial property transaction, in which case A must comply with s 320 CA 1985, that is, disclose his interest to the general meeting or run the risk that the transaction will be invalidated by s 322 CA 1985, if avoided by the company. This, however, seems unlikely.

In conclusion, it seems that D and E may have *locus standi* to sue in the company's name, but that, should they seek so to do, A, B and C will simply ratify the disputed transaction, leaving no wrong in respect of which litigation could proceed.

▌NOTE

Some further discussion of s 320 CA 1985 could be useful.

Question 12

Christie Ltd was incorporated in 1999. The articles of the company contain the following provisions:

1　So long as he remains a member, Marple shall be entitled to be a director of the company and to be the company secretary.

2　Marple shall be paid such remuneration as a director as the board shall determine and he shall be paid not less than £20,000 per annum as company secretary.

Marple holds 15% of the issued shares of the company, the remainder being held by his brothers, Battle and Poirot. The three brothers are the only directors of the company but Poirot takes no active part in management. Marple quarrels with Battle over the future of the company: Battle enters into an agreement with Poirot whereby, in consideration of a payment of £10,000, Poirot agrees to vote with Battle at all board and general meetings. After appropriate notice, an Extraordinary General Meeting is held and Art 1 is deleted by special resolution.

The remuneration of the directors has never been fixed; Marple received about £75,000 in total for the years 1999–2001 'for services rendered'. He received no money in 2002 for his services as a director of the company but has always been paid for his work as company secretary. The company is profitable but has never declared a dividend.

Marple is worried about his position and seeks your advice. Advise him.

Answer plan

Marple has, presumably, a number of concerns. First, the deletion of the article by virtue of which he had a right to be a director and to be the company secretary. Second, has he any entitlement to be paid while he continues to act as director and/or company secretary, and has he any claim for the period prior to the amendment of the articles? Third, is the voting agreement between Battle and Poirot valid?

In addition to any specific remedy open to Marple, consideration should also be given to overall remedies, for example, use of s 459 CA 1985 or, less likely, s 122(1)(g) of the Insolvency Act (IA) 1986.

Answer

In advising Marple (M), consideration must be given to his specific concerns relating to the change of articles, but also to the possibility of a more general remedy being open to him.

(a) Deletion of Art 1

Companies have an unfettered right to amend their articles by special resolution (s 9 CA 1985). M lacked a sufficient shareholding to block the passing of a special resolution to amend the articles of the company, so the deletion of Art 1 appears unchallengeable. However, shareholders, in voting to amend the articles, may not have an unfettered right to cast their votes with regard only to their own interests. There are *dicta* in the cases which suggest that, on a vote to change the articles, the shareholders (Battle and Poirot, hereafter B and P) must vote '*bona fide* for the benefit of the company' (*Allen v Gold Reefs of West Africa Ltd (1900)*). Could this apply in this case, so that M could seek the reinstatement of Art 1? There are two objections to such a proposal. First, the scope of this *dictum* is uncertain, although it is clear that, where the proposed change of articles is designed to appropriate the shares of the minority, the court will strike down the amendment unless it is objectively in the best interests of the company. For example, in *Dafen Tinplate Ltd v Llanelly Steel Co (1920)*, an amendment to the articles which allowed any shareholder to be required to sell his shares in the company was rejected by the court as going beyond that which was necessary to benefit the company. However, whether there is a *general* requirement that shareholders vote on proposals to alter the articles in a manner which is objectively in the best interests of the company is uncertain. In addition, B and P could argue that this proposal *is* in the best interests of the company.

A further argument of which M should be apprised is that the deletion of this article may not affect his rights, in that Art 1 gave him no rights! B and P could then argue that, since M was no worse off, there could be no objection to the deletion of Art 1. Certainly, despite Art 1, M could have been sacked by ordinary resolution (s 303 CA 1985). Where dismissal using the statutory format constitutes a breach of contract, the sacked director would be entitled to compensation. However, if Art 1 did not give M any enforceable contractual rights as a director, M would be no worse off if he was dismissed by ordinary resolution before or after the deletion of Art 1. M might try to argue that Art 1 created a contract between himself and the company, which entitled him to be both a director and company secretary, because s 14 CA 1985 provides that the articles constitute a contract between the shareholders and the company. However, the scope of the s 14 contract and the ability of M to enforce it in his capacity as director/secretary is likely to disappoint him. The traditional view is that a shareholder can enforce the articles by virtue of s 14 CA 1985 only insofar as the relevant article creates a 'membership' right, that is, a right attaching to each and every share and which relates to the holding of shares. This view derives from the decision of Astbury J in *Hickman v Kent or Romney Marsh Sheepbreeders' Association (1915)* and would appear to preclude the enforcement of a right which does not fall into this category. In this case, it is difficult to see that a right conferred on M to be a director or to be company secretary could be regarded as a membership right. For example, in *Eley v Positive Life Assurance Co (1876)*, where the articles provided that E was to be company solicitor for life, E was held to have no contractual right of employment as solicitor and, in *Beattie v E & F Beattie Ltd (1938)*, a provision requiring members to submit disputes to arbitration was held not to apply to a dispute between the company and a shareholder in respect of his directorship.

(b) Entitlement to be paid

While M continues to act as company secretary, he is entitled to be paid for this work. If he has a service contract, that will define his entitlement. If M had an express service contract in respect of his role as company secretary, the deletion of Art 1 would have no effect on that contract and any attempt to dismiss him in breach of the independent contract would allow M to sue for damages. Any amendment of Art 2 could not affect a separate service contract or any entitlement already earned (*Swabey v Port Darwin Gold Mining Co Ltd (1889)*). Section 9 CA 1985 could be used by B and P to amend the articles (for example, to change the salary in Art 2), even if the amendment resulted in breach of M's service contract, although damages would then be payable (*Southern Foundries (1926) Ltd v Shirlaw (1940)*). If the terms of M's service contract are expressed to be as set out in the articles, any amendment of the articles would amend the service contract (*Read v Astoria Garage Ltd (1952)*). If he has a service contract whose terms on the relevant issue (in this case pay) are deficient or non-existent, the articles may be treated as implied terms of the contract and, as terms, the articles would be enforceable under the normal rules of contract. If this applied here, M could rely on Art 2 to claim £20,000 a year. In such a case, it would seem that amendment of the articles does not change the service contract because the usual rule in contract is that contract terms cannot be changed without the agreement of all parties to the contract. If M has no separate contract but is relying upon s 14 CA 1985 to provide a contractual right to remuneration, he will be disappointed—see *Eley v Positive Life Assurance Co* (above)—in that the s 14 contract does not apply to rights which are not membership rights.

While M remains a director, has he any entitlement to be paid? If he has an express service contract, his rights are parallel to those outlined above in respect of his role as company secretary. If M has a service contract, the terms of which are expressly based on the articles (terms subject to change using s 9 CA 1985) or a service contract into which the articles are implied (terms subject to change only with M's consent), his entitlement to remuneration is determined by Art 2. In *Re New British Iron Co ex p Beckwith (1898)*, the directors were held entitled to claim the sum specified in the articles as remuneration because the relevant article was 'embodied in and formed part of the contract between the company and the directors'. This case was approved, *obiter*, by the House of Lords in *Guinness plc v Saunders (1990)*. If M does not have a service contract, he cannot rely on s 14 CA 1985 to confer a contractual right based on Art 2 (see the arguments above). However, even if M can claim that the article gives him a contractual right, his right is limited to that provided by the contract which, in this case, is what the board decide. Thus, if the board decide to pay M nothing, he will receive nothing. Further, the House of Lords in *Guinness v Saunders (1990)* held that, where a provision in the articles was the implied contract term as to pay, the contract term was the exclusive definition of a right to pay, even if, as in that case and here, it effectively deprived the director of any remuneration.

(c) The voting agreement

M may challenge the validity of any decisions by B and P acting as directors or shareholders, in that B has bought P's votes and P has exercised no independent judgment in voting. It has been repeatedly laid down that votes are proprietary rights which the holder can do with as he wishes and there seems little doubt that, as a shareholder, P can bind himself to vote in a particular way (*Alexander Ward & Co Ltd v Samyang Navigation Co Ltd (1975)*). However, in a limited number of cases, the courts have held that this freedom to deal with one's assets (votes) as one sees fit must be restricted in the wider interests of company law. Nevertheless, the situations where a shareholder is subject to an inalienable duty are mainly concerned with expropriation of company property or the shares of other members and do not seem to apply here. It can be concluded that in respect of the decision to delete Art 1, P's decision to sell his shareholder votes to B is unchallengeable.

The situation is different when M seeks to challenge P's sale of his votes as a director. P as a director owes fiduciary duties to the company. One duty is to act in good faith in the best interests of the company which requires the director to be free to vote at board meetings as he wishes; the director must be 'left free to exercise his best judgment in the interests of the company' (*Boulting v ACTAT (1963)*). Presumably, an agreement to fetter one's directorial discretion is a fraud on the minority, thus allowing M, a minority shareholder, to litigate. While the agreement between B and P can be challenged by M, it would appear to be binding as between B and P themselves (*Dawson International plc v Coats Paton plc (1989)*).

Not all agreements by directors to filter their discretion are improper. If the directors take a decision, *bona fide*, to act in a particular way in the future, such a decision may be perfectly proper (see, for example, *Fulham FC v Cabra Estates plc (1994)*).

(d) General remedies

Given the uncertainty of the remedies which apply to the specific difficulties faced by M, it would be wise to advise him of the possibility of pursuing a general statutory remedy. The statutory remedies open to shareholders are to apply for a just and equitable winding up under s 122(1)(g) IA 1986 or to seek a declaration of unfair prejudice under s 459 CA 1985. The just and equitable winding up route will be open to the court where the company is of the appropriate type— traditionally called a 'quasi-partnership' company—and it is plain that there is such a breakdown in the relationship of the corporators that the company cannot function as intended.

In *Ebrahimi v Westbourne Galleries Ltd (1973)*, the House of Lords ordered the winding up of a small company where one of the founder members was, lawfully, excluded from management. As in this case, the clear intention of the parties was that all would participate in running the company and all profits were paid as directors' fees and not as dividends, so that dismissal of one director from his post meant that the underlying assumptions upon which the company was founded were destroyed and winding up was necessary. Of course, winding up is a very drastic remedy and M might prefer to use s 459 CA 1985. In *Re Kenyon (Swansea) Ltd (1987)*, the court held that an attempt to exclude from management a director who had the legitimate expectation that he would continue to be involved in management was unfair prejudice. However, the fact that M hoped his involvement in management would continue may not be sufficient to found a 'legitimate expectation'. In *O'Neill v Phillips (1999)*, the House of Lords stressed that such expectations must be based on a contract independent of the memorandum and articles or where equitable considerations meant that such expectations should be honoured. If s 459 CA 1985 applied, the court could award a remedy—possibly the exclusion of B from management or, more likely, an order for the company to buy M's share at a fair price.

CHAPTER 3

THE COMPANY AND OUTSIDERS

INTRODUCTION

A company, if it engages in any business at all, must necessarily have dealings with persons who are not members of the company and may have dealings with members in a non-member capacity (for example, many shareholders of Sainsbury Ltd buy their groceries from the company). It is the ability of the company to deal with outsiders and the legal implications of such dealing that this chapter addresses.

There are two main issues. First, what is the company entitled to do in its capacity as a company and, if there are restrictions on its power to operate, what is the effect of overstepping these constraints? Second, since a company exists only as a matter of law and must necessarily act through human agents, what is the position where the human agent engages in an activity on behalf of the company which the company was authorised to do but which the agent was not authorised to transact on the company's behalf?

In both of these areas, there has been a considerable amount of statutory tinkering with the common law rules. With respect to the first issue (the powers of the company), this has simplified the law, but, in the second (the ability of individuals to bind the company), the law is something of a mess.

Checklist

Students should be familiar with:

- the rules relating to the determination of the powers of a company and the consequences of non-compliance with any limitations on these powers (*ultra vires*);
- the rules relating to the ability of representatives of the company (or those purporting to represent the company) to bind the company.

The latter issue overlaps with the provisions pertaining to the liability of a director for breach of his duty.

Question 13

The Consultation Document from the Company Law Reform Steering Group (*Modern Company Law for a Competitive Economy: Company Formation and Capital Maintenance* (London: DT1, 1999)) posed the following question:

> Do you agree that a company should henceforth have unlimited capacity, regardless of anything in its constitution, including its objects, but a member should continue to be able to take proceedings to restrain the doing of an act contrary to the constitution?

Discuss.

Answer plan

In answering this question, a student should consider:

- the history and purpose of the objects clause;
- the current law;
- the effect of unlimited capacity;
- the position of the shareholders; and
- the changes introduced by the Companies Act (2006).

Answer

Currently, every registered company must have a memorandum of association, which must be submitted to the Registrar of Companies prior to registration. Although not in force, the Companies Act 2006 substitutes one document—the constitution—for the memorandum and articles. The Companies Act (CA) 1985 specifies the minimum content of the memorandum in s 2 of the Act. Section 2(1)(c) CA 1985 provides that the memorandum must state the 'objects of the company', a provision which has been present in company legislation since 1856. The model memoranda in the Tables, designed to provide a pattern for company promoters, show that the intention was that the objects should be few and should specify the business which the company intended to pursue but not the means by which the business was to be run. Thus, the Tables did (and do) not envisage a listing of such things as 'this company can borrow money or enter into leases or purchase items necessary to facilitate the achievement of our specified object'. The legal effect of the objects clause was determined by the House of Lords in the famous case of *Ashbury Railway Carriage Co v Riche (1875)*, in which R sued the company for money owing to him in respect of his supervision of a project entered into by the company to build a railway in Belgium. The company sought to deny liability for this debt by pointing out that the objects of the company were to build railway rolling stock and not railways, and asking the court to hold that the objects clause defined the contractual capacity of the company, thus denying the company the capacity to engage in contracts relating to building railways. The House of Lords accepted the company's argument and held that since the company did not in law have the ability to enter into a contract to build a railway, it could have no capacity to employ R to supervise such a project—it was beyond the powers of the company, that is, it was *ultra vires*. Consequently, R had no contract and no contractual right to be paid.

The rationale behind this decision was that shareholders and creditors must know what they were putting their money into; if you invested in a company which said it was going to build railway carriages, you were entitled to expect it to be used for that purpose alone. While this might be true of shareholders, although one might argue that they would have no objection to their money being used in non-authorised but profitable purposes, it is difficult to see how this rule protects creditors. One could say that creditors whose debts are incurred in the company pursuing authorised debts are protected by the inability of the company to waste its money on paying debts incurred on unauthorised business, but this is a somewhat remote benefit. Interestingly enough, the decision in *Ashbury* was no more popular with companies than it was with *Riche*, and means were soon adopted to try to evade the effect of the decision. This unpopularity stemmed from the fact that a company might expand into new areas without realising the need to amend its objects so that the company, or others who had financed the change of direction, would find that they had entered into a series of unenforceable transactions. More aware directors might feel constrained as to the type of business the company could pursue. The difficulties of the rule itself are compounded by the doctrine of constructive notice, which means that the objects clause, once registered, is constructively (that is, in law) notified to everyone. Thus, a person who made transactions with a company cannot claim not to know that a transaction was not within the company's objects since, in law, he knew the contents of the objects clause. The doctrine of constructive notice in relation to the objects clause was abolished by s 711A CA 1985, as introduced by the CA 1989. The section, however, is not in force, but its absence does not appear to cause any appreciable difficulty for a third party due to the general reform of the *ultra vires* doctrine by the CA 1989.

Companies sought means to evade the effect of the rule. This self-help approach generally took the form of adopting extremely long objects clauses, embracing everything the founders of the company and their advisers could think of with a view to authorising every conceivable activity. The judicial attitude to such self-help was mixed. In *Cotman v Brougham (1918)*, the House of Lords reluctantly accepted the validity of an objects clause authorising the company to do almost anything. However, in later cases such as *Re Introductions (1970)*, the Court of Appeal held that a list of registered 'objects' could be divided by the courts into 'true' objects and mere powers. A mere power did not give the company an absolute right to do something; it only gave a right to do something provided it promoted a true object. The situation was a mess. The rule existed but companies sought to evade it—sometimes with success and sometimes without. Neither shareholders nor creditors seemed to be protected by the rule. Parliament sought to amend the effect of the *ultra vires* rule in a series of statutory reforms. Initially, a company remained authorised to engage in activities which were permitted by its registered objects, but a third party dealing with a company could, if certain conditions were satisfied, enforce an *ultra vires* contract. The current law can be found in ss 3A, 4 and 35 CA 1985.

Despite the recommendations of the Prentice Report, the Act does not abolish *ultra vires* either wholly or in part; rather it mitigates and marginalises the rule. Four sections which were inserted into the 1985 Act are relevant. First, s 3A CA 1985, which might ultimately have rendered the *ultra vires* rule obsolete for all but charitable companies. This section provides that a company can adopt as its object 'to carry on business as a general commercial company' and then says that in such a case the company has as its object 'to carry on any trade or business whatsoever'. This section, which overturns case law that had rejected similar objects clauses, is strangely worded but it clearly allows a company to adopt a general object so that a company which has such an object can be authorised to do practically anything. This general objects clause cannot be adopted by non-commercial companies, for example charities. Section 3A CA 1985 then confirms the common law by adding that such a company 'has power to do all such things as are incidental or conducive to the carrying on of any trade or business by it' (s 3A(b) CA 1985). Section 3A CA 1985 appears to be couched in objective terms so that companies using s 3A CA 1985 may register an additional object allowing the pursuance of activities which the directors believe to be incidental to the carrying on of trade or business. Section 3A CA 1985 allows trading companies to adopt an object which authorises the pursuance of any lawful activity, so rendering the *ultra vires* rule moribund. However, companies have not substituted this general object for their lengthy objects clauses, they have merely added it to the list. Second, the new s 4 CA 1985 allows a company to change its objects, for example to that authorised in a s 3A clause, by special resolution. This simplifies the previous scheme for the alteration of objects and was designed to encourage existing companies to move to the new all-purpose objects clause.

Section 35 CA 1985 provides for the enforcement of *ultra vires* transactions if certain conditions are satisfied. Section 35(1) CA 1985 provides that: 'The validity of an act done by a company shall not be called into question on the ground of lack of capacity by reason of anything in the company's memorandum.' This section, if it stood alone, would have given companies legal capacity comparable to that enjoyed by natural legal persons of full age and understanding; unfortunately, it does not stand alone. While s 35(1) CA 1985 says that the validity of an act done by a company cannot be called into question on the grounds of lack of capacity by reason of anything in the memorandum, it is thought to extend to an action not mentioned by the memorandum, that is, an act not restricted by the objects clause but not authorised by it either. Further, it is assumed that the section also covers a decision not to act by the company despite the reference to an act done.

Turning to the restriction on the operation of s 35(1) CA 1985: s 35(2) CA 1985 allows a member of a company to restrain the company from doing an act which, but for s 35(1) CA 1985, would be beyond the company's capacity. For example, if the objects of the company do not authorise the company to buy property, a member can, it seems, restrain the directors from buying property on behalf of the company. This provision is designed to retain a member's ability to ensure that his investment is used in a manner authorised by the objects clause. However, s 35(2) CA 1985 is itself restricted, in that it only permits a member to restrain the directors from a proposed action unconnected to any 'legal obligation' arising. The lack of capacity on the part of the company cannot be used by a member to restrain an action entered into by the directors on behalf of the company. Thus, a shareholder can stop a contract which it is proposed shall be entered into but cannot stop the carrying out of a contract which has been entered into.

Perhaps to reinforce the idea that a member should have some control over the use of his money, s 35(3) CA 1985 provides that the shareholders can by special resolution ratify a transaction which would be beyond the capacity of the company but for s 35(1) CA 1985. This allows shareholders to decide whether to authorise, albeit retrospectively, the company to spend their money on *ultra vires* activities. If the shareholders do not ratify a transaction entered into by the company, s 35(1) CA 1985 still protects the person dealing with the company. The failure of the directors to observe the objects clause is a breach of directors' duty and ratification of their action does not absolve the directors from liability. However, the shareholders can absolve the directors from liability by special resolution.

These statutory changes reduced the effect of the objects clause in a way which self-help could never achieve, even though they did not apply to statutory companies and registered charitable companies. Even with these changes there was one minor area where the objects clause, theoretically, retained some life—the *substratum* rule. This rule allows a shareholder to wind up the company where the company could no longer achieve its registered object (*Re German Date Coffee Co (1882)*). Since companies now adopt very long objects clauses setting out a mass of objects and have the option of using the s 3A object, it is difficult to imagine this rule operating in many circumstances.

In the light of the difficulties associated with the *ultra vires* rule and the complexity of the statutory reforms, the Company Law Steering Group proposed that private companies should no longer have an objects clause and would have unlimited capacity (a reform which has been applied to limited liability partnerships by the Limited Liability Partnerships Act 2000). Public companies must retain an objects clause because of the wording of the Second EC Directive on Company Law. Although, to date, not in force, the Companies Act 2006 abolishes the objects clause and this seems an entirely sensible suggestion. The *ultra vires* rule was designed to have an internal effect (to allow members to know where their money was going), but there is no need for this rule of internal management to have any effect on third parties who deal with the company. However, the Steering Group wished to retain the ability of shareholders to restrain the doing of an act contrary to the constitution of the company. The Companies Act 2006 simply provides that a company will have unlimited capacity but does not preclude the constitution restricting the power of the directors to engage in certain transactions. Hence, directors will be required to comply with constitutional restrictions or be in breach of their duties.

It seems entirely sensible that shareholders can restrain the actions of directors in appropriate cases, but this does raise the usual problem with directors' duties—who enforces them and how.

Question 14

The main business of Cowell Ltd is the production of 'reality tv' game shows, as provided for in the company's objects clause. The objects clause further provides that the company has a power to borrow money for any purpose and that all the objects are to be regarded as separate and distinct.

Following a downturn in viewer ratings and wishing to exploit new opportunities, Cowell's board of directors resolve that the company should 'prepare' for the likely success that will be generated by London hosting the Olympic Games in 2012. For this purpose, the directors decide to enter into the following arrangements on behalf of the company:

(a) To borrow money from BICC Bank plc with security granted over the company's assets in favour of BICC Bank.

(b) To use the funding obtained from BICC Bank in order to purchase presses for the manufacture of gym and weight lifting equipment from Livingstone Ltd.

Following a 'due diligence' search, Livingstone is aware that Cowell's objects clause does not contain any reference to the purchase of such presses.

Apprentice Ltd, a minority shareholder of Cowell, is concerned with these activities, in particular, (a) the validity of the two contracts, (b) whether the directors have exceeded the powers of the company and (c) the fact that directors of Cowell are negotiating with potential retailers to stock the equipment after manufacture.

Advise Apprentice as to its legal position.

Answer plan

Any answer requires an analysis of the principles dealing with the capacity of the company and the board of directors to enter into binding arrangements of the kind that have taken place and the action if any that can be taken by an aggrieved shareholder. Owing to the reform of the doctrine of *ultra vires*, by the Companies Act (CA) 1985, as amended by the CA 1989, a consideration of the 'external' and 'internal' aspects of corporate transactions will need to be undertaken.

Answer

EXTERNAL ASPECTS OF CORPORATE CAPACITY

The issue that arises here is whether the transactions between Cowell (C) Ltd and BICC Bank (B) plc and between C Ltd and Livingstone (L) Ltd are valid and binding. This is an external aspect of a company's capacity to enter into transactions.

Assuming that C Ltd has not adopted a s 3A clause (s 3A CA 1985—general commercial objects clause) and that the arrangements are not covered by its objects clause, the directors of C Ltd may discover that the company's 'new' business is *ultra vires*. However, s 35(1) CA 1985 provides that no act (which includes contractual arrangements) can be questioned on the ground of any lack of capacity found in the company's constitution. Further, where an act is considered to be beyond the company's capacity, such an act can be ratified by the company in general meeting, by the passing of a special resolution (s 35(3) CA 1985), although the absence of such a resolution does not affect the validity of an act under s 35(1) CA 1985. However, the passing of a such a resolution may have an effect on a minority shareholder seeking an injunction under s 35(2) CA 1985. Therefore, from an external perspective, the contracts between C Ltd and B plc and C Ltd and L Ltd are valid and enforceable. This is because the effect of s 35(1) CA 1985 is to abolish the doctrine of *ultra vires*—there is no limitation on a company's capacity to enter into contracts.

Similarly, where an act of a company is within the company's powers but outside the powers of the directors, a third party dealing with the company can assume there is no limitation on powers of the directors or those authorised by the directors (s 35A(1) CA 1985). However, s 35A(1) CA 1985 requires that the third party is acting in good faith, but mere knowledge on the part of the third party that the directors have exceeded their powers is insufficient to amount to a lack of good faith (s 35A(2)(b) CA 1985). To that extent, L Ltd's due diligence search in uncovering the lack of powers on the part of C Ltd's directors would not affect the application of s 35A(1) CA 1985. A general meeting can approve an act of the directors which is beyond the powers of the directors by the passing of an ordinary resolution. This is the position at common law and contrasts with the statutory requirement that ratification of an act beyond the company's powers requires a special resolution (s 35(3) CA 1985). At common law, prior to reform, an *ultra vires* act could not be ratified by the members.

Section 322A CA 1985 provides a different conclusion on the issue of contractual validity where a third party to a contract with a company is a director of the company or is connected to a director of the company, although there appears to be no indication from the question that the section should apply. Under s 322A CA 1985, any transaction between the company and the director is deemed voidable, at the instance of the company, where the transaction exceeds any limitation placed on the powers of the board of directors or is beyond the powers of the company. It will cease to be voidable however where the company ratifies the transaction or some other limit to rescission operates (s 322A(5) CA 1985). The section further provides that the third party, or the directors of the company who authorised the transaction, are liable to indemnify the company for any loss or damage resulting from the transaction and to account to the company for any gain made from the transaction.

The advice to A Ltd would be that the two contracts complained of are valid and binding on C Ltd. However, s 35(2) CA 1985 preserves the common law right of a shareholder to seek an injunction to prevent a company from entering into a proposed *ultra vires* act (*Parke v Daily News Ltd (1962)*; *Simpson v Westminster Palace Hotel Co (1860)*). There is an equivalent provision under s 35A(4) CA 1985 relating to acts beyond the powers of the board of directors. Obtaining an injunction, however, is limited by (a) any 'legal obligation' arising; (b) the right of the company to ratify an *ultra vires* act by the passing of a special resolution under s 35(3) CA 1985, a course of action the company in general meeting might choose to adopt if the majority shareholder(s) were in support of the directors' actions; (c) whether the acts are beyond the company's constitution (that is, *ultra vires*);

and (d) the fact that injunctive relief is discretionary. On this basis, given that the contracts between C Ltd and B plc and C Ltd and Ltd have taken place, an injunction would not be available, Further, given these limits, an injunction preventing C Ltd entering into future transactions with retailers would be unlikely to be granted. Interestingly, the existence of s 35(2) CA 1985 (and s 322A CA 1985) demonstrate that the doctrine of *ultra vires* is still part of company law, albeit in a highly modified form. This is further the case in respect of s 35(3) CA 1985 which is discussed later.

INTERNAL ASPECTS OF CORPORATE CAPACITY

The issue that arises here is whether action can be taken by A Ltd in respect of the activities of C Ltd's directors. This is seen as an internal matter in the sense of whether A Ltd has *locus standi* to take action against the directors who may have committed a wrong against the company.

Where transactions involving third parties are valid, action can be taken against the directors for breach of duty in failing 'to observe any limitations on their powers flowing from the memorandum' (s 35(3) CA 1985) or in respect of 'any liability for exceeding their powers' (s 35A(5) CA 1985). Alternatively, the directors may have breached a general fiduciary duty or common law duty owed to the company, although the question appears to demand a consideration of the statutory duty alone. It would be worth speculating whether the directors' activities have caused any loss to be suffered by C Ltd. For the purpose of any action under s 35(3) CA 1985 or 35A(5) CA 1985, it is considered that there would need to be an examination of the company's constitution, including the objects and powers contained in the company's objects clause (s 2(1) CA 1985—requirement for a company to have an objects clause).

Despite the reform of the *ultra vires* doctrine, it is the existence of ss 35(3) and 35A(5) CA 1985 that the past rules relating to *ultra vires* may still be relevant. There have been two reported decisions on s 35A CA 1985 but they were decisions dealing with the meaning of 'person' within ss 35A(1) CA 1985 and the extent to which any third party is protected by that subsection (*Smith v Henniker-Major & Co (2002)*; *EIC Services Ltd v Phipps (2004)*). In *Smith v Henniker-Major & Co (2002)*, in a mistaken but honest, breach of the articles of association, a director entered into a contract with the company at an inquorate meeting of the board of directors and he attempted to rely on s 35A CA 1985 to validate the transaction. The Court of Appeal held, by a majority, that although a requirement for a quorum of directors was a limitation on the power of the board of directors and that s 35A CA 1985 was wide enough to include a director of the company, s 35A CA 1985 could not protect a director relying on his own mistake in order to validate something which had no validity under the company's constitution. In *EIC Services*, the Court of Appeal held that a shareholder of a company could not rely on s 35A CA 1985 in respect of an issue of shares that was beyond the powers of the directors of the company. The share issue was void and unenforceable.

A brief consideration, therefore, of these past rules might be helpful for 'internal' purposes. For instance, the insertion of a 'separate and independent objects' clause renders express powers as substantive objects (*Cotman v Brougham (1918)*; *Re Horsley & Weight (1984)*). However, despite a so-called Cotman clause, some powers remain mere ancillary powers which must be exercised in furtherance of some authorised purpose of the company (*Re Introductions (1970)*; *Re Horsley & Weight (1984)*). Another consideration might be in respect of implied powers. In *Simmonds v Heffer (1983)*, where the memorandum was silent as to the making of donations, the court held that one of two donations by a company was *intra vires*, on the ground that there was an implied power to so do, so long as the donation was in furtherance of the company's business. We have already ruled out C Ltd's objects clause containing a s 3A clause ('general commercial objects clause') but were such a clause adopted, the effect of such a clause would suggest that the directors are in not in breach of s 35(3) CA 1985 or s 35A(5) CA 1985.

Assuming liability can be established against the directors, A Ltd, as a minority shareholder, is faced with the rule in *Foss v Harbottle (1843)*, namely, that it is a matter for the company to decide whether to take action for a wrong done to the company. That would be a matter of majority rule and, therefore, the power to sue would lie either with the company's directors or with the general meeting acting in accordance with Art 70 by the passing of a special resolution instructing the directors to sue or in accordance with a default power. Therefore, any action would be a matter for the company and not a minority shareholder. An exception to the rule in *Foss v Harbottle* is where the minority shareholder can establish a 'fraud on the minority', but there are a number of procedural and substantive hurdles standing in the path of the minority shareholder in pursuing a derivative claim based on a fraud on minority. In any event, under s 35(3) CA 1985, the general meeting can waive liability incurred by the directors by the passing of a special resolution, or by the passing of an ordinary resolution in respect of any liability incurred under s 35A(5) CA 1985.

CONCLUSION

You may wish to comment on the practical as well as the legal difficulties faced by the minority shareholder in the question. Action by a minority shareholder is very difficult and any action by the company, which might satisfy the minority shareholder, would depend on the action of the majority shareholder(s). In the question we are not told whether the majority shareholder(s) feel aggrieved at the activities of the directors. Nor does the question reveal whether the majority shareholder(s) are fully supportive of the activities of the directors.

▌NOTE

A further consideration of duties generally owed by directors could be possible here, for example, the fiduciary duty to act *bona fide* in the interests of the company or the common law duty of care and skill. Another possible consideration is whether a minority shareholder could petition for relief under s 459 CA 1985 (unfair prejudice).

In contrast to acts of a company, acts of a limited liability partnership are not limited by an objects clause. By virtue of the Limited Liability Partnership Act 2000, a limited liability partnership is not required to have an objects clause and its contractual capacity is unlimited. The Companies Act 2006 contains provisions reforming the area of corporate capacity. In particular, when in force, a company will no longer be required to have an objects clause, unless it chooses to have one in the articles of association. Further, the Act provides for the abolition of the right of a shareholder to seek an injunction, but retains, where appropriate, the duty of directors to observe the constitutional powers of the company.

Question 15

Ascot is a minority shareholder and non-executive director of both Epsom Eels Ltd and Newbury Nosh Ltd, companies set up to provide catering services at racecourses. He seeks your advice about each of the following:

(a) Alf, the company secretary of Epsom Eels, has been buying alcohol from Zak. Alf has charged the alcohol to the company but he has used it in another business with which he is connected. Zak has demanded payment from the company.

(b) Bryony, a shareholder in Newbury Nosh, has written derogatory comments about the board in the press. The other directors have suggested that it would be in the best interests of the company if either they or the company purchased Bryony's shares.

(c) Charlie, a shareholder in Epsom Eels, has discovered that the company entered into a transaction which was beyond the company's powers. Charlie has insisted that the company withdraw from the transaction and wishes to initiate litigation against the directors for disregarding the constitution of the company.

Answer plan

This question addresses a number of issues conveniently set out in the three parts of the question:

(a) Is the company bound by this contract (*ultra vires* and powers of agents)?

(b) Can the company or the directors insist on Bryony selling her shares to either the directors or the company (articles)?

(c) Can Charlie insist that the company withdraws from this transaction and can he obtain a remedy for a breach of duty by the directors?

Answer

(a) Is the company bound by the alcohol contract?

Zak, the supplier of alcohol, wants to be paid. He can claim against Epsom Eels (EE) if the company was authorised to purchase alcohol and the person who negotiated the contract was authorised to act on behalf of the company in a transaction of this type. There is little doubt that EE was authorised to enter into this contract given its line of business, but even if this was not the case, Zak could enforce the contract under s 35 Companies Act (CA) 1985. However, in order to enforce the contract, Zak must also establish that Alf had authority to enter into a contract for the supply of goods.

If Alf was given express authority to purchase alcohol, then EE must pay Zak even though Alf has converted the alcohol for his own use: EE could pursue a remedy against Alf if it chose to do so. If we assume that Alf does not have express authority, then Zak must show that he had usual or ostensible authority in order to make EE liable. Usual authority can be defined as the degree of authority which it would be normal for a person occupying a particular post or office to possess. Thus, Zak needs to establish what could be regarded as 'normal' transactions which a company secretary could undertake and see whether the purchase of goods is among them. In *Panorama Developments Ltd v Fidelis Furnishing Fabrics Ltd (1971)*, the usual authority of a company secretary (the position held by Alf) was held to include the hiring of cars to transport visitors to the company's premises. Consequently, the company was liable for the car-hire charges even when the secretary had used the cars for his own purposes. In that case, the court considered that the company secretary has usual authority to run the administrative side of a company's affairs: this could involve purchasing office equipment, hiring staff and generally ensuring the smooth running of the support side of a business. Thus, Alf could be said to have usual authority to purchase goods, but probably not goods relevant to the commercial operations of EE. It seems likely that Alf did not have usual authority to enter into this transaction. Could Alf have ostensible authority? When those authorised to run a company (that is, those with actual authority) hold a person out as having authority to undertake particular tasks, then a third party who relies upon that representation is entitled to assume that the person held out has authority to act—the person held out has ostensible authority. In the important case of *Freeman & Lockyer v Buckhurst Park Properties Ltd (1964)*, the Court of Appeal laid down four conditions for ostensible authority to operate:

- a holding out
- by those with actual authority
- on which the third party relied and
- with no restrictions on the authority of the person held out (or the ability to hold out) in the company's constitution (now subject to s 35A CA 1985).

We have no evidence to suggest any holding out in respect of this purchase by those with actual authority (the board), so it seems unlikely that Alf would have ostensible authority unless Zak could show that Alf had often purchased alcohol before and that EE had happily paid up in the past. There is no doubt that the board had the power to buy alcohol and it might be possible that the articles of EE authorised delegation of board powers to others. However, Zak cannot rely on this power of delegation to claim that he assumed that the board delegated power in this respect to Alf unless he could establish that he had read (rather than having constructive notice of) the articles (*British Thomson-Houston Co Ltd v Federated European Bank Ltd (1932)*). Even if Alf did have usual or ostensible authority, EE would not be bound if the transaction was so manifestly suspicious that Zak should have inquired as to the extent of Alf's authority (*Underwood Ltd v Bank of Liverpool (1924)*: bank liable to reimburse company when director signed cheques drawn on company's account into his own account). This purchase does not seem so suspicious as to require further inquiry. In conclusion, it seems unlikely that Zak can claim repayment from EE.

(b) Can Bryony be forced to sell her shares?

It may be that the articles of the company provide that a shareholder can be required to sell his or her shares to the company (or the directors) in certain defined circumstances. If this is the case then s 14 CA 1985, which gives contractual effect to the articles, would allow the company to rely on that provision, although the court would not enforce the provision if it provided for acquisition without compensation, even if the conduct of the shareholder was detrimental to the company. However, directors who are not shareholders would not be able to enforce such a provision as individuals because they are not parties to that contract. Even if the directors were shareholders, the traditional view is that they could not enforce the articles other than in respect of provisions which related to their rights as shareholders. For example, in *Beattie v E & F Beattie Ltd (1938)*, a provision requiring members to submit disputes to arbitration did not apply to a dispute between the company and a shareholder in respect of his directorship. Whether the s 14 contract does extend to rights conferred other than in a capacity as a member remains controversial, but it seems unlikely that the directors acting for themselves could enforce such a provision in the articles.

If there is no power in the articles to require Bryony to sell her shares to the company, the company could seek to amend the articles (s 9 CA 1985) to insert such a provision. A change in the articles must be passed by special resolution. Even if Newbury Nosh (NN) succeeded in amending its articles, the courts have the power to strike down the amendment since shareholders, in voting to amend the articles, do not have an unfettered right to cast their votes with regard only to their own interests. There are *dicta* in the cases which suggest that on a vote to change the articles the shareholders must vote '*bona fide* for the benefit of the company' (*Allen v Gold Reefs of West Africa Ltd (1900)*). The scope of this *dictum* is uncertain, although it is clear that where the proposed change of articles is designed to appropriate the shares of a minority shareholder, the court will strike down the amendment unless it is in the best interests of the company. For example, in *Dafen Tinplate Ltd v Llanelly Steel Co (1920)*, an amendment to the articles allowing any shareholder to be required to sell his shares in the company was rejected by the court as going beyond that which was necessary to benefit the company. A court might not overturn insertion in the articles of the right to require shareholders whose actions are detrimental to the company to sell their shares to the company at a fair price (for example, *Sidebottom v Kershaw, Leese & Co Ltd (1920)*). However, if the company has (or acquires) such a right, the court could still rule that making derogatory comments about the board is not sufficient to allow the company to exercise that right.

(c) Has Charlie any prospects of success in his claims?

A company is required to have an objects clause (s 2(1) CA 1985). It is this clause which determines generally the contractual capacity of the company. It should be noted that the draft Companies Act abolishes this provision and gives all private companies unlimited contractual capacity, but this does not help EE at this time. We are told that the transaction about which Charlie is complaining is beyond the powers of the company, so it is *ultra vires* and at common law unenforceable by or against EE. However, the common law has been amended by s 35 CA 1985. Section 35(1) CA 1985 provides that: 'The validity of an act done by a company shall not be called into question on the ground of lack of capacity by reason of anything in the company's memorandum.' While s 35(1) CA 1985 says that the validity of an act done by a company cannot be called into question on the grounds of lack of capacity by reason of anything in the memorandum, it is thought to extend to an action not mentioned by the memorandum, that is, an act not restricted by the objects clause but not authorised by it either. Hence, it appears that the party with whom EE contracted can enforce the contract and that Charlie can do nothing to prevent it. However, s 35(2) CA 1985 allows a member of a company to restrain the company from doing an act which, but for s 35(1) CA 1985, would be beyond the company's capacity. This seems to suggest that Charlie can restrain the company from proceeding with this contract. This provision, which is designed to allow a member to ensure that his investment is used in a manner authorised by the objects clause, is itself restricted, in that it only permits a member to restrain the directors from a proposed course of action. Once a legal obligation arises, the lack of capacity on the part of the company cannot be used by a member to restrain an action entered into by the directors on behalf of the company. Thus, Charlie cannot get an injunction to prevent the company from proceeding with the disputed contract. It should also be noted that a company can ratify an *ultra vires* contract (by special resolution) if it chooses, and if the board commands sufficient votes they might choose to do this.

While Charlie may not prevent the contract from proceeding, he is entitled to complain that the actions of the directors in ignoring the objects clause are a breach of directors' duty (s 35(3) CA 1985). Even if the shareholders have ratified the transaction, this does not prevent a claim against the directors for breach of duty. However, the directors' breach is itself ratifiable and the shareholders could choose to absolve the directors from liability (again, a special resolution is required). While the directors may be in breach of duty, Charlie has to establish that he is entitled to bring an action against them—he must show that he has *locus standi*. In *Foss v Harbottle (1843)*, Wigram VC laid down the basic principle that a shareholder could not sue in respect of wrongs done to a company, since where a wrong has been done to the company, the proper claimant is the company. Hence, if disregard of the constitution of the company is a wrong done to the company, then Charlie has no right to sue on behalf of the company (there are exceptions). However, if the wrong done by the directors breaches the personal rights of a shareholder, then the wrong is done to the shareholder and he is entitled to sue them. The right of a shareholder to have his investment applied *intra vires* has always been regarded as a right vested in each and every shareholder, so that Charlie, even if he owns only one share, could bring an action against the directors. However, it is not at all clear how s 35 CA 1985 and this exception to *Foss* interrelate. Section 35(3) CA 1985 permits a breach of duty which involves the directors authorising an act beyond the company's powers to be ratified and the directors absolved from liability. If the shareholders have relieved the directors from liability under s 35(3) CA 1985, can Charlie still rely on the common law to launch proceedings? Perhaps the statute and common law can be reconciled by saying that Charlie's common law right (like some exceptions to *Foss*) is discretionary and can be exercised only where the court thinks that it is in the best interests of the company. On the other hand, it could be argued that a personal right possessed by a shareholder cannot be overridden by the votes of a majority—there are, however, other areas of company law where individual rights are subject to majority rule (for example, changes in the articles).

NOTE

The Companies Act 2006 contains a number of provisions reforming the law on corporate capacity and minority shareholder action.

Question 16

The articles of Fish Ltd state that:

(a) the board of directors may delegate all or any of its powers;

(b) any transaction with a value of £40,000 or more must have the prior approval of the company in general meeting; and

(c) company cheques must be signed by two directors.

The board, recognising that the company is in need of new business, appoints Shark to the board, with particular responsibility for marketing, and instructs him to 'make things happen'. Without reference to the rest of the board, Shark immediately organises a 'sales conference' for potential clients at a luxury hotel in the Bahamas, at a total cost of £50,000. Shark pays a deposit of £5,000 to the hotel by means of a company cheque which he alone signs, having forged the signature of a second director, since he is keen to book the conference before the hotel implements a proposed price rise.

Shark has just reported his actions to the board. The board, horrified by the proposed expenditure, wishes to dismiss him from his post of Marketing Director and terminate his directorship, and intends to cancel the conference.

Advise Shark and the luxury hotel.

How, if at all, would your answer differ if the board had organised the conference without reference to the shareholders and the shareholders objected to the cost?

Answer plan

Shark (S) and the luxury hotel have different concerns. S does not want to be dismissed from either his executive post or his office of director, or at least wants compensation for loss of office. The luxury hotel is concerned with the enforceability of the contract negotiated by S—issues of agency and effect of forgery arise. In the alternative situation, the hotel is looking at the enforceability of a contract negotiated by the board—the impact of the articles on enforceability and s 35A CA 1985 are at issue.

Answer

S's DIRECTORSHIP

S should be advised that, in forging a signature on the cheque, he has committed a serious criminal act, for which he could be prosecuted. Even if prosecution, conviction and imprisonment ensued, this would not automatically terminate his non-executive directorship, although it might well terminate his executive directorship, since he would be unable to act as an effective marketing director from prison. Indeed, his conduct might be found to be evidence of fraud, which could lead to disqualification under the Companies Direction Disqualification Act 1986. Whether prosecution or imprisonment arises, S should be informed that he has broken the terms of his executive directorship by acting as he has and that it is likely to be a breach which entitles the company to terminate his contract of service. If this is so, there is no requirement to pay compensation, so that, even if there are more than four years of the service contract to run, there will be nothing, other than salary already earned, to pay S on termination of his executive role. The power to dismiss S from his executive post is vested in the company; as in most companies, this means that the power is vested in the board of directors (Art 70 of Table A).

As to his non-executive role, this would continue unless and until terminated by the company. The articles of the company do not give the board power to dismiss a director (there is nothing in Table A to this effect), so for the board to try to do so would be ineffective. However, there is no reason why the shareholders should not dismiss S by using s 303 CA 1985. Section 303 CA 1985 allows the shareholders to dismiss a director by ordinary resolution, provided that appropriate notice of the meeting has been given and the director has had the chance to put his case to the shareholders and to speak at the meeting. The shareholders can use their powers under s 303 CA 1985 even if a director has done nothing wrong and they just feel like a change—it is not a power which must be exercised for a proper purpose. However, termination of office using s 303 CA 1985 does not prevent the director from seeking compensation for loss of office (s 303(5) CA 1985).

THE LUXURY HOTEL

Regardless of who negotiated the contract with the hotel, there is little doubt that Fish Ltd (F) had the contractual capacity to enter into such a contract. It is likely that the ability to organise a sales conference falls within the implied powers of the company, since all companies have implied powers to undertake activities conducive or necessary to the pursuance of their objects. Consequently, the contract cannot be rejected on grounds of *ultra vires* and, even if such was the case, the contract would be enforceable by the hotel by virtue of s 35 CA 1985. However, simply because the company has the capacity to contract does not mean that the contract is binding on F. Since F is an artificial legal person, its decisions and actions have to be taken by natural persons acting on its behalf. These acts and decisions may fail to be taken by the board or the shareholders in general meeting or by agents or employees of the company. Whether a particular person (or persons) can bind the company to this contract is essentially a question of agency—the principal (F) is bound by acts entered into on its behalf by a person with actual, usual or ostensible authority so to do. In this company, it is the board of directors which has the power to make the decisions as to how the company is to operate (Art 70 of Table A) subject to the need for approval from the general meeting for contracts valued over £40,000. Does this mean that S's agreement cannot bind the company?

(a) Contract negotiated by S

The hotel wants the contract entered into by S, a single director, to be binding on F. In order to enforce the contract, the hotel must establish that S had authority to enter into this contract and bind F. Alternatively, F would be bound if it ratified an unauthorised act, but it seems obvious that the board has got cold feet about S's activities and has made it plain that it does not wish to ratify S's contract. Has S authority to bind the company?

Plainly, S has not got express authority to enter into this transaction unless the instruction to 'make things happen' confers express authority to do anything on S. Nor can the hotel rely on the articles to claim that S was impliedly authorised by the articles, in that the board could have delegated power to him, since the cases seem to accept such reasoning only where the third party has read the articles (*British Thomson-Houston Co Ltd v Federated European Bank Ltd (1932)*). This would raise difficulties for the hotel, since, if it had read them, it would know of the restriction on S's powers, although the hotel might be able to argue that it was entitled to assume that the general meeting had given permission in accordance with the principle enunciated in *Royal British Bank v Turquand (1856)*. It is unlikely that the hotel has read F's articles.

More promising for the hotel is the possibility that S has usual authority to enter into this transaction. The extent of S's usual authority to enter into a transaction is determined by reference to the position which he holds, that is, he has the powers which the holder of such a post within a company would usually possess. For example, a company secretary has usual authority to run the administrative side of a company's affairs. This could involve purchasing office equipment, hiring staff and generally ensuring the smooth running of the support side of a business. In *Panorama Developments Ltd v Fidelis Furnishing Fabrics Ltd (1971)*, the usual authority of a company secretary was held to include the hiring of cars to transport visitors to the company's premises, so that the company was liable for the car-hire charges even when the secretary had used the cars for his own purposes. The question for the hotel in this case is, what is the usual authority of a 'marketing director'? If it includes the organisation of a sales conference, then F is bound, even though it did not actually authorise S to act as he did.

S is a properly appointed director, so the problems of *de facto* appointments do not arise. There are no cases on the usual authority of a marketing director, so one can merely speculate on the scope of his usual authority. It can be assumed that S has authority for matters concerning marketing, but at some point the magnitude of the transaction might indicate that board approval is required—the sums involved in this case do not seem so large (but see the articles) that the hotel should instantly be suspicious; nor do there seem to be any suspicious circumstances which should have put it on its guard. If there are suspicious circumstances, the hotel will not be able to claim that it relied upon S's usual authority unless it 'made such inquiries as ought reasonably to be made' (*Underwood Ltd v Bank of Liverpool (1924)*, where the bank was held liable to reimburse the company when a director signed cheques drawn on the company's account in his own favour).

Even if, *prima facie*, S has usual authority, the hotel has deemed notice of the limitation on the powers of individuals contained in the articles, because registration of the articles is constructive notice of their contents to the whole world. However, if the hotel can rely on s 35A CA 1985 (see below), the restriction on S's power contained in the articles does not bind it. In addition to usual authority, an agent may have ostensible authority, whereby an agent of the company is held out by those with authority (for example, the board) as having wider powers than those normally possessed by an agent of that type (ostensible authority also has other meanings), but there seems to be no question of S possessing such authority. The scope of ostensible authority, if any, would also be curtailed by the articles unless the hotel could rely on s 35A CA 1985 to abrogate any restriction on S's authority. It is not clear whether s 35A CA 1985 applies to an action decided upon by a single director rather than one entered into by the board. The wording of the section seems to suggest that it applies only to actions by the board or those authorised by it, which of course could include a single direction.

The act of forgery committed by S should not destroy his usual authority, provided that he was simply carrying out an authorised task (conference organising) in an unauthorised way (*contra* the case of *Ruben v Great Fingall Consolidated (1906)*). However, even if S is found to have authority to enter into the hotel contract, F is not criminally liable for the forgery committed by S.

Thus, the hotel could enforce the contract against F only if not bound by the restriction in the articles.

(b) Contract negotiated by the board

There is no doubt that, if the board had decided to embark on organising a sales conference for less than £40,000, the company would have been bound. Even if such a decision had been a breach of directors' duty, for example if it had not been made *bona fide* or for a proper purpose, that would not affect the validity of the transaction as far as the third party was concerned. However, in this case, the board has exceeded its powers by not referring the contract to the shareholders. The validity of appointment of the board of F has not been raised, so it can be assumed that the board are all *de jure* directors.

At common law, the third party, the hotel, would have had constructive notice of the need for prior shareholder approval, although the hotel might have been able to rely on the case of *Royal British Bank v Turquand (1856)* to enforce the agreement. *Turquand* established that, where the board (or an individual) appeared to have authority to act, the company could not rely upon some internal irregularity in its own procedures to deny that liability. However, the hotel can rely on s 35A CA 1985 if it wishes to enforce the conference contract despite the wishes of the shareholders. Section 35A(1) CA 1985 provides that, 'in favour of a person dealing with a company in good faith, the power of the board of directors to bind the company ... shall be deemed to be free of any limitations under the company's constitution'. In interpreting this section, s 35A(2) CA 1985 provides some guidance. A person 'deals with a company' if he is a party to a transaction or other act to which the company is a party—the hotel has no difficulty in satisfying this test. Section 35A(2) CA 1985 then provides that it is assumed that a person dealt in good faith unless the company proves the converse. Cases on earlier versions of s 35A CA 1985, which would probably remain applicable, ruled that good faith was a subjective test. Nourse J in *Barclays Bank Ltd v TOSG Trust Fund (1984)* stated that 'A person acts in good faith if he acts genuinely and honestly in the circumstances of the case.' There seems to be no evidence of any lack of good faith on the part of the hotel in this case and the hotel would appear to be protected by s 35A CA 1985. Moreover, s 35B CA 1985 provides that the hotel is not under a duty to inquire as to whether the directors are exceeding their powers in entering into the disputed contract (that is, failure to inquire is not bad faith).

Thus, the hotel can be advised that its contract with F is enforceable against the company.

NOTE

A good student might wish to touch on any proposals for reform in these areas.

Question 17

Mansfield Park Ltd was incorporated in 1998. The objects of the company provide that Mansfield Park Ltd is to purchase a specific stately home, Mansfield Park, and convert it into luxury flats for rent, and that the company can also purchase and convert similar properties. The articles of the company include the following provisions:

(a) the qualification to hold office as director shall be the holding of shares in the company to the nominal value of £100;

(b) the board of directors may delegate all or any of their powers or functions to any director or directors; and

(c) any contract to purchase land for the company's use must be approved by the company in general meeting.

At the outset, the company had three shareholders, Austen, Bingley and Collins, who each held 25% of the company's share capital. Austen and Darcy were appointed as directors; Darcy has always acted as managing director but has never been formally appointed to the position. In 1999, Elton was appointed to manage the flats at Mansfield Park. In early 2002, Elton ordered a car costing £25,000 in the company's name, to be used by him primarily for company business. Elton, in conjunction with Austen, has just negotiated the purchase, at a price of £500,000, of another property for conversion, Kellynch Hall, which Elton has just inherited.

Darcy does not wish the purchase of the car or Kellynch Hall to proceed and wishes to dismiss Elton and restrict Austen to a non-executive role in the company.

Advise Darcy, Bingley and Collins.

Answer plan

First, it must be established whether Darcy, who has not taken any qualification shares, has any *locus* to act on his own account or on behalf of the company, or, if he does not have such *locus*, whether he acts in conjunction with Bingley and Collins in respect of these issues. The second issue is the ability of a manager to enter into a contract which can bind the company (car) and whether he can be sacked. Third, can Elton and Austen together bind the company to purchase Kellynch, and, if they can, does the fact that it belonged to Elton affect the validity of the contract?

Finally, have Bingley and Collins any rights of their own without acting through Darcy?

Answer

The first thing to note is that Darcy (D), who acts as managing director, has not, in breach of the articles, acquired any qualification shares. Consequently, he can have no rights as a shareholder. Does this failure on his part affect his ability to enforce the rights of the company, assuming that he has such a right, and is he in breach of his duty in failing to acquire the shares?

The power to run a company, which includes the right to sue errant directors, dismiss employees and seek to evade contracts, is determined by reference to the articles. This company has Art 70 of Table A, so that it is the directors who decide whether to exercise legal rights on the company's behalf. The directors of this company are, *prima facie*, Austen (A) and D. However, Mansfield Park has retained the rather outmoded requirement that the directors acquire qualification shares. Section 291 CA 1985 provides that, if such shares are not acquired by a director within two months of his appointment, the errant director has to quit his office and is not eligible for reappointment until the shares are acquired. Thus, it seems that D is not a director of the company and that the power to run the company is vested in A. Consequently, D cannot act for the company or initiate litigation, and is himself liable to a fine for acting as a director without acquiring shares. If he acquires the shares, he can be reappointed.

Until D acquires the shares, A is the sole director of the company and he may not wish the company to try to back out of the car contract, given that he appears to be allied to Elton (E) and is, it can be assumed, in favour of the purchase of Kellynch. Bingley (B) and Collins (C) cannot instruct A as to how he runs the company, because such instructions are operative only if given in the form of a special resolution, which they cannot muster (they hold 50% of the share capital, or 66% if only 75% is issued). However, B and C do have sufficient voting strength to obtain an ordinary resolution, which would enable them to dismiss A (s 303 CA 1985, which would terminate both the non-executive and executive roles). Should they do so, they may then seek to appoint new directors (or reappoint D), run the company themselves (they would then be treated as the directors, even if not formally appointed—s 741 CA 1985) or reappoint A with limited powers.

While A remains in charge, the shareholders cannot engage in legal activity on behalf of the company, because the famous case of *Foss v Harbottle (1843)* provides that the power to act on behalf of the company lies with the company itself and, given the usual practice of adopting Art 70 of Table A, the exercise of that power lies, in the main, with the directors. However, majority shareholders can exercise a residual power to sue where the wrong done to the company is committed by the whole board, and a minority shareholder can bring an action where *Foss v Harbottle* does not apply, an example of this being when the company has acted *ultra vires*. However, *ultra vires* is limited to cases where the company has exceeded its powers and is not in issue when the company itself is authorised but the particular human intermediary was not authorised to act.

The purchase of a car and the purchase of Kellynch clearly fall within the express or implied powers of the company, so that these contracts cannot be called *ultra vires*. Another exception to *Foss* arises when there is 'fraud on the minority', that is, where an unratifiable wrong has been done to the company and the wrongdoers control the company so that there is no effective champion of the company's rights. If the purchase of the car or Kellynch is such a wrong, then B and A have power to initiate litigation in the name of the company by means of a derivative action. This looks like being a remarkably long-winded way of outflanking A, whom they can sack, and it is difficult, although not impossible, to see why justice (a factor relevant in determining whether shareholders should be given *locus* to pursue the company's claims—see *Barrett v Duckett (1995)* for an example) should allow B and C to act for the company while ignoring their alternative remedy. However, B and C might argue that it was more appropriate for them to sue rather than sack, if sacking A might jeopardise the existence of the company, in that A's dismissal could trigger a claim by him for just and equitable winding up. Section 122(1)(g) of the Insolvency Act (IA) 1986 allows such an action if the company has the hallmarks of a 'quasi-partnership' company and the relationship of the parties has irretrievably broken down. This could well apply here.

If B and C dismiss A (or persuade him to fall in with their views), they may seek to pursue the remedies sought by D—to evade the car and Kellynch contracts. Since there is no doubt that a company such as this has an implied power to purchase a motor car for a senior employee, even if he also uses it for non-company business, the company is bound by this contract unless it can establish that the person who negotiated the contract, E, had no power to bind the company to a contract of this type. Since Mansfield Park, as an incorporated company, is an artificial legal person, its decisions and actions have to be taken by natural persons acting on its behalf.

Whether E can bind a company is essentially a question of agency—the principal (the company) is bound by acts entered into on its behalf by a person with actual, usual or ostensible authority so to do. E does not appear to have actual authority to enter into this contract but he may have usual authority—that is, the authority that can be assumed to arise from the position he holds within the company. A senior manager must have some ability to bind his company but there is little case law on the usual authority of senior employees. It is a moot point whether a third party is entitled to allege that he was entitled to assume that E had the power to buy a car of relatively high value on behalf of the company.

Alternatively, E may have possessed ostensible authority. Ostensible authority allows a person to bind the company: those with actual authority, the board, have indicated to the world that E possesses such power, that is, they have given the impression that he has the relevant power and the car dealer has no reason to doubt the impression that the board has given him. The fact that the directors can delegate all or some of their powers does not mean that a third party is entitled to assume that a power has been delegated; there must be some indication by the board that E has the authority to bind Mansfield Park.

If E does not have usual or ostensible authority, it seems that the company is not bound by the car contract and it should be noted that s 35A CA 1985 would not affect this. Section 35A CA 1985 merely permits a restriction, which would limit an authority which would otherwise exist to be ignored; it does not confer authority where none existed previously.

E can be sacked by his employer, the company, provided that the decision to sack him is taken by the appropriate organ of the company—the board. The consequences of this will depend upon whether he was in breach of his contract of employment, which would allow dismissal without compensation, or whether there was no such breach, so that the company would have to compensate him on normal legal principles.

Finally, have B and C, either as the new board (or a new set of directors appointed by them) or as shareholders, any power to challenge the purchase of Kellynch? The question of authority again arises—can A (the sole legitimate director) and E (a manager) bind the company? Clearly, the company has the ability to undertake such a purchase, since the objects of Mansfield Park permit the purchase and conversion of other properties of a similar type to Mansfield Park itself. Kellynch would appear to be such a property. Whether B and C can prevent the contract of sale proceeding to completion without exposing the company to an action for breach of contract depends upon the authority possessed by the negotiators and the effect, if any, of the close relationship of the vendor with one of these negotiators. Plainly, neither A nor E, either together or singly, had actual authority to bind the company. While a manager must be regarded as having some usual authority by virtue of his position (see above), it cannot extend to a transaction of this magnitude (*Armagas Ltd v Mundogas SA (1986)*) so that the company is bound only if A has usual authority or A and/or E had ostensible authority.

Generally, the usual authority of a single director who is not a managing director is very limited, and in this case, D, however improperly, has been acting as managing director, so that A cannot be regarded as filling that post. Perhaps it could be argued that, since D is not a director (he has no shares), then A is the board, and that since the board could negotiate this contract, A could bind the company by virtue of being the only director; or that A, as the board, could hold himself out as able to bind the company. If A has no authority, he cannot bind the company; if he has authority, E may still appear to be defeated by Art 3. Article 3 provides, in effect, that the purchase of land without the approval of the general meeting cannot bind the company. However, s 35A(1) CA 1985 provides that, 'in favour of a person dealing with a company in good faith, the power of the board of directors to bind the company ... shall be deemed to be free of any limitations under the company's constitution'.

E, as vendor of Kellynch, falls within the section, especially since s 35A(2) CA 1985 then provides that it is assumed that a person dealt in good faith unless the company proves the converse. Cases on earlier versions of s 35A CA 1985, which would probably remain applicable, ruled that good faith was a subjective test. Nourse J in *Barclays Bank Ltd v TOSG Trust Fund (1984)* stated that 'A person acts in good faith if he acts genuinely and honestly in the circumstances of the case'. Thus, the fact that the vendor is an employee of the company (even one who was involved in negotiations) does not mean that there is a lack of good faith on his part in this case and the vendor might well be protected by s 35A CA 1985. Neither s 320 CA 1985 nor s 322A CA 1985 apply to employees, so the transaction is not voidable on the basis of either of those sections. However, if E could be treated as a shadow director (see s 741 CA 1985), then s 320 CA 1985 (which applies to substantial property transactions) would apply and the sale would be voidable unless approved by the company in general meeting.

Entry into the land transaction is a breach of directors' duty on the part of A (and breach of his duty as employee on the part of E), but this simply gives the company a remedy against A and does not allow it to disregard the contract if it is rendered enforceable by s 35A CA 1985.

CHAPTER 4

DIRECTORS

INTRODUCTION

There are few aspects of company law which do not, in some way, involve a discussion of the directors and their powers. Every company must have at least one director (two in the case of a public company) and they have a multifaceted role within a company. The directors may be employees, they have duties as directors and they generally act on behalf of the company in its dealings with the outside world (that is, they act as agents). This variety of functions means that any question can include an aspect relating to the directors—a question on shares might raise issues of the power to allot (s 80 of the Companies Act (CA) 1985), a question involving litigation might touch on division of power within the company, almost any transaction might be challengeable as an improper use of directorial power and, as discussed above in Chapter 3, the validity of a company's contract can turn on the authority of the director who purported to act on behalf of the company. In addition, questions might arise, although rarely as the only issue, issues of the validity of the appointment, the amount of remuneration or the legitimacy of a dismissal of a director.

The most likely area for questions solely on directors is that of the extent of their duties. Students must not become too narrow minded in addressing the issue of directors' duties. For example, a question may require consideration of a contract between a director and the company—obviously, the usual rules on disclosure, the nature of the disclosure and the effect of non-disclosure (including possible ratification) arise, but students must also consider the nature of the contract. Ask yourself whether the transaction is a substantial property transaction (s 320 CA 1985) or whether it involves a loan, etc (ss 330–42 CA 1985) or a service contract (s 317 CA 1985). Entry into a contract may also be attacked as an improper use of directors' power. Any question on directors' duties may raise the issue of *locus standi*; is the person seeking to sue the director authorised to do so? *Locus* involves the case of *Foss v Harbottle (1843)* and its exceptions, and it may be that a litigant denied *locus* on behalf of the company has an alternative remedy under s 459 or 122(1)(g) of the Insolvency Act (IA) 1986.

Linked to questions of directors' duties may be questions about the liability of third parties who have been involved in misappropriating corporate property. The ambit of constructive trusteeship in respect of third parties arises in such cases. Reference to the provisions of the Companies Act 2006 (when in force) in this area may also be relevant to some of the questions. The Companies Act 2006 contain a statement of directors' fiduciary and common law duties. Although the statement sets out directors' general duties, with some amendment to the regulation of conflicts of interest, it is expected that they will be interpreted and applied in the same way as the common law and the equitable rules.

Question 18

The combination of *Percival v Wright (1902), Foss v Harbottle (1843)* and Art 70 of Table A effectively frees directors from any risk of litigation for breach of duty being brought by minority shareholders or creditors.

Discuss.

Answer plan

First, discuss what the decisions and statutory provision provide, then turn to the effect of the law on potential actions by minority shareholders or creditors. Sum up by determining whether directors are right to feel fearless.

Answer

All companies are required by law to have at least one director (s 282 Companies Act (CA) 1985), public companies must have at least two and Table A provides that all companies shall have at least two directors unless the company determines otherwise by ordinary resolution (Art 64). When a company is registered, the shareholders of the company possess the authority to determine how the company will operate and be operated, and they are not required to bestow all or any of their powers on the board of directors. The shareholders generally give away their power to run the company in the articles but the degree of delegation is a matter for the shareholders to determine, either in the articles or subsequently. In practice, most companies adopt Art 70 of Table A, which effectively gives the power to operate the company, which would otherwise be vested in the shareholders in general meeting, to the directors. Consequently, the shareholders (majority or minority) cannot complain if the directors exercise the powers which have been delegated to them unless the articles of the company, or other provision giving power to the directors, restrict the apparently unfettered use of such powers. The articles can, of course, be changed by special resolution (s 9 CA 1985) but this will not avail a minority shareholder (who will be unable to muster the requisite number of votes) or a creditor (who has no right to attend company meetings or vote off the officers of the company). Directors who upset their shareholders can be dismissed by ordinary resolution (s 303 CA 1985) but a minority shareholder may find even this lowered hurdle too high to scale. Article 70 of Table A contains a provision permitting the shareholders to instruct the board how to act, provided that such directions are given by special resolution—this is of little practical value to minority shareholders and of none at all to creditors. It can be concluded that, in most companies, the directors have a relatively unfettered right to run the company, although their right to do so is hedged by fiduciary and statutory obligations.

A minority shareholder or a creditor might seek to restrain the proposed acts of the board or sue in respect of past acts, alleging breach of a fiduciary or statutory duty. Potential litigants have two cases with which to contend: *Percival v Wright (1902)*, which provides that the board, in exercising its powers (or duties), is generally responsible to the company and not to individual shareholders or creditors (or the employees); and *Foss v Harbottle (1843)*, which held that a breach of duty owed to a company can be litigated only by the company. Since the power to litigate on behalf of the company will normally reside in the board (by virtue of Art 70 or its equivalent), the directors would appear to be able to determine whether to sue themselves in respect of wrongs which they have done to the company. While the board might be willing to sue a director (or former director) with whom the majority had fallen out, it is difficult to imagine a united board voluntarily agreeing to sue itself or one of its members. The issues which must be considered are whether *Percival v Wright* precludes a director from owing a duty to a shareholder or creditor and whether *Foss v Harbottle* is subject to exceptions.

In *Percival v Wright* (1902), the directors of a company were privy to confidential information which, once released, was likely to increase the value of the company's shares. P, a shareholder, offered to sell his shares to the directors, who accepted his offer. When the confidential information was released, P sought to have the contract of sale set aside and to recover the shares, on the ground that the lack of disclosure was a breach of fiduciary duty by the directors. Swinfen-Eady J, in rejecting P's claim, held that the directors did not, simply by being directors, owe a fiduciary duty to an individual shareholder; they did owe such a duty to the *company* but they had not broken it. This case remains the law, despite being the subject of fierce criticism, and was confirmed by the Court of Appeal in *Peskin v Anderson (2001)*. Hence, a director owes fiduciary and other duties to his company by virtue of his office but owes none to a shareholder or creditor on that basis.

However, this rule does not preclude a director from being found to have chosen to undertake some responsibility to a shareholder (fiduciary, contractual or tortious (the last of these under *Hedley Byrne* principles)) on a personal level; that is, the duty arose because of an arrangement between two people who happen to be a director and shareholder (or creditor). For example, in *Allen v Hyatt (1914)*, the directors induced the shareholders to give them options to purchase shares without disclosing the possibility that the directors would be able to resell the shares at a profit. The Privy Council found that the directors had, by their words and actions, made themselves agents for each shareholder and owed the usual obligations of an agent to his principal. These obligations include a duty to account for any benefits accruing from the agency so that the directors had to account for the profits they had made on the exercise of the options and the subsequent resale of the shares. However, in most cases there is no question of the directors undertaking responsibility to an individual shareholder, so that *Percival v Wright* is the norm.

The fiduciary obligations owed to the company can be summarised as a duty to act in the best interests of the company, even if this is not in the best interests of the director. It is the fact that the directors should act in the interests of the company which has allowed some mitigation of the effect of *Percival v Wright*. The interests of the company are generally concurrent with the economic interests of current and future shareholders but not any particular shareholder. However, when the company is the subject of a takeover bid, the interests of the company have been treated as concurrent with the interests of current shareholders, so that directors have a duty to give them honest advice about the merits of the bid (first established in *Gething v Kilner (1972)*). The New Zealand courts have gone further, expressing the view that a director can incur liability to an individual shareholder without the need for agency and in circumstances other than that of a takeover bid. In *Coleman v Myers (1977)*, Woodhouse J held that whether liability could arise depended 'upon all the surrounding circumstances and the nature of the responsibilities which in a real and practical sense the director has assumed towards the shareholder'. In *Coleman*, the managing director of a family owned and run company, who had persuaded shareholders to sell him a majority shareholding on the basis of the published valuation of the company's assets, was required to account to those shareholders when the assets were sold at a price substantially above book value. The English courts have not been prepared, as yet, to follow *Coleman*.

What, then, of creditors? There are *dicta* which suggest that directors should have regard to the interests of creditors. It should be noted, however, that the *dicta* which suggested that directors owe a duty to creditors seem incapable of support, following the decision of the Privy Council in *Kuwait Asia Bank EC v National Mutual Life Nominees Ltd (1991)*. In this case, the appellant bank, which was registered in Bahrain, was a major shareholder (holding approximately 40% of the shares and nominating two out of five directors) in a New Zealand money broking company (AICS) which had gone into insolvent liquidation. The respondent company, NMLN, was, in accordance with New Zealand law, trustee for AICS's depositors and had incurred considerable liabilities and expense in connection with the insolvency. NMLN was seeking a contribution to its liabilities from a number of defendants, including the directors of AICS. The Privy Council, in considering whether the New Zealand courts had jurisdiction over the bank, advised that a director does not owe a duty to the creditors of his company simply by virtue of his office, although he may by agreement or representation undertake such a responsibility. Lord Lowry, in his speech, relied upon a number of nineteenth-century decisions (none in the House of Lords) in support of this view but, somewhat surprisingly, made no reference to the more recent cases (including one in the House of Lords) which had appeared to acknowledge the possibility of such a duty existing (see *Winkworth v Edward Baron Development Co Ltd (1996)*).

None of the recent cases appears to have been cited by counsel. If the *Kuwait Asia Bank* case is construed literally, it would appear to be strongly persuasive of the view that directors cannot incur liability to corporate creditors.

Members and interested outsiders may find that the directors have the power to run the company and do not owe any duty to individual shareholders and creditors. A director's only duty is to the company. A further difficulty facing shareholders who wish to sue directors is that, even where a wrong has been done to the company, the proper claimant is the company (you cannot sue to enforce another person's rights or remedy their wrongs), so that, as indicated above, it is the company (the operation of whose powers are vested in the board) which decides whether to sue the board or a director (*Foss v Harbottle (1843)*). However, there are a limited number of cases where a shareholder, but not a creditor, has *locus* to sue to enforce the rights of the company (a shareholder can always sue a director to enforce his own personal rights, if any)—such a claim is called a derivative claim (or, until the **Civil Procedure Rules 1998**, a derivative action). For a shareholder to bring a derivative claim is somewhat unattractive; the shareholder has to pay for the litigation (although the courts have the power to order the company to indemnify the shareholder—*Wallersteiner v Moir (1974)*) and any remedy which is ordered accrues to the company and not the shareholder. Moreover, it is not easy to establish that an exception to *Foss* has arisen. To do so, the shareholder must establish a *prima facie* case of fraud on the part of those in control of the company and, unless such a case is established, the shareholder must be denied *locus* (*Prudential Assurance v Newman Industries (1981)*). The shareholder must also show that authority cannot be obtained for proceedings to be brought in the name of the company (*Birch v Sullivan (1957)*; *Fraser v Oystertec plc (2004)*). Under the Civil Procedure Rules 1998, permission of the court is required in order to continue to bring a derivative claim. This will be enhanced by a two stage procedure contained in the Companies Act 2006, when in force.

Fraud in this context extends beyond legal fraud to embrace an apparent lack of probity (equitable fraud). Hence, in *Daniels v Daniels (1978)*, where legal fraud was not alleged, a sale of a corporate asset to a director at a price which appeared to be substantially below its market value was held to fall within the exception. That is, while simple negligence could not form the basis of an exception to *Foss v Harbottle* (1843), a sale at an undervalue which had benefited a director to the extent of £115,000 could be treated as equitable fraud. Even when 'fraud' and control by the wrongdoers (which embraces effective as well as legal control) have been established, the courts have a discretion to deny *locus* to a shareholder. Denial of *locus* has arisen when the shareholder has himself behaved improperly (*Nurcombe v Nurcombe (1985)*), the shareholders or directors who are not party to the wrongdoing have indicated that they do not wish an action to proceed (*Smith v Croft (No 2) (1988)*) or where the shareholder is acting for an ulterior motive rather than to enforce the company's rights (*Barrett v Duckett (1995)*). The logic underpinning these cases is that, if the company is not going to benefit from the action, it is foolish to allow it to be dragged into litigation against its will. Hence, where a case could be brought, but a majority of independent shareholders are against it for a *bona fide* reason, for example the unlikelihood of any real benefit to the company, their views should prevail over those of a minority shareholder. Further, in *Cooke v Cooke (1997)*, the court stayed proceedings of a derivative action, because the claimant had also petitioned for relief under s 459 CA 1985, making substantially the same factual allegations. It was assumed that the s 459 petition was the most appropriate means of dealing with the issues.

As the previous paragraphs illustrate, a director can indeed assume that, while he retains the support of his fellow directors, he will be free of litigation in respect of his running of the company. However, s 459 CA 1985 is more likely to prove a more troublesome provision for directors than anything else in company law. Section 459 CA 1985, which allows a shareholder to litigate if he has been unfairly prejudiced by some act or proposed act of the company, gives *locus* to a single shareholder (but not creditors), who, if successful, obtains any remedy awarded by the court, although there is no question of the company being required to fund such an action.

Directors may also need to be mindful of the for the reforms contained in the Companies Act 2006. Although to data not in force, the Act provides that a derivative claim may be brought by a shareholder of a company if the cause of action arises as a result of an actual act or omission through either (a) negligence, default, breach of duty or breach of trust by a director of the company, or (b) a director putting himself in a position where his personal interests conflict with his duties to the company. The first part of this proposal would have the effect, therefore, of ending the rule found in *Pavlides v Jensen (1956)*, which prevents a minority shareholder bringing a derivative action where the negligent conduct complained of does not benefit the directors personally. The Act also provides that in bringing a derivative claim, it will no longer be necessary for an applicant to show that the wrongdoing director(s) control a majority of the company's shares.

NOTE

A discussion of relevant provisions of the Company Act 2006 could be made, such as the codification of directors' duties.

Question 19

Directors of companies have onerous fiduciary and statutory duties imposed upon them, which makes their limited liability for negligence all the more puzzling.

Comment.

Answer plan

A straightforward question requiring a synopsis of the fiduciary and statutory duties imposed on directors with a comment as to whether these duties can be classified as onerous, followed by a similar synopsis on the liability of a director for negligence with a comment as to whether it is 'limited'. A concluding paragraph should be added, to link up the arguments on the relative weight of directorial burdens. Some discussion of proposed reforms might be expected.

Answer

All companies must have at least one director (s 282 of the Companies Act 1985); there must be two in a public company. There are few statutory restrictions upon who is eligible to be a director: youth is no bar—a day old baby can be a director; nor is age (subject to s 293 CA 1985 in respect of public companies); nor is there any entrance examination. The only automatic bar to a directorship is being an undischarged bankrupt. Most companies adopt Art 70 of Table A, which effectively gives the power to operate the company, otherwise vested in the shareholders in general meeting, to the directors, although their right to do so is hedged by fiduciary, statutory and common law obligations. The Companies Act 2006, when in force, lays down some general principles applicable to directors which would replace the common law and equitable rules. These principles seek to clarify existing law. What, then, is the nature of these duties, and to what extent is there an imbalance between those imposed by common law and the rest? Is this disparity, if proven, justifiable?

FIDUCIARY AND STATUTORY DUTIES

As Lord Porter put it in *Regal (Hastings) Ltd v Gulliver (1942)*, 'Directors, no doubt, are not trustees, but they occupy a fiduciary position towards the company whose board they form.' As a fiduciary, each director is individually subject to equitable duties—fiduciary duties—which require him to exercise his powers in a way which has regard to the interests of the person to whom the duties are owed and not to abuse his position of trust and influence within the company. Indeed, in respect of corporate property, the director's fiduciary duty goes further and, in common with a trustee, a director cannot, without the unanimous approval of the shareholders, derive any benefit from the use of corporate property. Fiduciary duties are owed to the company, that is, current and future shareholders as a body, and not to individual shareholders (*Percival v Wright (1902)*; *Peskin v Anderson (2001)*), although a director may voluntarily undertake a fiduciary duty towards a shareholder by acting as his agent (*Allen v Hyatt (1914)*).

Fiduciary duties can be subdivided into the general and the applied. The general duties cast on a director consist of an obligation to act *bona fide* in exercising his powers and a requirement that certain powers are used only for 'proper purposes'. The obligation to act *bona fide* is subjective, so that, provided that a director honestly believes he is acting properly in deciding how to operate the company, he is not in breach of this duty (*Re Smith & Fawcett Ltd (1942)*). Since a director must make decisions on the basis of his own honest belief in what is best for the company, it is a breach of fiduciary duty for a director to fetter his freedom to exercise his powers. Consequently, an agreement by a director that he would always vote for proposals put forward by X would be a breach of fiduciary duty. However, where a director has *bona fide* agreed to pursue a particular course of action and has contracted to that effect, he is bound by that contract and cannot argue that he has thereby fettered his discretion (*Fulham FC v Cabra Estates plc (1994)*). Moreover, a director must exercise his powers not only honestly, but also for a purpose consistent with that for which the powers were conferred on him. A leading case in point is the Privy Council decision of *Howard Smith Ltd v Ampol Petroleum Ltd (1974)*.

In *Ampol*, the directors of HS, a company in need of further finance, issued shares to members who held a minority interest in the company, but offered none to the majority shareholder (A), who had made an unwanted takeover bid. The effect of the issue was to reduce A's shareholding to below 50%. This allotment of shares was challenged by A as an improper use of the directorial power to issue shares. The Privy Council ruled that, when the use of a power is challenged, the court should first consider the nature of the power (that is, why was this power conferred on the directors whose exercise thereof is in question?) and then examine the substantial purpose for which it was exercised. If, considering the issue objectively, the power was not exercised for the proper purpose, the exercise of the power is void. The court ruled that the power to allot shares is given to directors to raise funds for the company and that, while the directors intended this allotment to raise capital, the primary purpose of the issue was to defeat A's bid and not to raise money. Consequently, this allotment was void—the facts of this case could now also fall within ss 80–96 CA 1985.

Other cases on this area have held that an improper use of directorial power can be ratified by ordinary resolution (*Bamford v Bamford (1970)*). It is uncertain which powers must be exercised for proper purposes.

In addition to the general obligations, a director is also subject to the requirement to put the interests of the company before his own interests. This responsibility has given rise to a number of areas of litigation, some of which have been supplemented by statutory provisions. An obvious source of conflict between corporate duty and personal interest concerns corporate contracts which directly or indirectly benefit the director. The House of Lords in *Aberdeen Rly Co v Blaikie Bros (1854)* ruled that a director could not benefit directly or indirectly from a contract made by his company. This has been modified to provide that a director cannot benefit from a contract between himself and his company or between his company and a third party without making adequate disclosure of his own interest in that contract. Disclosure should be to the general meeting, unless the articles allow disclosure to the board; Art 85 of Table A permits disclosure to the board.

Section 317 CA 1985 provides rules for the nature of the disclosure to the board. It can be argued that disclosure to one's fellow directors is not an onerous duty. Failure to make adequate disclosure in compliance with the common law or the articles allows the company to rescind the contract (where the director has received a direct benefit) or make the director liable to account (indirect benefits). The effect of failure to comply with s 317 CA 1985 is obscure. Perhaps because disclosure to the board might allow a cosy cartel among directors, certain sections impose further obligations in respect of particular contracts upon directors. Section 319 CA 1985 places restrictions upon the service contract which a director can make, s 320 CA 1985 affects 'substantial property transactions' and s 330 CA 1985 prohibits a company from making loans to directors. The general thrust of these provisions is not to prohibit contracts between directors and their companies but, rather, to ensure that such contracts are valid only if affirmed by the shareholders in general meeting.

The general duty to put corporate interest above private profit is augmented in respect of corporate property; in common with a trustee, a director cannot, without the unanimous approval of the shareholders, appropriate (even innocently) corporate property. If he does so appropriate, he is liable as a constructive trustee (*JJ Harrison (Properties) Ltd v Harrison 2001*)). It is obvious that, if a director appropriates the company's tangible property, he will be liable to return the property to the company. The same is true of appropriation of intangible corporate assets, for example the benefit of a contract possessed by the company. This liability for misappropriation is extended to commercial opportunities which are within the company's grasp. For instance, in *Cook v Deeks (1916)*, a company, X, was about to sign a contract to build a railway when the railway company was persuaded by some of the directors of X to award the contract to a new company which they had formed. The directors were held liable to hold the benefit of the contract as constructive trustees for X. Misappropriation of corporate assets is an unratifiable breach of directors' duty.

Difficulties can arise in determining what is corporate property in the area of corporate opportunities (*Boardman v Phipps (1967)*; *Bhuller v Bhuller (2003)*). Further, because of the onerous obligations in respect of corporate property, the courts have distinguished between misuse of property and misuse of the position of director and the line between the cases can be hard to draw (*Industrial Development Consultants Ltd v Cooley (1972)*; *Balston Ltd v Headline Filters Ltd (1990)*; *Island Export Finance Ltd v Umunna (1986)*; *CMS Dolphin Ltd v Simonet (2001)*; *Bhuller v Bhuller (2003)*). In most cases where a director has benefited from his position, for example by using information received in a corporate capacity, liability is imposed not for breach of a trustee-like duty but, rather, for breach of a lesser fiduciary duty. This fiduciary duty provides that a director should not benefit from his position as director, which duty extends after the ending of the directorship, at the expense of the company. This is not an absolute prohibition, so a director can benefit from his position if there is no real conflict of interest.

An interesting decision in this area is to be found in *Framlington Group plc v Anderson (1995)*. In this case A, C and L had all been employed by the claimant group as private client fund managers and had been directors of companies within the group. A, C and L agreed to take up employment with R plc and the claimant company negotiated a sale of the business, represented by the clients, who would move their business to R plc when A, C and L moved; A, C and L were not party to these negotiations and had been specifically told not to be become involved in any negotiations on behalf of the claimant group. Subsequently, A, C and L entered into contracts with R plc which entitled them to shares in R plc (in addition to their salary) in proportion to the amount of business transferred by the claimant company's clients on their change of employer. The claimant company, which had not been aware that share benefits would be payable to A, C and L, claimed to be entitled to the shares transferred to them, alleging that such shares were secret profits arising from their directorships of companies within the claimant group.

Blackburne J found no conflict between the duty owed by the directors and their own interests. A, C and L were free to leave the claimant group at any time and were able to solicit clients if they left, hence their deal with R plc was a sale of an asset (client goodwill and their freedom to exploit it) in return for shares and a salary. There is no obligation on a director leaving a company to take up other employment to reveal to his current company the nature of his remuneration package, nor is there any duty as a fiduciary not to compete with the company with which one has previously been connected.

While the decision may be justified on the basis that there was no real conflict between personal interest and fiduciary duty, the notion that, since the directors were not party to the negotiations between the claimant group and R plc, they were free to arrange a deal for themselves which might be adverse to their current company seems somewhat surprising.

If a director does benefit from his position and there is a conflict of interest, the profit made by the director can be retained by the company if the company, by ordinary resolution, so decrees, either before or after the conduct complained of (*Regal (Hastings) Ltd v Gulliver (1942)*). However, there is uncertainty over ratifiable and unratifiable breaches of duty, a position which is widely felt to be unsatisfactory. What is clear is that fiduciary duties are extensive and pervasive.

CARE AND SKILL

In contrast, the common law duty of care and skill borne by directors was traditionally very modest. However, it must be noted that directors can incur liability for wrongful trading by virtue of s 214 of the Insolvency Act (IA) 1986 irrespective of any common law liability, but only if the company goes into insolvent liquidation. At common law, directors are expected to carry out their duties with an appropriate degree of care and skill. The traditional formulation of the nature and extent of this duty is that given by Romer J in *Re City Equitable Fire Insurance Co Ltd (1925)*, in which he held that a director:

- need display only such skill as may reasonably be expected from a person of his knowledge and experience;

- need not give the affairs of the continuous attention; and

- is entitled to leave the day to day running of the company to the officials of the company and is entitled to assume, in the absence of suspicious circumstances, that such officials are performing their duties honestly.

These propositions remain good law with regard to non-executive directors, but executive directors will generally be constrained by their service contracts to devote a set percentage of their time to the affairs of the company. The most important aspect of a director's duty of care relates to the amount of skill he must exercise. Directors are not subject to the Supply of Goods and Services Act 1982, which requires service providers to display reasonable care and skill. It is plain that a director who does his honest best may be held to have exercised sufficient care and skill to evade liability for negligence—the test of liability is subjective and not objective. Certainly, a director need possess no particular skill on appointment (*Re Brazilian Rubber Estates & Plantations Ltd (1911)*). Each case turns on its own facts and the issue is, did the relevant director, given his qualities, display adequate care and skill?

The courts are beginning to be a little more robust in determining the standard of care which a company can expect. In *Dorchester Finance Co Ltd v Stebbing (1989)*, the company had three directors: S, P and H; S and P were chartered accountants and H had considerable accounting experience. P and H left the running of the company to S, doing little more than calling in periodically and signing blank cheques for S to use; no board meetings were held. The issue before the court was a claim by the company against all three directors for negligence. Foster J, in determining the appropriate degree of care and skill to be expected from S, P and H, took into account their experience of accountancy and business. The judge found that the complete failure by P and H to do anything in respect of the running of the company was, even for non-executive directors, negligent, as well as in breach of several sections of the Companies Act 1948. Signing blank cheques was also negligent, in that, allied to their lack of control, it allowed S to run the company as he pleased. In addition, S ran the company without any care and skill and was plainly in breach of this duty; he was also liable for breach of fiduciary duty (misapplication of corporate assets).

This change of emphasis can also be seen in *Norman v Theodore Goddard (1991)*, in which a chartered surveyor (B), who was a director of a Jersey-based company, had been tricked by a co-director (Q), a solicitor, into authorising the payment of the company's money to a company controlled by Q. Q's partners were liable to reimburse the money and were seeking a contribution from B, alleging that he had failed to display sufficient care and skill as a director. Hoffmann J found on the facts that B's conduct in trusting Q was reasonable and that B had not been negligent. However, he held *obiter* that the duty of care and skill at common law was co-extensive with that imposed by s 214 IA 1986, that is, that a director should display such care when carrying out functions in relation to the company as would reasonably be expected from a person carrying out those functions. This seems to have a more objective ring about it than Romer J's view, which assessed a director's conduct by reference to the relevant director's abilities and not by reference to those of *a* person carrying out directorial functions. The Companies Act 2006 contains a dual objective/subjective standard for the duty of care, skill and diligence as part of the codification of directors' duties. Cases on s 459 CA 1985 have also held that gross negligence by a director may be unfairly prejudicial to the shareholders (*Re Macro (Ipswich) Ltd (1994)*).

CONCLUSION

Despite recent developments, there is little doubt that the fiduciary and statutory duties of directors greatly outweigh the duties of care and skill. Perhaps it is not inappropriate that we can demand honesty and fair dealing from our directors but cannot necessarily expect skill. Equally, it could be argued that people should not allow shareholders to entrust money to their care without exercising some degree of care in looking after it.

NOTE

Further discussion of proposed reforms and/or the approach of other jurisdictions to the 'proper purpose' doctrine could be included.

Question 20

Epsom is a director and employee of Ludlow Ltd and is a shareholder in two other companies. He holds 10% of the shares of Aintree Ltd and 15% of the shares of Newbury Ltd. He is also owed £2,000 salary by a former employer, Fontwell Ltd. All these companies are connected with the racing industry.

He seeks your advice about the following:

(a) Fontwell Ltd is incompetently managed and is apparently moving towards insolvency.

(b) The directors of Ludlow have proposed an allotment of shares to their employees and hope thereby to defeat a hostile takeover bid.

(c) The board of Aintree decided that it was in no immediate need of a substantial piece of land which it owned and, being unable to sell it, leased it to the company's managing director at market rates. He intends to use the land to develop a new business unconnected with racing.

(d) Newbury Ltd has five directors but management of the company was carried on by two of them and the rest took no interest in the running of the company and rarely attended board meetings. One of the executive directors has recently absconded with some of the company's money.

Answer plan

A large number of issues are raised, which allows little scope for lengthy discussion of any one issue. After general introductory comments, two issues arise in respect of each company:

• has Epsom (E) *locus* to bring an action in respect of these activities?;

• are the actions, or proposed actions, of the directors of the relevant companies a breach of their duties as directors?

Answer

It can be assumed that the acts about which E seeks advice are not beyond the powers of the company concerned, that is, they are not *ultra vires*. Two issues arise in respect of each company—first, has E the ability to litigate either on his own account or on behalf of the company (the *locus* point)? Second, is there a cause of action open to him?

(a) Fontwell

E is owed money by Fontwell Ltd (F)—he is a creditor of the company. A creditor of a company has no right to intervene in the running of the company and has no *locus* to complain about the alleged inefficiency of the management either on his own account or on behalf of the company. E has no rights under s 459 Companies Act (CA) 1985, which confers rights only on shareholders. E has the usual remedy open to a creditor owed more than £750, namely to make a statutory demand for the sum and, if it is unpaid, to seek to wind up the company on the ground that it is unable to pay its debts (s 122(1) of the Insolvency Act (IA) 1986). A threat of liquidation may galvanise the company into trying to pay E's debt, although such a payment could be set aside if the company went into liquidation within six months and the payment was found to be a 'preference' (s 239 IA 1986). If the company was to go into liquidation before E had enforced his claim, he would be a preferred creditor for the first £800 of his debt by virtue of s 175 IA 1986 (that is, he would take priority over all other creditors except those with a fixed charge) and an unsecured creditor for the balance, in respect of which he would rank behind anyone holding any charge over the assets of the company. E's position does not look promising unless he moves swiftly or is confident that there will be assets available to satisfy his debt if the company goes into liquidation.

(b) Ludlow

As an employee of Ludlow, E has no *locus* to challenge or to enforce the proposed allotment of shares, either on his own account or on behalf of the company. Section 309 CA 1985 provides that the directors must have regard to the interests of the employees in performing their functions, but this section confers no *locus* upon employees who wish to claim that the directors are not paying due regard to their interests. In addition, there is no evidence that this allotment is not in the interests of the employees. If any offer to allot shares is accepted by E, he is a party to a contract and, as such, would seem to have the usual contractual remedies if the company failed to keep its side of the bargain. However, if the allotment of shares is in some way improper, for example if it is made for an improper purpose, the contract may be unenforceable and the directors (including E), by proposing to make such an allotment, might be in breach of their fiduciary duty

(*Howard Smith Ltd v Ampol Petroleum Ltd (1974)*). However, only a shareholder or the company could raise the invalidity of the allotment and such an allotment can be ratified by the company in general meeting, although the disputed shares cannot be voted (*Bamford v Bamford (1970)*). There is no question of E being forced to buy the shares.

The directors should be warned that, in issuing shares, they must comply with the provisions of the CA 1985 and their own fiduciary obligations. Section 80 CA 1985 provides that the power to allot shares can be exercised by the directors only if they have been authorised so to act, either in the articles or by a resolution of the shareholders, which authorisation can be for an indefinite period in the case of a private company which has so determined by elective resolution (s 80A CA 1985). If an allotment is not authorised, it is still valid (s 80 CA 1985) but the directors are liable to a fine. The directors of Ludlow Ltd (L) should comply with s 89 CA 1985 (pre-emption) in allotting shares, unless they are to be held under an employee share scheme, but failure so to do does not invalidate the allotment. The directors who breached s 89 CA 1985 and L would be liable to compensate those shareholders who were not offered the shares for any loss thereby suffered (s 92 CA 1985). L, being a private company, may have chosen to exclude the right of pre-emption (s 91 CA 1985). If the proposed allotment to employees is at a discount or is otherwise not fully paid, the allotment remains valid but the allottees would be liable to make up the discount (s 112 CA 1985, although an allottee can be relieved of liability by the court: s 113 CA 1985) and the directors and L would be liable to a fine (s 114 CA 1985).

However, the most likely challenge to the allotment of shares would be the potential takeover bidder. An outsider cannot challenge the validity of the allotment but a shareholder could do so on the basis that the directors, in making the allotment, were not acting for a proper purpose (*Bamford v Bamford (1970)*); that is, they were in breach of fiduciary duty. If the challenge was successful, the allotment would be invalid but capable of ratification by the shareholders in general meeting (*Bamford v Bamford (1970)*). A leading case on the improper use of directorial power is the Privy Council decision in *Howard Smith Ltd v Ampol Petroleum Ltd (1974)*, which concerned the allotment of shares. In *Ampol*, the directors of HS, a company in need of further finance, issued shares to members who held a minority interest in the company but offered none to the majority shareholder (A), who had made an unwanted takeover bid, thereby reducing A's shareholding to below 50%. This allotment of shares was challenged by A as an improper use of the directorial power to issue shares.

The Privy Council ruled that, when a use of power is challenged, the court should first consider the nature of the power (that is, why was this power conferred on the directors whose exercise is in question?) and then examine the substantial purpose for which it was exercised. If the power was not exercised for the proper purpose, the exercise of the power is invalid. The court stated that the decision as to whether the power was properly exercised is determined objectively. In this case, the court ruled that the power to allot shares was given to directors to raise funds for the company and that, while the directors intended this allotment to raise capital, the primary purpose of the issue was to defeat A's bid and not to raise money. Consequently, this allotment was invalid and A, the majority shareholder, had no desire to ratify the allotment. This would seem to apply here. Thus, whether E can enforce any contractual right to the shares will depend upon whether the validity of the allotment is challenged and, if it is, whether the shareholders ratify the actions of the directors.

(c) Aintree

E is a minority shareholder in Aintree Ltd (A) and, as a shareholder, he can enforce any rights conferred upon him as a shareholder. Unfortunately, as a shareholder he would seem to have no individual right to complain about the conduct of the board in letting property to one of their number: even if it is a breach of fiduciary duty, the directors owe their duty to the company and not to individual shareholders—that is, current and future shareholders as a body (*Percival v Wright* (1902); *Peskin v Anderson* (2001))—although a director may voluntarily undertake a fiduciary duty towards a shareholder, for example by acting as his agent (*Allen v Hyatt* (1914)). There seems no question of E being owed a fiduciary duty as an individual. Section 322 CA 1985 provides that, if a transaction between a director and a company is a substantial property transaction, it is voidable unless approved by the shareholders in general meeting (a director-shareholder could vote on a resolution to ratify). Approval of such a transaction can be informal: see *Niltan Carson Ltd v Hawthorne* (1988), where knowledge and acquiescence by the majority shareholders was held to constitute approval of the activities of the director. A transaction is a substantial property transaction if a director acquires an interest in a non-cash asset, the value of which is over £100,000 or 10% of the asset value of the company (subject to its value exceeding £2,000), which seems likely to be the case here.

However, the section provides that an unapproved substantial property transaction is voidable at the instance of the *company*. Thus, it seems that E has no *locus* to challenge the lease. If the lease is perceived as being in some way a device to defraud the company, E might, as an exception to *Foss v Harbottle* (1843), be able to bring a derivative action on behalf of the company, but, since the lease is at market value, the conduct of the board seems unimpeachable. Section 459 CA 1985 might prove a more effective statutory remedy for E if he can establish that the conduct of the directors is unfairly prejudicial to the shareholders. E would seem to have no cause of action in respect of the managing director taking up another business, either. Even if such conduct was in breach of the director's service contract, E, as a minority shareholder, has no right to litigate the matter, although he could raise it at a meeting of the company.

(d) Newbury

As a minority shareholder in Newbury Ltd (N), E has no *locus* to complain about any lack of care and skill on the part of those members of the board who failed to attend meetings either on their own account or on behalf of the company. The duty of care and skill is not owed to individual shareholders and a want of care and skill does not form an exception to *Foss* in order to allow E to bring a derivative claim on behalf of the company (*Pavlides v Jensen (1956)*). Indeed, it can be said that the conduct of the non-executive directors may well not constitute a breach of the duty of care and skill owed by directors. The traditional formulation of the nature and extent of this duty is that given by Romer J in *Re City Equitable Fire Insurance Co Ltd (1925)*, in which he held that a director is entitled to leave the day to day running of the company to the officials of the company and is entitled to assume, in the absence of suspicious circumstances, that such officials are performing their duties honestly. Consequently, failure to prevent fraud by the absconding director, unless the circumstances gave rise to suspicion which was not followed up, is unlikely to be actionable even by the company. The absconding director is liable to reimburse the company and any director who knowingly assisted his acquisition of corporate assets would be liable to the company. Such conduct, were it to be present, would be an unratifiable breach of a director's duty, thus allowing E to sue on behalf of the company, by bringing a derivative claim.

▌NOTE

An answer could touch on proposals to reform some of these areas of law depending on the provisions of the Companies Act 2006 (when in force). For instance, the Act provides for the abolition of the rule in *Pavlides v Jensen* and the abolition of the requirement for wrongdoing directors to have a majority of the company's shares.

Question 21

The business of World Con Ltd is construction and property development. The company's articles are based on Table A. The managing director of the company is Leeson and five other directors sit on the board of directors. Between them, the directors own 45% of the shares of the company.

Last month, Leeson, on World Con's behalf, placed an order for five tons of engineering bricks from Maxwell Ltd. Unknown to World Con's board of directors, Leeson received a 'thank you' present from Maxwell of £50,000 for placing the order. The bricks were shortly sold by World Con to an innocent buyer at half their original price.

During the same month, Leeson was approached by a director acting on behalf of Saunders plc, a property developer and former client of World Con, with a view to entering into a contract for the building of a student halls of residence for UK University on a private–public partnership (PPP) basis. A week later, Leeson informed the director of Saunders that World Con was interested only in construction projects of a purely commercial nature, but that another company, Nadir Ltd, was interested in doing the work.

Subsequently, Nadir obtained a contract from Saunders to build the halls of residence and made a £10m profit from the contract. Leeson is a majority shareholder and director of Nadir since its incorporation in 2005.

These activities have come to light and World Con seeks your advice as to what action is available to the company in respect of any breach of the no-conflict rule.

Advise World Con accordingly.

Answer plan

The question requires an analysis of directors' duties and the means by which a company can take action against a director for breach of duty in respect of the no-conflict rule. Assuming that a duty has been breached, there is also a requirement to consider the remedies available to the company in the event of breach and whether action can be taken against any third party who may have participated wrongly in a director's breach of duty.

Answer

The fiduciary (and common law duties) that directors owe are owed to the company, that is, the company's current and future shareholders as a body, and not to any individual shareholder (*Percival v Wright (1902)*; *Peskin v Anderson (2001)*), although a director may voluntarily undertake a fiduciary duty towards a single shareholder by acting as his agent (*Allen v Hyatt (1914)*). In *Percival v Wright (1902)*, the directors of a company were privy to confidential information which, once released, was likely to increase the value of the company's shares. P, a shareholder, offered to sell his shares to the directors, who accepted his offer. When the confidential information was released, P sought to have the contract of sale set aside and to recover the shares, on the ground that the lack of disclosure was a breach of fiduciary duty by the directors. Swinfen-Eady J, in rejecting P's claim, held that the directors did not, simply by being directors, owe a fiduciary duty to an individual shareholder; they did owe such a duty to the *company* but they had not broken it.

In *Peskin v Anderson (2001)*, the directors were held not to owe a duty to former shareholders to inform them of the disposal of a company asset, which resulted in existing members each receiving a windfall of £34,000, as there was no special factual relationship generating a fiduciary obligation such as a duty of disclosure.

These fiduciary (or equitable) duties require a director to exercise his powers in a way which has regard to the interests of the person to whom the duties are owed and not to abuse his position of trust and influence within the company. In respect of corporate property, the director's fiduciary duty goes further and, in common with a trustee, a director cannot, without the approval of the shareholders, derive any benefit from the use of corporate property.

THE CONTRACT BETWEEN WORLD CON (WC) LTD AND MAXWELL (M) LTD

A director is under a duty to avoid a conflict of interest arising as between his duty to the company and his own personal interest. The House of Lords in *Aberdeen Rly Co v Blaikie Bros (1854)* ruled that a director could not benefit directly or indirectly from a contract made by his company, for example, where he enters into a service contract, or where a director benefits indirectly from a contract between his company and a third party (such as being in receipt of a bonus or commission) without making adequate disclosure of his own interest in that contract. Disclosure should be to the shareholders, unless the articles allow disclosure to the board (for example, Art 85 of Table A). Further, s 317 of the Companies Act (CA) 1985 provides rules for the nature of the disclosure to the board, but the penalty for failing to comply with s 317 CA 1985 is a criminal one, not a civil one. For the civil consequences of non-disclosure, we need to turn to general equitable rules, which provide (a) that the contract is voidable at the option of the company (*Aberdeen Rly Co v Blaikie Bros (1854)*) and (b) the director can be held accountable for any secret profit made (*Boston Deep Sea Fishing Ice Co v Ansell (1888)*). Given that L did not disclose his interest in the contract between WC Ltd and M Ltd, the contract becomes voidable, although whether WC Ltd can rescind the contract depends on whether the right to exercise rescission has been lost. On the facts, it would appear the company cannot rescind the contract, as restoration of the parties' property (a condition of rescission) would not be possible, the goods having being sold to an innocent purchaser.

However, whether the contract is voided or not, the company can compel the director to account for any secret profit he made from breaching the no-conflict rule. Alternatively, a director can be sued in damages (more precisely, equitable compensation) where, in breaching the no-conflict rule, he causes the company to suffer a loss. In *Mahesan v Malaysia Government Officers' Co-operative Housing Society (1978)* a housing society company claimed from the manager of the society the difference between the amount the society paid for the land and what it was later sold for, the original price not being its market value. Although we do not know the market conditions behind the original purchase of the goods or any external factors affecting the subsequent sale of the goods, the quick nature of the sale of the engineering bricks suggests that goods were not acquired at market value. The question does not reveal the amount of the loss suffered by WC, but it is likely to have been greater than the amount of L's secret profit. In *Attorney-General for Hong Kong v Reid (1994)*, the Privy Council recognised a proprietary remedy by way of a constructive trust in favour of the company against the director or other agent in respect of a bribe, so that the company would be able to claim any profit the director made from his use of the bribe.

THE CONTRACT BETWEEN NADIR (N) LTD AND SAUNDERS (S) LTD

As Lord Porter stated in *Regal (Hastings) Ltd v Gulliver (1942)*, 'Directors, no doubt, are not trustees, but they occupy a fiduciary position towards the company whose board they form.' As a fiduciary, each director is individually subject to equitable duties—duties which require him to exercise his powers in a way which has regard to the interests of the person to whom the duties are owed and not to abuse his position of trust and influence within the company. Indeed, in respect of corporate property, the director's fiduciary duty goes further and, in common with a trustee, a director cannot, without the approval of the shareholders, derive any benefit from the use of corporate property. The general duty to put corporate interest above private profit is augmented in respect of corporate property; in common with a trustee, a director cannot appropriate corporate property. If he does so appropriate, he is liable as a constructive trustee (*JJ Harrison (Property) Ltd (2003)*). It is obvious that, if a director appropriates the company's tangible property, he will be liable to return the property to the company. The same is true of appropriation of intangible corporate assets, for example, the benefit of a contract possessed by the company. This liability for misappropriation is extended to commercial opportunities which are within the company's grasp. In *Cook v Deeks (1916)*, a company, X, was about to sign a contract to build a railway when X was persuaded by three of the four directors of X to award the contract to a new company which they had formed. The directors were held liable to hold the benefit of the contract as constructive trustees for X. Neither could the directors be excused by the subsequent shareholder ratification of their actions (the three directors held 75% of the shares in X), for misappropriation of corporate assets is an unratifiable breach of a director's duty. The fiduciary duty provides that a director should not benefit from his position as director, a duty which extends after the ending of the directorship, but is this an absolute prohibition? Some cases (see the comments in *Regal (Hastings) Ltd v Gulliver (1942)*) suggest that a director must account for any benefit deriving from the use of information gained in a corporate capacity, even if this is also available elsewhere, but another view suggests that a director can benefit from information if there is no real conflict of interest between himself and his company in his use of the information. Where there is a conflict of interest, the fact that the company was unlikely to be able to use that information itself does not justify a director using it for his own benefit. In *Industrial Developement Consultants Ltd v Cooley (1972)*, C, the managing director of the company, was party to negotiations by the company for the design and construction of a gas terminal. It became clear that the company was unlikely to obtain the contract and C feigned illness, resigned his directorship and successfully tendered for the contract on his own account. The judge held C liable to account for the profit he had made on the contract. Although the company was unlikely to get the contract, C was not entitled to use information concerning it and obtained in corporate service, for his own benefit. In contrast, in *Island Export Finance Ltd v Umunna (1986)*, a former director who successfully tendered for a contract with the Cameroon postal authorities was not in breach of his fiduciary duty despite the fact that he had gained useful information and contacts with the authority while negotiating a contract with it on the company's behalf some two years ago. The court noted that there was a lack of a 'maturing business opportunity' for the director to exploit. Further examples of cases involving a director's liability for a misuse of corporate property or opportunity include the recent cases of *Bhullar v Bhullar (2003)*, *Ball v Eden Project Ltd (2004)* and *LC Services Ltd v Brown (2003)*. In *LC Services Ltd v Brown (2003)*, a director, in breach of duty delivered a copy of a company database to a rival company for whom he worked and removed company documents and company maintenance procedures. He had misused confidential information. In *Ball v Eden Project Ltd (2004)* the court held that, despite B's claim for compensation in respect of a dispute with the company over remuneration, that did not entitle the director to register the company's mark in his own name and deprive the company of the use of its property.

Judging by the cases in this area, it would appear that L has breached the no-conflict rule by appropriating an opportunity that belonged to the company. The information does not appear to be in the 'public domain' and the fact that WC Ltd might not be interested in the opportunity may not absolve L from liability as the information might be considered 'worthwhile and commercially attractive' to the company (*Bhullar*) or the director is under a duty to pass on the information (*Industrial Development Consultants Ltd v Cooley (1972)*; *Bhullar v Bhullar (2003)*). If, however, he had obtained approval from the shareholders, he might be able to escape liability (*Regal (Hastings) Ltd v Regal (1942)*). For misuse of corporate property, L would be liable to account for any profit made. In the question, any profit that has been made has been made by N Ltd, a company controlled by L. In these circumstances, to allow recovery by WC Ltd, the court may be prepared to lift the corporate veil (*Trustor AB v Smallbone (1999)*) or to hold the third party liable as a constructive trustee (see below).

LIABILITY OF THIRD PARTIES

Liability can be imposed on third parties who have been involved in a director's breach of duty (*Selangor United Rubber Estates v Cradock (1968)*—third party liable as a constructive trustee). Whether such liability can exist in respect of the facts of the question depends on whether M Ltd or N Ltd had knowingly participated in a breach of duty or trust by the director on the basis of 'knowing receipt' or 'knowing (or dishonest) assistance'; the appropriate remedy is either restoration of property misapplied and held by the third party or damages representing the value of the misapplied assets (*Royal Brunei Airlines Sdn Bhd v Tan (1995)*; *Twinsectra Ltd v Yardley (2002)*; *Barlow Clowes International Ltd v Eurotrust International Ltd (2006)*). In *Twinsectra Ltd v Yardley (2002)*, the House of Lords held that in order to show that defendant has been dishonest for purpose of liability as an accessory it must be shown that his conduct was dishonest by the ordinary standards of reasonable and honest people and that the defendant realised that by those standards his conduct was dishonest. It is not necessary to show dishonesty on the part of the third party in respect of knowing receipt (*Bank of Credit and Commerce International (Overseas) Ltd v Akindele (2001)*). A consideration of the facts of the question suggest that M Ltd and N Ltd have participated in respect of L's breach of duty either on the basis of knowing receipt or knowing (or dishonest) assistance. This is, however, unlikely to be the position in the case of the purchaser of the engineering bricks who acted innocently.

CORPORATE ACTION

It should be noted that the proper claimant to address a wrong done to the company is the company itself (*Foss v Harbottle (1843)*). The power to sue on the company's behalf normally resides with the directors (Art 70 Table A—the wide power of management), but it can lie with the general meeting, either through the passing of a special resolution directing the directors on how to act or through taking action under a default power where the directors have committed the wrong to be suffered by the company.

NOTE

The Companies Act 2006 contain a codification of directors duties, including the duty relating to interests in company contracts or misusing corporate property and opportunities. The Act restates the case law duties but amends the procedure on authorisation for directors to follow in order to avoid liability for a breach of the no-conflict rule. To date, these provisions are not in force.

Question 22

The board of Kington Ltd, which consists of Cecil, Dot and Epsilon, have authority to issue shares and the articles of the company exclude the right of pre-emption. Cecil is also a non-executive director of Pembridge Ltd, a company in the same line of business as Kington, which owns 14% of Kington's shares. Anson plc purchased 26% of Kington's shares from the company, on the understanding that, if any further shares were created, they would be allotted to Anson to facilitate its eventual acquisition of the company. The remaining 60% of the Kington shares are owned by the James family, who proposed Dot and Epsilon as directors. Kington is short of work and the board hope to sell its business to Pembridge. If the deal goes ahead, Dot and Epsilon would join the Pembridge board, but 50% of the Kington workforce would be made redundant. The board recommended acceptance of a takeover bid by Pembridge, and members of the James family, who hold 30% of the Kington shares, have agreed to sell their shares to Pembridge. The directors of Kington propose to create further ordinary shares and allot them to Pembridge for cash, thus giving Pembridge 53.3% of Kington's share capital; Anson's shareholding would be reduced to 21.6%.

Advise Anson.

Answer plan

Anson would oppose the plan for two reasons: first, the reduction in its shareholding to a figure below that capable of blocking a special resolution; and, second, the destruction of its hopes of taking over Kington. Anson has a number of lines of attack. Consider:

(a) the allotment of shares—improper purpose, variation of class rights, s 459 of the Companies Act (CA) 1985;

(b) the role of the Kington board;

(c) the non-supporting members of the James family.

Try to marry practical with legal advice.

Answer

Anson (A) has three choices open to it when faced with the proposals made by the board of Kington (K). It could launch a rival bid to that made by Pembridge (P), offer to sell its shares to P or try to destroy or modify the current proposals. Even if it was to launch a rival bid, there is no guarantee that it would be successful and there may be practical reasons not to proceed with such a plan, for example lack of funds. An offer to sell shares to P might be rejected and may not be in line with A's business plans. It should be noted that P has no right to force A to sell. However, if P had made an offer for all the shares in K and its offer had been accepted by holders of 90% of the shares, ss 428–30F CA 1985 permit P to acquire the remaining shares compulsorily and these sections also give a right to the holder of the unpurchased shares to be bought out. Where shares are purchased under the provisions of ss 428–30F CA 1985, the price payable is that offered to those who have accepted the offer. Obviously, P cannot obtain 90% of the shares without A's agreement. If A does not wish to make a counter-offer or sell its shares, it may wish to oppose the proposed scheme; can it do so?

(a) The allotment of shares

A company which has issued its full complement of shares can increase its share capital, if authorised by its articles (Art 32 of Table A so authorises this), in accordance with s 121 CA 1985. Section 121 CA 1985 permits a company to increase share capital by ordinary resolution, and thus A cannot block the creation of further shares. In issuing shares, directors must comply with the provisions of the CA 1985 and their own fiduciary obligations. Section 80 CA 1985 provides that the power to allot shares can be exercised by the directors only if they have been authorised so to act either in the articles or by a resolution of the shareholders, which authorisation can be for an indefinite period in the case of a private company which has so determined by elective resolution (s 80A CA 1985). Hence, the board of K have the necessary authority. K has excluded the right of pre-emption, which, as a private company, it is permitted to do (s 91 CA 1985), so that shares do not have to be offered to existing shareholders. The proposed allotment is for cash at, it is assumed, a non-discounted price. The requirements of the CA 1985 appear to be satisfied.

The validity of the allotment is more likely to be questioned on the basis that the directors, in making this allotment, were not acting properly. Directors are not required to obtain the highest possible price for any shares allotted (provided that there is no discount) but, in choosing to allot shares, the directors are subject to the fiduciary duty—to exercise the power for a proper purpose (*Bamford v Bamford (1970)*). An improper allotment is invalid and capable of challenge by A, even though such an allotment is ratifiable by ordinary resolution (*contra Foss v Harbottle (1843)*), unless and until it is ratified. If the allotment is ratified before any court action is brought, the court would refuse to hear A's application. Is the allotment by the directors of K in breach of their fiduciary duty? Consider the Privy Council decision in *Howard Smith Ltd v Ampol Petroleum Ltd (1974)*, which concerned the allotment of shares. In *Ampol*, the directors of HS, a company in need of further finance, issued shares to members who held a minority interest in the company but offered none to the majority shareholder (A), who had made an unwanted takeover bid, thereby reducing A's shareholding to below 50%. This allotment of shares was challenged by A as an improper use of the directorial power to issue shares. The Privy Council ruled that, when a use of power is challenged, the court should first consider the nature of the power, that is, why was this power conferred on the directors whose exercise thereof is in question? It should then examine the substantial purpose for which it was exercised. If the power was not exercised for the proper purpose, the exercise of the power is invalid.

The court stated that the decision as to whether the power was properly exercised is determined objectively. In this case, the court ruled that the power to allot shares was given to directors to raise funds for the company and that while the directors intended this allotment to raise capital the primary purpose of the issue was to defeat A's bid and not to raise money. Consequently, this allotment was invalid and A, the majority shareholder, had no desire to ratify the allotment. This would seem to apply here, with the proviso that A, without the help of at least some of the James family, cannot block ratification. On a vote to ratify, the shareholders, whose votes are in dispute, cannot exercise the right to vote. The fact that the employees of K would be adversely affected by the takeover would tend to support the impropriety of the allotment (s 309 CA 1985), although an attempt to allot shares to preserve *bona fide* workers' jobs has been held to be improper (*Hogg v Cramphorn Ltd (1967)*). In *Hogg v Cramphorn (1967)*, the allotment of shares was later ratified by the passing of an ordinary resolution at a general meeting of the company.

If A cannot block the allotment of shares by raising the validity of the director's acts, it may seek to do so on the basis that it had an agreement that any new shares would be allotted to it and that failure to do so is breach of contract or a variation of its class rights. If there is a valid contract between K and A relating to the allotment of shares, it would seem to give A a contractual right to the new shares, but if it is described as an understanding, it may be difficult to enforce as a contract. The understanding might be deemed to be a class right and, where a company proposes to vary the rights attaching to a class of shares, it must comply with its own internal procedures and the provisions of ss 125–27 CA 1985.

A faces two difficulties. First, can its parcel of ordinary shares be regarded as a class distinct from the other ordinary shares? Second, is the dilution of its shareholding and the disregard of its understanding a variation of any class right? In *Cumbria Newspapers Group Ltd v Cumberland and Westmoreland Herald Ltd (1987)*, Scott J postulated three situations. First, where there are rights attaching to a particular group of shares; second, where rights were conferred on a shareholder in his capacity as a shareholder (as in the *Cumbria* case); and, third, where rights were conferred on a particular individual. Only the first two categories create class rights. Applying this case, A might have class rights if the understanding could be called a right conferred on A in its capacity as a shareholder. If this is not the case, the mere fact that there are two opposing groups of shareholders is unlikely to be regarded as creating two classes of share (see the Court of Appeal decision in *Greenhalgh v Arderne Cinemas (1946)*). Indeed, even if A can be treated as constituting a separate class of ordinary shareholder, the diminution in voting strength is unlikely to be seen as a variation of class rights. In *Greenhalgh v Arderne Cinemas (1946)*, G's ordinary shares had been subdivided into five, thereby quintupling his votes. The company then proposed similarly to subdivide the rest of the ordinary shares, thereby affecting the efficacy of G's votes and, as here, depriving him of negative voting control. The Court of Appeal held that, provided that the rights attaching to G's shares remained the same (they did—he was not losing votes), there was no variation of his class rights, notwithstanding the fact that the result was to alter the voting equilibrium of the shareholders.

Greenhalgh was distinguished by Foster J in *Clemens v Clemens Bros Ltd (1976)* on non-existent grounds. In *Clemens*, the majority shareholder (55%), who was the dominant director, authorised the allotment of shares to other directors, thereby depriving the minority shareholder (45%) of her negative voting control. The judge set the allotment aside. While this case has parallels with A's position, there is an important distinction. In *Clemens*, the disputed allotment was made by the majority shareholder and the judge felt able to classify the allotment as a breach of the fiduciary duty imposed on a shareholder. A should be warned that it is unlikely that *Clemens* will be followed here. If there is no variation of class rights, ss 125–27 CA 1985 do not apply. A should argue that the understanding does create a separate class of shares and that the allotment is a variation which must be approved by the appropriate majority of the relevant class (in compliance with s 125 CA 1985). Since A is the sole member of the class, the majority will not be forthcoming.

A will be best advised to challenge the validity of the allotment under s 459 CA 1985. This section provides that a shareholder can seek an order that a proposed act of the company would be unfairly prejudicial to him and, if successful, the court can make such order as it thinks fit (s 461 CA 1985). There has been something of a torrent of case law on this provision and it has proved a flexible tool in judicial hands for the righting of injustice to minority shareholders. Section 459 CA 1985 provides a remedy independent of the existence of (or lack of) any other remedy, provided that there has been unfair prejudice, although any remedy is at the court's discretion. Cases have shown that an attempt to dilute the voting strength of a shareholding may be unfairly prejudicial (see *Re OC (Transport) Ltd (1984)*) even if, as in this case, that is not in breach of company law. A court would consider the basis on which A acquired its shares—did A have a legitimate expectation that it would retain negative voting control such that it would be inequitable to deny that right? If so, any dilution is likely to be unfairly prejudicial—or had A done anything to justify deprivation of negative voting control? If unfair prejudice is proven, the court could order A to be bought out at a fair price, could require shares to be allotted to A to preserve the voting equilibrium or could allow A to take K over, although the last remedy is unlikely.

(b) The conduct of the directors

A may feel aggrieved by the conduct of the board of K. Cecil (C) is a director of P already and Dot (D) and Epsilon (E) are to join the board of P. All three have recommended acceptance of the P bid. Surprisingly, being a director of two rival companies (P and K are in the same field) is not a breach of director's duty (*London & Mashonaland Exploration Co Ltd v New Mashonaland Exploration Co Ltd (1891)*), but it is clear that rival directorships are not a breach of duty by a director only when the director is not involved in management at all. In the case of *Euro RSCG SA v Conran (1992)*, the court held that it would be difficult to envisage a situation where a person who was a director of two competing companies would not be in breach of his duty of loyalty and good faith if he took any part in running either company. However, this potential breach of fiduciary duty by C is actionable by the company and not by A (*Foss v Harbottle (1843)*).

The directors of K, in recommending P's takeover bid, probably owe a duty to individual shareholders and not, as is usual, merely to the company. Whether this is because the directors, by offering advice, have voluntarily undertaken a duty towards shareholders (akin to *Allen v Hyatt (1914)*) or whether it is because directors automatically owe a duty to current shareholders as the manifestation of the company in a takeover context is not clear. The duty seems to be one of honesty and fair dealing—putting the case for the bid fairly (*Gething v Kilner (1972)*)—and there is no requirement to support the highest bid (*Dawson International plc v Coats Paton plc (1989)*), although the board should do nothing to prevent members from getting the best possible price (*Heron International v Lord Grade (1983)*). If the duty owed to the shareholders is broken, the breach is actionable by the shareholders: in *Gething*, the judge ordered the withdrawal of a misleading circular issued to shareholders, but in other cases it has been suggested, *obiter*, that damages could be awarded. If the directors of K could be said to be in a special relationship with their shareholders, it would be possible to impose liability under *Hedley Byrne v Heller (1964)*, but the assessment of damages in the case of a private company would be difficult.

▌CONCLUSION

Apart from the legal advice offered to A, it would be well advised to seek to mobilise the James family to block the allotment of shares and promise that, if it is not yet in a position to make a bid, it will soon do so at a price better than that of P (not that such a promise would be enforceable). Alternatively, it should sell out to P if the price is right rather than risk being a minority shareholder in a hostile environment.

Question 23

Sell-U-Home Ltd, which operates a chain of estate agents, has a subsidiary, Fix-U-Up Ltd, which offers financial services to homebuyers. Julian, a director of Sell-U-Home, asks Fix-U-Up to enter into the following transactions:

(a) to lend Julian £75,000 to enable him and his wife to purchase a holiday home;

(b) to pay Julian's monthly account at a local hotel (where he frequently entertains clients) on the understanding that Julian will repay Fix-U-Up in respect of any private use of the hotel; and

(c) to guarantee a hire-purchase contract, under which Julian's son, Sandy, is to acquire a car.

Advise the directors of Fix-U-Up, which is in a shaky financial state, as to whether it may comply with Julian's requests, and, if so, with what conditions must it comply.

Answer plan

This question would only be set for students with access to the relevant statutory material, in which case it is relatively straightforward. Statutory interpretation is all that is required and the question could even be tackled by a student who has done no revision on this area but knows that there are statutory provisions on loans. Consider any general points on directors' duties and, then, in respect of the three situations, consider:

(a) is the proposal prohibited?;

(b) if so, does an exception apply?;

(c) what are the conditions for the operation of an exception?; and

(d) consequences of no exception or non-compliance with conditions in (c).

Answer

The directors of the subsidiary company, Fix-U-Up (F), have an unfettered discretion to run the company as they see fit. However, they are, in law, required to comply with instructions given to them by their shareholders by special resolution and, in practice, may find it prudent to comply with the wishes of a director of their (one assumes) major or sole shareholder, Sell-U-Home (S). In exercising their powers, the directors of F must comply with the usual duties imposed upon directors, particularly the obligation to act *bona fide* in the interests of F and to exercise their powers for proper purposes. Failure to comply with these fiduciary duties could result in action by F, but since F is controlled by S, this is unlikely unless Julian (J) was acting without the approval of S or the remainder of its board. If F were to go into liquidation, the liquidator would also have the power to sue the directors of F for breach of fiduciary duty (for example, acting for an improper purpose in making these 'loans') and it would be no defence to an action that they complied with the unofficial instructions of J, although this might allow the court to relieve them from the consequences of their actions (s 727 of the Companies Act (CA) 1985). Indeed, these loans might be seen as wrongful trading by the directors and, if F were to go into insolvent liquidation, the liquidator could seek contribution from the directors to swell the company's assets (s 214 of the Insolvency Act (IA) 1986).

In addition to the general duties imposed on directors, ss 330–46 CA 1985 contain specific provisions dealing with loans and related transactions. These sections restrict the ability of a company to make loans (or guarantee a loan) to a director of the company, or a director of a holding company, or a shadow director (s 330(1) CA 1985). Further, where the company is a relevant company, the prohibition is extended to quasi-loans and credit transactions (or guarantees thereof) to the same people or to a person 'connected' to such a person (s 330(2) CA 1985). A company is a relevant company if it is either a public company or a member of a group in which one of the members is a public company (s 331 CA 1985). F and S are not public companies (both bear the name Ltd), but it is possible that there is a further company in their group which is a public company, so the possibility that F is a relevant company cannot be excluded, even though it seems unlikely. A connected person includes a spouse and children under the age of 18 (s 346 CA 1985) of a director of a company, so that J son may be a connected person. Perhaps the purchase of a car would tend to suggest a child who may be over 18 and, consequently, not connected. J wife (see (a) below) is a connected person. J may also be deemed to be a shadow director of F, since he seems to be a person on whose instructions the board of F are accustomed to act and the rules on loans apply to shadow directors.

We must now turn to the three proposals to be considered by the board of F.

(a) The loan to J and his wife

Section 330 CA 1985 provides that a company shall not make a loan to a director of a holding company. J is such a director and his wife is a connected person, so the loan, unless it falls within an exception, is prohibited. The consequences of such a loan are that the transaction would be voidable at F's behest unless restitution of money or any asset which is the subject of the transaction is impossible, or the company has been indemnified, or restitution would affect the rights of a *bona fide* purchaser for value (s 341 CA 1985). This would allow F to recover the money, if lent, from J and his wife. Section 341 CA 1985 also provides that a director (or connected person) who authorised the loan must account to the company making the loan for any gain made as a result of the loan and indemnify the company against loss. Thus, if the loan was made, the holiday home bought and then resold at a profit, the profit would be payable to F. There are exemptions from liability. One which might apply here is s 341(5) CA 1985, which exempts from liability any director or connected person who did not know the circumstances which constituted a contravention of the Act. This applies to persons who do not know the *circumstances* which were the contravention; not knowing about the relevant law is not a defence. There are also criminal penalties (fine and/or imprisonment) for breach of s 330 CA 1985 but only where the lending company is a relevant company. The criminal penalties apply to the company, to the directors of the company or to any person (J here) who procures the illegal transaction.

Section 330 CA 1985 provides that a loan to a director may fall within one of the exemptions in ss 332–38 CA 1985. The only section which might be relevant is s 338 CA 1985. This provides that a loan made by a money lending company may be exempted from s 330 CA 1985. Section 338(2) CA 1985 defines a money lending company as a company whose ordinary business includes the making of loans. F is a company which offers financial services to homebuyers and, as such, it may make loans. However, if it organises loans from third parties, for example building societies, and arranges security for loans, for example endowment policies, it would seem not to be *making* loans but facilitating loans; it is thus not a money lending company. Even if F is a money lending company, the loan is not exempt unless s 338(3) CA 1985 is complied with—the loan must be made in the ordinary course of business (this seems unlikely here) and the loan must be on the same terms as that which would be made to a non-director applicant of the same financial standing as Julian (one could call this 'standard loan terms'). A non-relevant company can lend an unlimited amount under this provision but a relevant company is limited to loans of up to £100,000 unless it is a banking company (which F is not). The second condition set out in s 338(2) CA 1985 (the 'standard loan terms') does not necessarily apply where the money is lent for the purchase or improvement of a house (s 338(6) CA 1985). However, this restriction will not apply to J, since it is limited to loans for the purchase, etc, of the director's only or main residence.

An exempt transaction must be revealed in the accounts of the company.

(b) J's monthly account

Payment of J's monthly account is not a loan and is thus not prohibited at all under s 330(1) CA 1985, although it may be a breach of fiduciary duty by the directors of F to enter into such a transaction. In addition, there will be tax to pay on the benefit received by J. If F is a relevant company, the payment may be prohibited by s 330(2) CA 1985, which provides that a relevant company cannot make a quasi-loan to a director of a holding company. A quasi-loan is defined in s 331(2) CA 1985 to include an agreement whereby a person (F in this case) agrees to pay a sum to a third party (the hotel) and expenditure incurred by another (J) for which the company will be reimbursed. Thus, J's private usage of the hotel which the company pays for and which he has agreed to reimburse is a quasi-loan. The business usage of the hotel would not be a quasi-loan, since J has not agreed, and is not liable, to reimburse F for this sum, although s 337 CA 1985 would apply. Section 337 CA 1985 states that providing a director with funds to meet business expenses (or reimbursement thereof) does not fall within s 330 CA 1985, provided that there is adequate disclosure in advance of the provision of funds (matters to be disclosed are set out in the Act) and the transaction is approved by ordinary resolution. Failure to make adequate disclosure or failure to approve results in the money being repayable by the director. Relevant companies are limited in the amount of expenditure outstanding at any one time which it can reimburse (currently £20,000). Should F be paying for J to entertain clients of S anyway? Perhaps there is an improper purpose issue here.

The quasi-loan will be exempt from s 330 CA 1985 if the quasi-loan (including any other quasi-loan) is for less than £5,000 and is repayable within two months of it being incurred (s 332 CA 1985), as seems likely to be the case here. Arguably, s 338 CA 1985 would also apply if F was a money lending company (see above).

An exempt transaction must be revealed in the accounts of the company.

(c) Guarantee of the hire-purchase contract

If Sandy is over 18, he is not a connected person and whether the transaction should be approved by the board of F depends upon the power of F to guarantee hire-purchase contracts, the ambit of the powers of the board, and whether this a proper purpose. If Sandy is a connected person, the guarantee of a credit transaction (which includes a hire-purchase contract—s 331(4) CA 1985) is prohibited if F is a relevant company (s 330(4) CA 1985). This seems improbable but not impossible. The usual penalties apply in such a case unless the guarantee is exempt. There seems to be one section which could exempt the guarantee—s 335 CA 1985 (s 338 CA 1985 does not apply to guarantees of credit transactions; s 334 CA 1985 only applies to loans of small amounts to directors). Section 335 provides that s 330(4) CA 1985 does not apply to a transaction entered into by the company in the ordinary course of business and it is made on the same terms as would be offered to an applicant who was not connected with the company. It seems unlikely that F's business ordinarily includes the guaranteeing of such contracts as this.

▌ABILITY TO SUE

Failure to comply with these statutory duties could result in a civil action. However, since the power to sue is vested in F, and F is controlled by S, such an action is unlikely unless J was acting without the approval of S. If F were to go into liquidation, the liquidator would also have the power to sue the directors of F for breach of the Act and it would be no defence to an action that they complied with the instructions of J, although this might allow the court to relieve them from the consequences of their actions (s 727 CA 1985).

▌NOTE

The answer given is based on current and relevant parts of Pt X CA 1985, but the Law Commissions (1999) have made recommendations in relation to Pt X, suggesting, *inter alia*, that:

- the definition of 'connected person' should be extended to include cohabitants, including same-sex cohabitants, and their infant children living with them;
- restrictions placed upon loans and similar transactions should be extended to all companies, not just 'relevant' companies; and
- civil remedies should be used to replace many of the criminal sanctions.

Other recommendations for change were made by the Company Law Review Steering Group. The Companies Act 2006 does contain changes to Pt X CA 1985 based on these recommendations. To date, these are not in force. However, some parts of Pt X CA 1985 have been repealed and are in force (from 6 April 2007), namely ss 311 and 323–29 CA 1985.

Question 24

Certain persons, notably directors, are in a position to gain valuable information about a company. To what extent, if at all, does the law prevent such persons from using that information for their own personal profit?

Answer plan

This is a general question, requiring a student to select information carefully and not simply reproduce vast amounts of information. It is important to consider both the civil and the criminal law in this context.

Answer

While this question is not limited to directors, it is obvious that directors are a group well placed to acquire valuable information about their company, so directors are primarily considered. All companies are required by law to have at least one director (s 282 of the Companies Act (CA) 1985), public companies must have at least two and Table A provides that all companies shall have at least two directors unless the company determines otherwise by ordinary resolution (Art 64). A single director cannot also be the company secretary. Limitations on the ability of a director (or others) to use information gained by virtue of his connection with the company fall into two principal categories—criminal sanctions and civil penalties—although there are other minor constraints.

CRIMINAL LAW

Information about companies is an important factor in determining the value of company shares. Such information is available to those closely connected with the company, giving them the opportunity to deal in the shares of the company before that information is generally known. Use of inside information (insider dealing) is generally regarded as reprehensible, first, in that it lowers investor confidence in the Stock Exchange (though not all condemn insider dealing on this ground). Second, insider dealing may constitute fraud on the shareholders, for example, if they are persuaded to sell their shares to the directors or others at an undervalue relative to the value of the shares once the information known to the directors is widely known. Where fraud is provable, which is difficult, directors who defraud shareholders can be prosecuted. More importantly, the Criminal Justice Act (CJA) 1993 (which replaces earlier legislation) makes insider dealing a criminal offence. While fraud is difficult to prove, it is wider in its scope than the CJA 1993, which does not apply to unlisted securities, that is, shares in private companies and shares in unquoted public companies, or face to face, as opposed to market, dealings.

The CJA 1993 provides that, if a person deals in securities (the Act covers dealings in things other than shares, for example gilts) listed on a regulated market, for example the Stock Exchange, he is guilty of an offence if:

(a) he is an insider (or a tippee);

(b) he is privy to specific and precise information which relates to the shares themselves or the state of the company which issued them; and

(c) the information has not been made public;

(d) the information is of the sort which, if it had been made public, would be likely to have had a significant effect on the share price; and

(e) the dealing is intended to make a profit or prevent a loss.

The definition of 'insider' includes directors and a tippee is a person who has obtained information, directly or indirectly, from an insider. Liability under the CJA 1993 is entirely criminal and no civil remedy is available to shareholders who have sold shares without knowing that the purchaser was privy to inside knowledge which might have affected the share price. Experience of the provisions concerning insider dealing suggests that so few criminal cases are brought that it is either a very effective provision (so no one breaks the law) or that it is very hard to discover if insider dealing has occurred. The rules requiring a director to disclose any interest in the shares of the company aid any investigation of a director's share dealing, provided, of course, proper disclosure is made.

Under the Financial Services and Markets Act 2000, the Secretary of State and the Financial Services Authority have powers of investigation in respect of suspected cases of insider dealing.

In addition to the criminal penalties under the CJA 1993, the Stock Exchange Code for Securities Transactions, which forms part of the Listing Rules, limits the right of a director of a company to deal in its shares and requires disclosure of all authorised dealings.

CIVIL LAW

Directors, and possibly senior employees, have a fiduciary relationship with their company but are not to be equated with trustees. As Lord Porter put it in *Regal (Hastings) Ltd v Gulliver (1942)*, 'Directors, no doubt, are not trustees, but they occupy a fiduciary position towards the company whose board they form'. As a fiduciary, each director is automatically and individually subject to equitable duties—fiduciary duties—which require him to exercise his powers in a way which has regard to the interests of the person to whom the duties are owed and not to abuse his position of trust and influence within the company. In addition to this automatic fiduciary duty which attaches to a director in all he does and at all times (*IDC v Cooley (1972)*), a director may, in particular circumstances, incur further duties. For example, a director-employee owes to the company the duty of loyalty and good faith which is imposed on all employees, and, in respect of corporate property, the director's duty can be equated with that of a trustee: a director cannot, without the unanimous approval of the shareholders, derive any benefit (even innocently) from any use of corporate property. Fiduciary and other duties are owed to the company, that is, current and future shareholders as a body, and not to individual shareholders (*Percival v Wright (1902)*). In *Percival v Wright* (1902), the directors of a company were privy to confidential information which, once released, was likely to increase the value of the company's shares. Percival (P), a shareholder, offered to sell his shares to the directors, who accepted the offer. When the confidential information was released, P sought to have the contract of sale set aside and to recover the shares, on the ground that the lack of disclosure was a breach of fiduciary duty by the directors. Swinfen-Eady J, in rejecting P's claim, held that the directors did not, simply by being directors, owe a fiduciary duty to an individual shareholder; they did owe such a duty to the company. This case remains the law, despite being the subject of fierce criticism, and has been reaffirmed by the Court of Appeal in *Peskin v Anderson (2001)* but it does not preclude a director from being found to have chosen to undertake some responsibility to a shareholder (fiduciary, contractual or tortious). For example, in *Allen v Hyatt (1914)*, the directors induced the shareholders to give them options to purchase shares without disclosing the possibility that the directors would be able to resell the shares at a profit. The Privy Council found that the directors had, by their words and actions, made themselves agents for each shareholder and owed the usual obligations of an agent to his principal. These obligations include a duty to account for any benefits accruing from the agency so that the directors had to account for the profits they had made on the exercise of the options and the subsequent resale of the shares.

To what extent do the duties imposed on directors and owed to the company impinge upon their ability to use information obtained by virtue of their position for their own profit? The civil law, unlike the CJA 1993, makes no distinction between public and private companies, nor is the law limited to market dealings in the shares of a company. Consider three categories:

(a) obligations akin to trusteeship;

(b) fiduciary duties;

(c) competing interests.

(a) Trusteeship

In common with a trustee, a director cannot, without the unanimous approval of the shareholders, use corporate property to make a personal profit. A director who does use corporate property to make such a profit is a constructive trustee of any benefit derived for the company (*JJ Harrison (Properties) Ltd v Harrison (2001)*). This constructive trusteeship can also be imposed on a third party who has knowingly received, or dishonestly assisted in the misuse of, corporate property (*Royal Brunei Airlines Sdn Bhd v Tan (1995)*; *Twinsectra Ltd v Yardley (2002)*; *Barlow Clower International Ltd v Eurotrust International Ltd (2006)*). It is obvious that, if a director appropriates the company's tangible property, however innocently, he will be liable to return the property to the company. The same is true of appropriation of intangible corporate assets, for example the benefit of a contract entered into by the company. This liability for misappropriation has been extended to commercial opportunities which are within the company's grasp. For example, in *Cook v Deeks (1916)*, a company, X, was about to sign a contract to build a railway when the railway company was persuaded by some of the directors of X to award the contract to a new company which they had formed. The directors were held liable to hold the benefit of the contract as constructive trustees for X. There seems no reason why a person other than a director should not be subject to a 'trustee' duty where the facts demand it.

As yet, there is no judicial decision that information alone can be treated as corporate property and thus subject to the 'trustee' duty imposed on a director (or others). The most important case in point is *Boardman v Phipps (1967)*, in which the House of Lords considered the liability of a fiduciary (a solicitor) who had used information properly obtained by virtue of his connection with a trust to make a personal profit in dealings in the shares of a company in which the trust had a substantial minority shareholding. In his dealings, the fiduciary, B, had also benefited the trust. The House of Lords required B to account for his profits to the trust because of his breach of fiduciary duty. Some of their Lordships suggested, *obiter*, that information could be treated as property and, if such is the case, the obligations of a director in respect of corporate information would not be limited to a general fiduciary duty but would be akin to the stricter duty imposed on trustees.

(b) Fiduciary duties

What could be called the general fiduciary duty of a director—to act *bona fide* for the benefit of the company—has given rise to specific applications of the duty, particularly the requirement manifestly to put the interests of the company before his own interests. This responsibility has given rise to a number of areas of litigation, some of which have been supplemented by statutory provisions. One obvious source of potential conflict between corporate duty and personal interest, in that the director is privy to confidential information by virtue of his office, is corporate contracts. The House of Lords in *Aberdeen Rly Co v Blaikie Bros (1854)* ruled that a director could not benefit directly or indirectly from a contract made by his company. This has been much modified when a director contracts with his company, for example when he enters into a service contract, or a director benefits indirectly from a contract between his company and a third party. Such contracts are valid if the director adequately discloses his interest in the contract (for example, in accordance with the articles, see Art 85 of Table A).

The position is less clear when a director benefits by the use of information obtained in his capacity as a director but there is no contract involving the company. Where a director has benefited from his position, liability can be imposed for breach of fiduciary duty but the ambit of this obligation is uncertain. Some cases (see *dicta* in *Regal (Hastings) Ltd v Gulliver (1942)*) suggest that a director must account for any benefit deriving from the use or information gained in a corporate capacity, even if also available elsewhere, but the better view is that a director can benefit from information if there is no real conflict of interest between himself and his company in his use of the information. Where there is a conflict of interest, the fact that the company was unlikely to be able to use that information itself does not justify a director using it for his own benefit. For example, in *IDC v Cooley (1972)*, C, the managing director of the company, was party to negotiations by the company for the design and construction of a gas terminal. It became clear that the company was unlikely to obtain the contract and C feigned illness, resigned his directorship and successfully tendered for the contract on his own account. The judge held C liable to account for the profits he had made on the contract. Even though the company was unlikely to get the contract, C was not entitled to use information concerning it and obtained in corporate service, for his own benefit. In contrast, in *Island Export Finance Ltd v Umunna (1986)*, a former director who successfully tendered for a contract with the Cameroon postal authorities was not in breach of his fiduciary duty despite the fact that he had gained useful information and contracts with the authority while negotiating a contract with it on the company's behalf some two years previously. The company had failed to pursue the contracts the director had made or seek further contracts—it had effectively washed its hands of the Cameroons and Hutchinson J saw no reason why the former director should account for his profits to his former company.

If a director does use information obtained in a corporate capacity and there is a conflict of interest, the profit made by the director can be retained if the company, by ordinary resolution, so decrees, unless the director's conduct and/or the subsequent ratification amounts to equitable fraud. It is not clear whether a company can absolve a director from liability in advance, rather than relieve him from the consequences of breach thereafter, although *dicta* in *Regal (Hastings) Ltd v Gulliver* (1942) would suggest that a resolution of the company, either antecedent or subsequent, could be effective.

(c) Competing interests

There is no general prohibition against a director of a company having a competing interest, such as a directorship in a rival company (*London and Mashonaland Exploration Co Ltd v New Mashonaland Exploration Co Ltd (1891)*; *Bell v Lever Bros (1932)*), a rule which has generated a great deal of criticism, see more recently the judgment of Sedley LJ in *In Plus Group Ltd v Pyke (2004)*. However, a director with a competing interest runs a risk of either breaching a fiduciary duty where he misuses confidential information (*LC Services Ltd v Brown (2003)*; *cf. In Plus Group Ltd v Pyke (2004), Coleman Taymar Ltd v Oakes (2001)*) or breaching a contractual duty where he is prohibited from having a competing interest by the terms of a service agreement (*Thomas Marshall (Exporters) Ltd v Guinle (1978)*). Liability, however, may be subject to (i) the law on restraint of trade and (ii) whether the pursuit of a competing interest arose during the course of, or after the director left, office or whether it involved actual competing as opposed to the taking of preliminary steps (*Balston Ltd v Headline Filters Ltd (1990); LC Services*). A director who seeks to use confidential information to compete with the company can be restrained by injunction. The position of employees and agents is similar to that of directors and employees and agents are under a general duty not to compete in the course of their employment or agency relationship (*Hivac Ltd v Park Royal Scientific Instruments Ltd (1946); Faccenda Chicken Ltd v Fowler (1987); Take v BSM Marketing (2006)*).

█ CONCLUSION

While there are many situations where the power of a director to use information obtained in a corporate capacity is subject to legal restraint, it is only when there is someone within the company who is willing and able to pursue the matter that any effective remedy exists.

NOTE

The Companies Act 2006 contains provisions relating to the ability of a director (or former director) to use information acquired while acting as a director. The Act also widens the scope of board authorisation of conflicts of interest. At the time of writing, these provisions are not in force.

Question 25

A friend of yours has been approached by a relative and asked to join the board of the family company. You have no doubts as to your friend's honesty and feel he would never act improperly, but he lacks any business sense and has no financial expertise. He seeks your advice about such issues as disqualification and the possibility of an action for wrongful trading in the event of the company going into insolvent liquidation. Are there any other risks consequent upon his lack of relevant expertise which you feel you should mention?

Answer plan

This straightforward question divides neatly into three sections:

(a) a discussion of disqualification;

(b) a discussion of wrongful trading; and

(c) mention of other actions which can arise if a director fails to display care and skill.

Finally, an appraisal of the relative likelihood of all or some of these actions being brought should be made.

Answer

Since your friend is honest, discussion of his liability, if any, in the event of the company going into insolvent liquidation can exclude breach of fiduciary duty, which tends to involve a want of probity or fair dealing. He has raised two specific concerns—disqualification and wrongful trading. These will be considered first.

(a) Disqualification

Section 1 of the **Company Directors Disqualification Act (CDDA) 1986** permits a court to disqualify a person from being a director, or being directly or indirectly concerned in the management of a company, in a number of prescribed circumstances. Sections 2–6, 8 and 10 CDDA 1986 set out the grounds for disqualification; ss 2–5, 8 and 10 CDDA 1986 give specific grounds—namely, conviction of *indictable* offence in connection with the management of a company, persistent breaches of company legislation, fraud in relation to the running of a company, adverse report by a company inspector, etc—but the majority of reported cases involve s 6 CDDA 1986. Section 6 CDDA 1986 provides that a person shall be disqualified (for a minimum of two years) from corporate management where he is or has been a director of a company which has become insolvent *and* his conduct as a director of that, or any other company, makes him unfit to be concerned in company management (this second condition also applies to s 8 CDDA 1986—adverse report by inspector). An application for disqualification under any section can be sought by the Secretary of State for Trade and Industry and some sections also confer the ability to disqualify under that section on specified persons. An application under s 6 CDDA 1986 cannot be heard, unless the court gives leave, more than two years after the company has first become insolvent (as defined in s 6 CDDA 1986). Acting as a director, etc, while disqualified is a criminal offence, punishable on indictment, by a fine and/or imprisonment for up to two years s 13 CDDA 1986.

The crucial question for your friend is whether any incompetence he might display could result in him being disqualified. In determining cases on the CDDA 1986, especially s 6 CDDA 1986, the courts have stressed that the Act, while designed to protect the public and while not a purely penal statute, can result in penal consequences for a disqualified person, in that a person may be precluded from trading through a limited company. Indeed, even to be the subject of an application for disqualification could have a serious effect on a person's reputation. Consequently, it is not surprising that judges, in interpreting the provisions of the CDDA 1986, have recognised these possible practical consequences whilst also seeking to give effect to Parliament's intention to limit the activities of unfit directors. Leaving aside the procedural aspects of the CDDA 1986, in what circumstances have the courts exercised their powers of disqualification and what is the courts' view of the appropriate period of disqualification? Guidance is provided by Sched 1 to the Act—factors to take into account include breach of fiduciary duty, misuse of assets, responsibility for breaches of mandatory requirements and, where the company is insolvent (necessary for s 6 CDDA 1986), the extent of the director's responsibility for the insolvency.

The leading case on s 6 CDDA 1986 is *Re Sevenoaks Stationery (Retail) Ltd (1990)*. In this case, C, a chartered accountant with an MBA and experience in the City as a merchant banker, had been a director of five companies which had gone into insolvent liquidation between 1983 and 1986, with a total deficit in excess of £650,000. C admitted that he had failed to keep proper books of account, prepare profit and loss accounts or make annual returns; one of the companies had, to his knowledge, traded while insolvent. The Court of Appeal held that the words 'unfit to be concerned in the management of a company' should be treated as ordinary English words, which should be simple to apply in most cases. Each case turned on its own facts, said the court, but a director need not display total incompetence to be unfit. The court approved earlier cases which had held that simple commercial misjudgment should not merit disqualification while a lack of commercial probity and an appropriate degree of incompetence could do so (see, for example, *Re Lo-Line Electric Motors Ltd (1988)*). In *Sevenoaks*, five years' disqualification ensued.

Since each case turns on its own facts, your friend cannot be given definite advice about the type of conduct, or lack of action, likely to lead to disqualification, but other cases make it clear that leaving everything to others who turn out to have defrauded the company may be enough to render a person 'unfit'. In *Re City Investment Centres Ltd (1992)*, the Official Receiver was seeking an order for the disqualification of the three directors, S, D and B, under s 6 CDDA 1986, based upon the conduct of the directors in connection with City Investment Centres (CIC) and other companies of which they were or had been directors. All of the companies were concerned with the 'over the counter' market in shares. There was little doubt that S (who was the moving spirit in all these companies) was liable to disqualification and he was duly disqualified for 10 years. D and B sought to escape disqualification by saying that they left all relevant matters to S. D had had 35 years' experience as an employee of the Council of the Stock Exchange, which included knowledge of disciplinary proceedings—he was called the compliance director. Morritt J had no doubt that D's conduct in allowing CIC to take over the assets and liabilities of other companies controlled by S without proper valuation of the assets (the assets proved illusory, the liabilities were not), allied to the failure of CIC to deliver shares which had been paid for because S had removed funds from the client account without any check by D and his failure to prevent or question CIC lending money to other ailing companies controlled by S, compounded by his inadequate supervision of the unqualified accounts staff, justified disqualification. The fact that D did not realise that CIC was trading while insolvent and that he relied upon S did not avail him—six years' disqualification were ordered. B's previous experience had been in connection with marketing and he had no relevant financial experience. He, too, simply relied upon S's word: when S took money from CIC's accounts, he believed S's statement that it was profit to which S was entitled, etc. While it was agreed that B did not know that CIC or other companies in the group were trading while insolvent, he should, said the judge, have known.

Morritt J was unimpressed by B's argument that nothing was his fault and that he merely marketed the companies services: '...this attitude displays a woeful ignorance of the duties attaching to the office of a director of a company.' B's duty was to question and check, where appropriate, S's conduct; his failure resulted in considerable loss to the Crown and other creditors—again, six years' disqualification were ordered. But this case can be contrasted with *Re Polly Peck International plc (No 2) (1994)* and *Secretary of State for Trade and Industry v Taylor*

(1997), where directors, forming a minority, were able to escape a disqualification order. However, in *Re Westmid Packing Services Ltd (1988)* the Court of Appeal considered that former directors of a company could not be excused from performing their obligations just because they may have been 'dazzled, manipulated and deceived' by a dominant member of the board who controlled the company.

The appropriate period for disqualification was discussed in *Sevenoaks*, where Dillon LJ suggested that a 10–15 year disqualification should be reserved for particularly serious cases (for example, where this was a second disqualification) and 2–5 years for not very serious cases, leaving 6–10 years for serious cases which do not merit the top bracket. In *Secretary of State for Trade and Industry v McTighe (No 2) (1996)*, the Court of Appeal imposed a disqualification order of 12 years for what was described as a 'particularly serious case'. In *Re City Truck Group Ltd (2007)*, the High Court described the fraudulent conduct of the two directors as belonging to the 'top bend' and a disqualification order for 12 years was imposed. The finance director had orchestrated a massive factoring fraud and had deliberately avoided the payment of crown debts. The chairman, who was also the company's majority shareholder, was held liable for consenting to and benefitting from the fraud.

(b) *Wrongful trading*

While disqualification would prevent your friend from being a director, it would not have direct financial consequences; a finding that a director had engaged in wrongful trading would do so. The concept of wrongful trading was introduced by s 214 of the Insolvency Act (IA) 1986 and it allows a court to declare a director liable to contribute to the assets of the company if the director knew, or ought to have concluded, that there was no reasonable prospect of the company avoiding insolvent liquidation, and he did not take every step he ought to have taken to minimise the potential loss to the company's creditors. Thus, on insolvent liquidation, the liquidator can seek a court order for one or more directors of the company to contribute to the assets of the company which will be available to creditors. Section 214 IA 1986 does not authorise an order requiring a director to contribute towards the costs of liquidation or post-liquidation debts. An order is to contribute to the assets of the company and the section does not authorise an order that a particular creditor be paid, nor only those creditors whose debts were incurred after the director should have known that the company would go into insolvent liquidation (*Re Purpoint Ltd (1991)*).

A director cannot be liable under s 214 IA 1986 unless he both knew, or ought to have concluded, that insolvency could not be avoided *and* he failed to take every step which he ought to have taken to minimise loss to creditors. The section only envisages the imposition of liability on a director who has not realised what he should have done and has not done what he should have done. In determining whether a director has met the standard expected of him, s 214 IA 1986 provides guidance as to the setting of the standard. Section 214 (4) IA 1986 states that a director is to be judged by what a reasonably diligent person with the 'general knowledge, skill and experience that may reasonably be expected of a person carrying out the same functions as are carried out by that director' (that is, the director potentially subject to an order) and the 'general knowledge, skill and experience' of the director whom it is sought to make liable. This somewhat obscure provision seems to mean that what a director should have known or done is to be judged by reference to a theoretical director who possesses those skills that may 'reasonably be expected' of a director, unless the director is better qualified than this theoretical director, when he is to be judged by reference to his own qualifications. The Act is silent as to what qualifications one can reasonably expect from a director. Given that there is neither a minimum age for a director nor a test of competence, it could be argued that one cannot reasonably expect a great deal. Certainly, in *Re Elgindata Ltd (1991)*, the judge concluded that poor management was one of the risks which an investor had to bear.

There is one case which should be drawn to the attention of your friend—*Re Produce Marketing Consortium Ltd (1989) (PMC)*. In *PMC*, the company was engaged in the import of fruit. It traded successfully for some 9–10 years and remained profitable until 1980. Thereafter, between 1980 and 1984 the company built up an overdraft and in 1984 had an excess of liabilities over assets and a trading loss. Between 1984 and 1987, when insolvent liquidation ensued, the trading loss continued, as did the excess of liabilities over assets, but the overdraft approximately halved, due to an increase in indebtedness to the company's principal supplier. By February 1987, one of the directors realised that liquidation was inevitable, but the company was allowed to trade until October—this decision being justified as allowing disposal of the company's supplies of perishable goods which were held in cold-store. The judge found that the directors should have concluded by July 1986 that liquidation was inevitable because, although accounts were not available until January 1987, their knowledge of the business was such that they must have realised that turnover was down and that the gap between assets and liabilities must have increased. Since the IA 1986 provides that the directors are to be judged by reference to what they know and what they ought to know, Knox J held that they ought to have known the financial results for the year ending 1985 in July 1986 at the latest, so that the fact that these results were not known until 1987 was no excuse. Moreover, the directors had failed to take all steps to minimise loss—they had not limited their dealings to running down the company's stocks in cold-store, even if this was a justified step. Knox J held that both directors must contribute £75,000 to the assets of the company, this being the loss which could have been averted by speedy liquidation.

While an action for wrongful trading may be a remote possibility, it is potentially extremely disadvantageous. A well-advised friend should check the regularity and accuracy of the management accounts before consenting to be a director. Presumably, non-executive directors are less vulnerable for action under s 214 IA 1986.

(c) Other risks

Directors also owe a common law duty of care and skill, but it is traditionally very modest. At common law, directors are expected to carry out their duties with an appropriate degree of care and skill. The traditional formulation of the nature and extent of this duty is that given by Romer J in *Re City Equitable Fire Insurance Co Ltd (1925)*, in which he held that a director:

- need display only such skill as may reasonably be expected from a person of his knowledge and experience;
- need not give the affairs of the company continuous attention; and
- is entitled to leave the day to day running of the company to the officials of the company and is entitled to assume, in the absence of suspicious circumstances, that such officials are performing their duties honestly.

These propositions remain good law with regard to non-executive directors, but executive directors will generally be constrained by their service contracts to devote a set percentage of their time to the affairs of the company. The most important aspect of a director's duty of care relates to the amount of skill he must exercise. Directors are not subject to the Supply of Goods and Services Act 1982, so they need not display reasonable care and skill. It is plain that a director who does his honest best may be held to have exercised sufficient care and skill to evade liability for negligence—the test of liability is subjective and not objective, although the Company Law Review Steering Group, in its 'trial draft' of directors' duties, suggested a dual objective/subjective standard in relation to the duty of care (*Modern Company Law for a Competitive Economy: Developing the Framework* (DTI, 2000)). The Companies Act 2006 adopts the dual objective/subjective standard as part of the codification of directors' duties although the relevant provision is not, to date, in force. Certainly, your friend can be advised that he need possess no particular skill on appointment (*Re Brazilian Rubber Estates & Plantations Ltd (1911)*) and whether he has been negligent is a question of fact. The courts are beginning to be a little more robust in determining the standard of care which a company can expect (see, for example, *Dorchester Finance Co Ltd v Stebbing (1989)*). Apart from the modest standard of competence which a director need demonstrate, the ability to sue an errant director is usually vested in the company and not in individual shareholders, so that a director of a solvent company may need not fear legal action while he remains on good terms with co-directors.

▌CONCLUSION

Your friend can be advised that there is little doubt that greater public and parliamentary scrutiny of the benefits enjoyed by directors can be anticipated (see, for instance, the work of the Law Commissions (1999) and the Company Law Review Steering Group (2001)). However, given the number of companies (almost one and a half million), the risk of being a director who is subject to any of the adverse happenings outlined above may seem acceptable. The Companies Act 2006 provides for a more objective test on directorial competence (in line with the proposal of the Law Commissions (1999)), so the position may well change when the Act is in force.

Question 26

The rules pertaining to the ability of a director to enter into an enforceable contract with the company of which he is a director give shareholders no effective control over such contracts.

Comment on this view.

Answer plan

A relatively straightforward question, requiring a summary of the existing rules relating to contracts between a director and his company, the extent to which there is, or is not, effective control and a comment on the desirability of the present situation. The major difficulties in such a question are sticking to the point and not discussing all aspects of the duties imposed on directors, and in gathering together information which may have arisen at different points in a course.

Answer

'Directors, no doubt, are not trustees, but they occupy a fiduciary position towards the company whose board they form.' (*Regal (Hastings) Ltd v Gulliver (1942)*.) Since a director is not (except when dealing with corporate property) to be treated as a trustee, he is not debarred from deriving some benefit from his directorship—most directors are remunerated for their efforts—but, as a fiduciary, a director does not have an unfettered right to profit from his position. As a fiduciary, each director is individually subject to equitable duties—fiduciary duties—which require him to exercise his powers in a way which has regard to the interests of the person to whom the duties are owed and not to abuse his position of trust and influence within the company. Fiduciary duties are owed to the company, that is, current and future shareholders as a body, and not to individual shareholders (*Percival v Wright (1902)*; *Peskin v Anderson (2001)*). Consequently, one difficulty faced by a minority shareholder who is unhappy with contracts between the company and a director is the lack of ability to litigate other than in exceptional circumstances (*Foss v Harbottle (1843)*). The minority shareholder's inability to litigate will not matter if there is appropriate control over a director's contracts at an earlier stage, that is, when the contract is made. Nor will it matter if the company chooses to take action against a director when it discovers a secret contractual benefit at a later stage.

The general fiduciary duty, which is essentially a duty of fair dealing, has been more precisely formulated in respect of particular aspects of the director-company relationship. Consequently, a director has a duty to put the interests of the company before his own interests. Obviously, this impinges upon his ability to contract with the company he serves. For example, a director who wishes to sell his own property to the company wishes, as vendor, to obtain the highest possible price, while his duty as a director is to negotiate the lowest possible price on behalf of the company. The potential for conflict between private interest and directorial duty has led to the formulation by the judges of various principles which have been supplemented by statutory provisions.

(a) Under equity

An early case in point is the House of Lords' decision in *Aberdeen Railway Co v Blaikie Bros (1854)*. In *Blaikie*, the company wished to purchase iron chairs for use on railway stations. The contract was awarded to Blaikie Bros, a partnership in which a director of the company was a partner. The company repudiated the contract and its repudiation was upheld. The Lord Chancellor, Lord Cranworth, said: '... no one having [fiduciary] duties to discharge shall be allowed to enter into engagements in which he has or can have a personal interest conflicting, or which possibly may conflict, with the interests of those he is bound to protect.' Later cases have modified this view where any possible conflict of interest is 'so small that it can as a practical matter be disregarded' (*Movitex v Bulfield Ltd (1988)*) and have stressed that a potential conflict can arise only where there is 'a real sensible possibility of conflict' (*Boardman v Phipps (1967)*). Where a director enters into a contract in circumstances where there is a conflict of interest or there is a sensible risk of such a conflict, the contract is voidable at the company's option, even if the contract is entirely fair and reasonable. Thus, a company can rescind a contract from which a director benefits, directly or indirectly, if he has entered into it in breach of fiduciary duty even if the contract terms are fair and are no less favourable to the company than those obtainable from non-directors. This would not appear to be fair to directors. However, a company, while a company, can rescind a contract entered into by a director when he is in breach of his fiduciary duty; the law does not say that a director can never benefit from a contract with a company of which he is a director.

A director can benefit from a contract between himself and the company he serves provided that he makes adequate disclosure of his own interest before the contract is entered into. Originally, disclosure to the shareholders was required to remove any issue of conflict, but companies soon began to adopt articles which provided that disclosure to the directors would suffice. It remains the law that disclosure must be to the shareholders unless the articles provide otherwise: Art 85 of Table A permits disclosure to the board. Since disclosure to the board is not as onerous as disclosure to the shareholders, s 317 CA 1985 provides rules for the nature and degree of disclosure where the articles of a company allow disclosure to the board. The requirement of disclosure is strict. In *Neptune (Vehicle Washing Equipment) Ltd v Fitzgerald (1995)*, a sole director who failed to disclose his interest in a contract between himself and the company to the board, that is, to himself, was in breach of the section. The judge ruled that he should have revealed his interest in the minutes of board meetings and that his knowledge of his interest did not exempt him from the provisions of the Act.

In addition to the requirements of s 317 CA 1985, companies may adopt their own disclosure rules: Arts 84–94 of Table A provide guidelines as to the type of disclosure requirements companies might adopt. The Table A provisions limit the ability of an interested director to vote on his own contracts, but a company may, of course, choose to adopt a different set of disclosure requirements from those that Table A envisages which allow an interested director to vote. As with failure to make adequate disclosure to the shareholders, failure to make disclosure in accordance with the requirements of the articles allows the company to rescind any contract.

On a vote to adopt or reject a contract entered into without adequate disclosure, an errant director who is also a shareholder is permitted to vote unless the articles provide otherwise (*NW Transportation Co Ltd v Beatty (1887)*). Failure to comply with s 317 CA 1985 is a criminal offence but it is less clear if a company can set aside a contract with a director who has complied with the articles of the company but not with s 317 CA 1985. In *Guinness plc v Saunders* (1990), members of the House of Lords were split upon whether simple breach of s 317 CA 1985 would render a contract voidable. In *Hely-Hutchinson v Brayhead Ltd (1968)*, the majority of the Court of Appeal took the view that breach of s 317 CA 1985 would not render the contract voidable, but that failing to disclose could render the contract voidable under general equitable principles. The views on s 317 CA 1985 were *obiter* in both cases. There is discussion of s 317 CA 1985 by the Law Commissions in *Company Directors: Regulating Conflicts of Interests and Formulating a Statement of Duties* (1999). Among several proposals for reform, the Law Commissions proposed (a) that s 317 CA 1985 should not apply to a company with only one director, thus overturning the decision in *Neptune (Vehicle Washing Equipment) Ltd v Fitzgerald (1995)*, and (b) that breach of s 317 CA 1985 should no longer be a criminal offence—the contract instead becoming voidable under the civil law. The first of these recommendations has been adopted by the Companies Act 2006, which contains some other changes to s 317 CA 1985.

Since most companies treat disclosure to the board as compliance with a director's fiduciary duty, the shareholders have little control over directors' contracts. Shareholders must be informed of contracts which benefit a director in the annual accounts (s 232 CA 1985). Perhaps because disclosure to the board might allow a cosy cartel among directors, a number of statutory provisions affect the ability of a director to contract with his company.

(b) Statutory intervention

There are a number of statutory provisions which could be described as designed to ensure fair dealing by directors. Section 319 CA 1985 places restrictions upon the service contract which a director can make, s 320 CA 1985 affects 'substantial property transactions' and s 330 CA 1985 prohibits a company from making loans to directors. The general thrust of these provisions is not to prohibit contracts between directors and their companies but, rather, to ensure that such contracts are valid only if affirmed by the shareholders in general meeting. Sections 320 CA 1985 and 330 CA 1985 extend to shadow directors, that is, those 'in accordance with whose directions or instructions the directors of the company are accustomed to act', but this does not include those giving advice to the directors 'in a professional capacity' (s 741 CA 1985).

Section 319 CA 1985 prohibits any term in a contract with a director whereby he is to be employed as an executive or non-executive director for a period of more than five years without provision for termination (or where termination is possible only in specified circumstances), unless the term is first approved by the company in general meeting (see *Atlas Wright (Europe) Ltd v Wright (1999)*). One consequence of s 319 CA 1985 is that directors now tend to have contracts for less than five years, thus removing the necessity of exposing the contract to the shareholders for their approval, but which contain a provision for reappointment for a similar period on the same terms, that is, including a reappointment term. Certain large investors have expressed disapproval of 'rolling' contracts or contracts whereby the directors are appointed for too lengthy a period. The Combined Code, which sets out best practice in the corporate governance of listed companies, says that 'there is a strong case for setting notice periods at, or reducing them to, one year or less'. The Law Commissions (1999) have recommended that 'rolling' contracts should come within s 319 CA 1985 and that, generally, the length of a contract requiring approval under s 319 CA 1985 should be reduced from five to three years.

Sections 320–22 CA 1985 provide that if a transaction between a director and a company is a 'substantial property transaction', it is voidable unless approved in advance by the shareholders in general meeting (a director-shareholder could vote on a resolution to ratify). Approval of such a transaction can be informal: see *Niltan Carson Ltd v Hawthorne (1988)*, where knowledge and acquiescence by the majority shareholders was held to constitute approval of the activities of the director. A transaction is a substantial property transaction if a director acquires an interest in a non-cash asset from the company, or the company acquires an interest in a non-cash asset from a director, where the value of the asset is over £100,000 or 10% of the asset value of the company (subject to its value exceeding £2,000). However, the section provides that an unapproved substantial property transaction is voidable at the instance of the *company*. Thus, it seems that a shareholder has no *locus* to challenge an unapproved transaction. A transaction entered into in breach of these sections ceases to be voidable even by the company if it is too late to avoid it or the company in general meeting has affirmed it. Where there is breach of s 320 CA 1985, the consequences can be harsh. In *Re Duckwari plc (No 2) (1998)*, a director who, without proper disclosure, sold property to the company at a fair market price was required to compensate the company when the land was resold at a substantial loss. The loss was due to the fall in the property market and not any fraud or malpractice by the director. It should be noted that, where a board lacks the authority to enter into a transaction (for example, a substantial property transaction), the provisions of s 35A CA 1985, which would normally confer authority on the directors and thus validate the contract, do not apply and the transaction remains voidable (s 322A CA 1985).

Sections 330–46 CA 1985 provide a highly elaborate set of provisions affecting the ability of a company to make loans to, or enter into related transactions with, directors. These provisions provide both civil remedies and, where the company is a relevant company, criminal penalties. These sections restrict the ability of a company to make loans (or guarantee a loan) to a director of the company, or a director of a holding company, or to a shadow director (s 330(1) CA 1985). Further, where the company is a relevant company, the prohibition is extended to quasi-loans and credit transactions (or guarantees thereof) to the same people or to a person 'connected' to such a person (s 330(2) CA 1985). A company is a relevant company if it is either a public company or a member of a group in which one of the members is a public company (s 331 CA 1985). A connected person includes a spouse and children under the age of 18 (s 346 CA 1985) of a director of a company. Sections 332–38 CA 1985 provide a number of exceptions to the basic prohibition, some of which operate only with the approval of the shareholders in general meeting. For example, s 337 CA 1985, which allows a company to provide a director with funds (limited to £20,000 maximum for a relevant company) to carry out his duties on behalf of the company, provides that the provision of funds is disclosed to and approved by the shareholders in advance or at or before the next annual general meeting (AGM) of the company (s 330(4) CA 1985 specifies what is to be disclosed to the shareholders). Failure to obtain the necessary approval or inadequate disclosure will result in the director having to repay the sums provided within six months of the AGM. Loans, etc, to directors must be disclosed in a company's accounts.

CONCLUSION

The position at common law was such that the shareholders had little or no control over contracts entered into by directors. The position has been modified by statute, but not to any significant degree. Disclosure and approval in advance may now be required, but breach of these provisions is likely to render the contract voidable at the option of the company and not the shareholders. Additionally, there is but a limited ability for shareholders to object to contracts in advance. Perhaps contracts between a company and a director should be void unless approved in advance by the shareholders in general meeting, and this should include all service contracts, including terms as to salary. It may be worth noting that, in addition to the comments made on ss 317 and 319 CA 1985, the Law Commissions also proposed other changes to Pt X of the Act, especially in the light of the highly elaborate nature of the provisions relating to contracts with directors. They proposed that:

• transactions coming within s 320 CA 1985 should be subject to a condition precedent that the company obtains shareholder approval;

• the restrictions placed upon loans and similar transactions should apply to all companies, not just 'relevant' ones; and

• civil remedies should replace many of the criminal sanctions.

Other recommendations for change were made by the Company Law Review Steering Group. The Companies Act 2006 does contain changes to Pt X CA 1985 based on these recommendations. To date, these are not in force. However, some parts of Pt X CA 1985 have been repealed and are in force (from 6 April 2007), namely ss 311 and 323–29 CA 1985.

CHAPTER 5

SHAREHOLDERS AND THEIR RIGHTS

INTRODUCTION

In considering the shareholders and their rights, three issues arise—who is a shareholder, what rights shareholders have and against whom these rights are exercisable. The first issue concerns the validity of the allotment, or transfer of shares, and is addressed primarily in Chapter 6, below, although it has been touched on in Chapter 4. Thus, in this chapter, the question of whether a person *is* a shareholder will not be central to any question.

The other issues, the nature of rights of shareholders and their enforcement, can arise in many contexts. Such matters have already formed part of questions in previous chapters, for example when considering *ultra vires* and division of power within a company, and will arise in later chapters, for example when appraising rights to dividends and the variation of class rights. In this chapter, it is the ability of shareholders (generally a minority shareholder) to do something either when dissatisfied with corporate management or when generally unhappy with the way the company is operating, which may involve the board and/or the majority shareholder, or when unable to co-exist happily with his fellow shareholders. A majority shareholder is able to dismiss the board (s 303 of the Companies Act (CA) 1985) and may be able to give the board instructions on how the company is to be run (Table A, Art 70) or even change the articles (s 9 CA 1985), and so has less need, but may still wish, to use the remedies discussed in this chapter. Since it is the company who generally has the sole right to challenge the actions of the board, any question which demands advice for a shareholder is necessarily asking you to consider not merely the cause of action open to a shareholder, but also how, if at all, the shareholder can enforce his rights (a *locus* question, which issue also played a prominent role in Chapter 4, above).

Where, as is common, the company is the only potential claimant, you should necessarily appraise alternative remedies. Possible general alternative remedies being just and equitable winding up (s 122(1)(g) of the Insolvency

Act (IA) 1986) and an 'unfair prejudice' action (s 459 CA 1985). Both statutory provisions have generated considerable case law, much of it recent. In rare cases, a shareholder may also be able to persuade the Department of Trade and Industry (DTI) to initiate an investigation into a company. These remedies can also apply to situations where a shareholder wishes to challenge the actions of fellow shareholders in the limited cases where shareholders owe duties to fellow shareholders.

As with questions on the directors, it is possible to combine questions on shareholder remedies with almost any other part of a company law syllabus. Students may also find that there is a need to consider some of the proposals for reform made by the Law Commission (*Shareholder Remedies*, LC 246 (1997)) and the provisions of the new Companies Act 2006.

Question 27

Despite the wide interpretation given by judges to s 459 of the Companies Act 1985, it is unlikely to be applied to a complaint about the mismanagement of a company. In such cases, the rule in *Foss v Harbottle (1843)* still represents a substantial, unjustifiable barrier to litigation by minority shareholders.

Comment on this view.

Answer plan

This requires a general introduction to the problem of locus, then discussion of the two main issues:

(a) what is the rule in *Foss v Harbottle (1843)* and does it have the effect claimed?; and

(b) the width of the interpretation of s 459 of the Companies Act (CA) 1985 and the likelihood of it being applied to private and public companies,

ending with a conclusion as to the validity of the view expressed in the question.

The crucial thing to beware is writing an answer which is simply a discussion of s 459 CA 1985 followed by a discussion of *Foss v Harbottle (1843)*. It is important to use material selectively so that it is tailored to the question.

Answer

What courses of action are open to a minority shareholder who is unhappy with the way a company is being operated? The simplest remedy available to a shareholder in a public company is to sell his shares and seek a better investment, although if others are equally unhappy the sale price may represent a loss. However, it is unlikely that a shareholder will find a ready market for a minority shareholding in a private company unless the directors or other shareholders wish to buy the shares (or it is a company running a football club where people buy shares for non-investment reasons). Further, the price of shares in a private company may well not represent the asset value or earnings potential of the company, therefore, making a sale, even where possible, an unattractive option. If the shareholder wishes to stay with the company but improve its operation, he could seek to change the directors of the company (s 303 CA 1985, ordinary resolution required) or to instruct the board how to operate (Table A, Art 70 or s 9 CA 1985, both special resolution) but both require the support of others. Assuming that the unhappy shareholder cannot persuade others to join him, he can consider two approaches. First, he could seek to initiate litigation on his own account, or, second, he could attempt to sue on behalf of the company. In respect of both approaches, the courts have been greatly influenced by the view that a company is a democracy, that a shareholder who is outvoted should abide by the result of a vote and that a court should intervene only when the interests of justice clearly demand it. As Lord Wilberforce put it, 'Those who take interests in companies limited by shares have to accept majority rule.'

A person can sue on his own account when a wrong has been done to him. Such a wrong would arise in respect of mismanagement, if such was a breach of a common law or statutory duty owed to the shareholder. Unfortunately, at common law, a shareholder is unlikely to be able to establish such a wrong if his complaint relates to simple mismanagement. The reason is two fold. First, mismanagement may not be a breach of directors' duty, since the standard of care and skill required of honest directors is traditionally very modest. Second, the duty of care and skill is owed to the company and *not* to an individual shareholder (*Percival v Wright (1902); Peskin v Anderson*). Section 214 of the Insolvency Act (IA) 1986 may impose a higher standard of care on directors, but the section does not give shareholders a right to sue to restrain incompetence; rather, it imposes personal liability to creditors on directors when the company has gone into insolvent liquidation and there has been 'wrongful trading'. Even where the alleged mismanagement consists of irregularity in conducting the affairs of the company, a shareholder may find that a wrong has not been done to him but only to the company. For example, an internal irregularity which is capable of ratification by ordinary resolution is not regarded as a wrong done to a member and, hence, an individual shareholder cannot sue those responsible for the irregularity (*MacDougall v Gardiner (1875)*).

In contrast, where the wrong complained of consists of breach of a personal right vested in a member, the member can sue.

There is no clear test of what is a personal right (breach cannot be ratified so individual member can sue) as opposed to a right to have the business of the company carried out properly, breach of which may be ratifiable (where a wrong is ratifiable, a member cannot sue). A right conferred on an individual by a contract or by a statute would be a personal right, and some provisions in the articles are also deemed to be personal rights (by virtue of s 14 CA 1985) while others are not (see *Hickman v Kent or Romney Marsh Sheepbreeders' Association (1915)*). Consequently, if the alleged mismanagement consists of ignoring provisions in the articles, it may or may not allow a member to sue (but note that some commentators treat the right to have the business of the company conducted in accordance with the articles as a personal right).

Certainly, where the alleged mismanagement consists of breaches of procedures laid down in the articles, an individual shareholder is unlikely to be able to claim that a wrong has been done to him (*MacDougall v Gardiner (1875)*). For example, if a meeting is called with short notice or by an inquorate board, the decisions taken at that meeting would not be set aside at the instance of a minority shareholder if they were passed by a substantial majority so that the irregularity was irrelevant to the result of the meeting (*Bentley-Stevens v Jones (1974)*). The justification given for denying a shareholder the right to sue, other than when a personal right is breached, is two fold. First, where there is a mere irregularity, there is little point in allowing litigation where the majority can ratify, and, second, to allow litigation on every procedural irregularity would open the famous floodgates of litigation. Where there is no common law right to initiate litigation about mismanagement, a shareholder may find a remedy by using s 459 CA 1985 (see below).

The circumstances in which a member can sue to enforce the rights of the company are even more limited. In *Foss v Harbottle (1843)*, Wigram VC laid down the basic principle that a shareholder could not sue in respect of wrongs done to a company (by insiders or outsiders); this remains the basis of the modern law—the wrong has been done to the company, so the proper claimant is the company. This decision has been approved by the Court of Appeal and the Privy Council in *Burland v Earle (1902)*. *Foss v Harbottle (1843)* itself, and later cases, have confirmed that there are limited exceptions to this basic principle. Most of the so called exceptions are cases where *Foss v Harbottle (1843)* does not apply, for example where the company acts *ultra vires*, or where a shareholder's personal rights are breached. The principal exception to *Foss v Harbottle (1843)*, whereby a shareholder can bring a derivative claim to enforce the company's rights, arises where there is fraud on the minority by those in control of the company; if mismanagement falls into this category, a minority shareholder could sue on behalf of the company.

One difficulty with this exception is that 'fraud' must be proved. Moreover, in *Prudential Assurance Co Ltd v Newman Industries (1981)*, the Court of Appeal, *obiter*, stressed that a court should not allow a derivative claim by a shareholder to commence unless the shareholder could establish a *prima facie* case that the company was entitled to the remedy claimed *and* that it was an appropriate case for a person to litigate on behalf of the company when the company has chosen not to litigate. In *Prudential*, the company had not sued two directors whom, it was alleged, had misled the company. Vinelott J had allowed a derivative claim, at the behest of the claimant, to proceed without investigating closely the question of whether Prudential, a minority shareholder, had *locus*. He took the view that the merits of the case and the question of *locus* could be heard together, and both issues would be determined at the conclusion of the case. The Court of Appeal rejected this approach and said that the law should not permit a 30 day hearing to see if there should be a 30 day hearing. The costs in this case were enormous and the Court of Appeal clearly felt that, if a shareholder was allowed to drag a company into expensive litigation (which the company might have to fund and which in this case it had reluctantly chosen to fund), the courts should save companies from their 'friends'.

Even where a shareholder crosses the *prima facie* barrier on the issue of fraud, he may still be denied *locus* if he is an inappropriate claimant, for example where he participated in the fraud or had benefited from it (*Nurcombe v Nurcombe (1985)*) or was seeking to sue for an ulterior motive (*Barrett v Duckett (1995)*), or where he has failed to establish that it is the fraudsters who are blocking litigation by the company (the control issue). Thus, in *Smith v Croft (No 2) (1988)*, Knox J held that, where the decision by the company not to litigate had been made 'by an appropriate independent organ', the shareholder was not allowed to bring a derivative claim— for in such a case it was not the fraudsters who were blocking litigation but others unconnected with the fraud. He pointed out that the appropriate independent organ might have good reason to refuse to litigate, for example, by reason of unnecessary expense or the unlikelihood of any judgment being satisfied. What constituted an independent organ would depend on the facts of the case, but, where a majority of shareholders had indicated no desire for litigation, their votes would be

> disregarded if, but only if, the court is satisfied either that the vote or its equivalent is actually cast with a view to supporting the defendants rather than securing a benefit to the company, or that the situation of the person whose vote is considered is such that there is a substantial risk of that happening.

While a difficult test to apply, it clearly militates against action by a minority shareholder in a case of mismanagement. Assuming that the votes of the directors are disregarded, it would be a bold decision for a court to rule that the remainder of the shareholders had rejected litigation for an improper purpose, particularly in a public company, where shareholding is widespread. Even where a shareholder has *locus* and sues successfully on behalf of his company, the benefits accrue to the company and not the shareholder.

Does s 459 CA 1985 provide the answer for a shareholder who regards the management as incompetent? There is no *locus* problem with the section, since 'A member of a company may apply to the court' and the definition of a 'member' includes 'a person who is not a member of a company but to whom shares in the company have been transferred or transmitted by operation of law'. Consequently, for example, a person who had inherited shares, and whom the directors were refusing to register as a member, would have *locus*.

In common with an action for breach of personal rights, any relief can benefit the petitioner, although the benefit may be indirect, for example where the court orders the articles of the company to be changed. A shareholder must bear the cost of a s 459 petition himself. However, merely because that court will hear an application does not mean that a member has been unfairly prejudiced. Two cases are pertinent. In *Re Elgindata Ltd (1991)*, the petitioner had joined the company on the basis of detailed written agreements which were reflected in the articles. The court accepted that it could find, but refused so to do on the facts, that the petitioner had interests other than those set out in the agreements. The courts are unlikely to do so unless there are clear reasons why the legal agreement between company and shareholder should not prevail. Hence, a shareholder who is unhappy with the management of the company may simply find that, provided that the incompetent directors are complying with the memorandum and articles, he can expect no more. While it is unlikely to be a specific provision in the articles, a member of a company could claim that he, in common with all shareholders, legitimately expects the company to be properly managed and that mismanagement is unfairly prejudicial. Certainly, mismanagement allied to attempts to do down a shareholder has been held to be unfairly prejudicial (*Scottish CWS Ltd v Meyer (1959)*—a case decided under s 210 CA 1948, which was later replaced by s 459 CA 1985), as has mismanagement linked to breaches of company law (*Re A Company (No 00789 of 1987) ex p Shooter (1990)*), but simple incompetence is unlikely to be within the section.

In *Re Elgindata Ltd (1991)*, the petitioner alleged, *inter alia*, that incompetence by management was unfairly prejudicial. In a lengthy judgment, Warner J held that in an appropriate case a court could find that serious mismanagement might be unfairly prejudicial but that courts would be extremely reluctant to accept that managerial decisions could be so (but see *Re Macro (Ipswich) Ltd (1994)*). A more recent case in point is that of *Re Saul Harrison & Sons plc (1995)*, in which the holder of non-voting shares claimed that the directors of the company were keeping the company running purely to earn substantial salaries when a reasonable board would, given the company's prospects, have liquidated the company and distributed its assets. The action was based partly on an allegation of fraud and partly on an allegation of incompetence. The company was a long established, family owned and run company, dealing mainly in paper and textile wiping cloths, which had in recent years suffered declining profitability. In support of her claim for unfair prejudice, the petitioner claimed that when, in 1990, the company negotiated a sale of its premises prior to the passage of a Bill which would have authorised compulsory acquisition, it was the ideal time to wind up the company and distribute its assets rather than, as had happened, acquire new premises. She also claimed that the directors had failed to wind up the company in order to continue to receive large salaries as directors. The Court of Appeal upheld the judge's decision to strike out the petition. In deciding what is fair or unfair for the purposes of s 459 CA 1985, one judge held that 'it is important to bear in mind that fairness is being used in the context of a commercial relationship'. The relationship of shareholders is primarily governed by the memorandum and articles of the company and commercial fairness can be seen as predominately a question of complying with them. The approach in *Re Saul Harrison* was approved by the House of Lords in *O'Neill v Phillips (1999)*, where the House stressed that compliance with the rules of company law cannot be unfairly prejudicial unless the company was 'using the rules in a manner which equity would regard as contrary to good faith'.

Even if conduct is not in accordance with the memorandum or articles and the powers thereby conferred, it is not necessarily unfair. For example, trivial and technical infringements of the articles will not attract the statutory remedy. Where, however, the memorandum and articles do not represent the understandings upon which the shareholders are associated (a principle recognised in the leading case of *Ebrahimi v Westbourne Galleries Ltd (1973)*), it may be unfair to a shareholder for those who control a company to exercise the powers set out in the memorandum and articles if to do so denies the legitimate expectations of the shareholder. Such expectations may derive from a contract independent of the memorandum and articles but is not restricted to such cases; as in *Ebrahimi*, it is a question of whether equitable considerations require express or implied promises not contained in the memorandum and articles to be honoured. One judge concluded that, where there is no reason to look beyond the memorandum and articles to determine the relationship of the shareholders, compliance with them cannot be unfair. In this case, the petitioner had no legitimate expectations beyond the general expectation that the memorandum and articles would be complied with and its powers exercised properly. Neill LJ agreed on the question of legitimate interests and the primacy of the company's constitution but added an important rider. He accepted that serious mismanagement could constitute unfair prejudice, albeit in exceptional circumstances, since in most cases a shareholder must accept that managerial decisions in the best interests of the company as a whole may dictate conduct which is prejudicial to some individuals. On the facts of this case, the accusation of mismanagement was not made out.

In conclusion, a shareholder who regards a company as incompetently managed is unlikely to have a remedy under s 459 CA 1985. Nor is an action for breach of personal rights likely to be attended by success, and so he will continue to find *Foss v Harbottle (1843)* a barrier to litigation on behalf of the company.

However, a proposal by the Law Commission, *Shareholder Remedies* (1997), may go some way to alleviating this problem, if implemented by statute. The Law Commission proposed that negligence without qualification can be the subject matter of a derivative action, thus replacing the rule in *Pavlides v Jensen (1956)*. The Companies Act 2006 does contain a procedure for bringing a derivative claim along the lines suggested by the Law Commission, but to date, is not in force.

Question 28

Whatever the difficulties of enforcement, shareholders have means at their disposal to control the conduct of directors. What is needed by minority shareholders is a system whereby the actions of the majority shareholders can be controlled. To what extent do shareholders currently have control over the conduct of their fellow shareholders? Should the current position be changed?

Answer plan

What is needed is a brief consideration of the problems that majority shareholders can cause to minority shareholders, followed by an evaluation of the degree of control currently exercisable and an appraisal of any necessity for change.

Answer

Directors of a company, even when acting within the powers conferred upon them, are required to comply with fiduciary, common law and statutory obligations in exercising those powers. A shareholder may encounter difficulties in enforcing his rights (due to *Foss v Harbottle (1843)*) but the existence of the obligations is certain. However, a minority shareholder may not be unhappy with the conduct of the directors but feel that the conduct of other shareholders in the company (generally a majority or another class) is prejudicial to his interests. For example, the majority shareholder may vote to change the articles, or block a decision to sue an errant director, or ratify the actions of that director; or voting shareholders may change the rights attaching to non-voting shares, contrary to the wishes of the minority or the non-voting shareholders. What, if anything, can the disgruntled shareholders do? Of course, the majority shareholder must comply with the provisions of the Companies Acts, the provisions of which may set out particular majorities which are required for certain ends to be approved. For example, s 9 CA 1985 (changing the articles) requires a special resolution, a vote to relieve a director from the consequences of entering an *ultra vires* contract requires a special resolution (s 35 CA 1985) and some variations of class rights require the class to be varied to approve the variation (s 125(3) CA 1985). But is there a general fiduciary duty imposed on shareholders which is akin to that imposed on directors?

A shareholder may be liable to a fellow shareholder by virtue of a function he exercises within the company. For example, a shareholder may be treated as a director if he 'occupies the position of director, by whatever name called' or as a shadow director if he is 'a person in accordance with whose directions or instructions the directors of the company are accustomed to act', unless the directors only 'act on advice given by him in a professional capacity' (s 741 CA 1985). After a number of rather narrow decisions on who is a shadow director, the Court of Appeal in *Secretary of State for Trade and Industry v Deverell (2000)* took a more purposive approach to the interpretation of s 741 CA 1985. A shareholder who is a shadow director may be subject to either all the usual obligations imposed on directors or merely those statutory provisions that are specifically stated to be applicable to shadow directors. For example, shadow directors are subject to the rules on loans to directors and can be liable for wrongful trading. However, these statutory duties arise from the directorial functions exercised by the shareholder, not from his position as a shareholder. Further, a shareholder may incur liability as a constructive trustee if he receives property misapplied by a fiduciary or assists in such misapplication without receiving anything himself, provided that, in either case, the appropriate degree of knowledge of the wrongdoing was possessed. Again, this liability is not imposed because the shareholder is a shareholder but because of his knowledge of the breach of fiduciary duty.

There are a number of cases which suggest that shareholders have a duty as shareholders to vote '*bona fide* for the benefit of the company as a whole' (see *Allen v Gold Reefs of West Africa (1900)* for the first use of the phrase), but closer analysis of these cases does not, in my view, support the idea that a fiduciary duty is imposed on majority shareholders in all cases. Shareholders are generally free to vote however they wish, even to ratify wrongful acts committed by themselves while acting as directors if need be (*North West Transportation Co Ltd v Beatty (1887)*), and they can sell their votes to another, thereby pledging themselves to vote to the order of another. No distinction appears to be drawn between shareholders who have only residual powers in respect of corporate management (the norm where a company has adopted Table A) and those who effectively run the company, for example where the board is in deadlock and unable to act (*Barron v Potter (1914)*).

While it is difficult to discern a general duty cast upon shareholders, there are circumstances where the court will require shareholders to vote '*bona fide* for the benefit of the company' and not just consider their own interests. There is no definitive list (or definition) of such circumstances, but some cases suggest that, wherever the majority has acted in a manner which constitutes fraud on the minority, it will be deemed to be in breach of fiduciary duty. This is a difficult test to apply without a clearer indication of what constitutes fraud, but there are certain areas where 'fraud on the minority' is likely to exist; that is, shareholders can expect to be treated as subject to a fiduciary duty.

First, shareholders voting to absolve from liability a fiduciary who has misappropriated corporate property (or to appropriate corporate property to their own use) are subject to the duty to vote *bona fide* for the benefit of the company. Since misappropriation can hardly be beneficial to the company, a vote to absolve is, traditionally, ineffective (*Cook v Deeks (1916)*). However, the inefficacy of such a vote must be looked at in the light of *Smith v Croft (No 2) (1988)*. In this case, Knox J held that, where the decision by a company not to litigate, for example not to sue a director who had misappropriated corporate property, had been made 'by an appropriate independent organ', no action could ensue and a minority shareholder would not be allowed to bring a derivative claim on behalf of the company because the majority of shareholders, assuming them to be the independent organ, did not wish to pursue the errant director. The judge pointed out that the appropriate independent organ might have good reason to refuse to litigate, for example unnecessary expense or the unlikelihood of any judgment being satisfied. However, in determining what constituted an independent organ, he said that where a majority of shareholders had indicated no desire for litigation, their 'votes would be disregarded if, but only if, the court is satisfied either that the vote or its equivalent is actually cast with a view to supporting the defendants rather than securing a benefit to the company', which seems to retain the possibility of ignoring the vote to discontinue action against a director if the vote was not designed to secure a benefit to the company. Consider also s 322A CA 1985, which provides that a transaction entered into by a company with a director, which the directors do not have the power to negotiate (or the company lacks the capacity to enter into), are voidable at the company's option. Suppose that the directors misappropriate corporate property (beyond their powers); s 322A CA 1985 suggests that this is ratifiable by the company and the section does not suggest that shareholders or director-shareholders, in voting to ratify, are subject to any fiduciary duty at all.

Second, when shareholders vote to expropriate the shares of another member, they are subject to a fiduciary duty and must vote '*bona fide* for the benefit of the company' (*Brown v British Abrasive Wheel Co (1919)*). This does not mean that a majority cannot approve an expropriation but that they must have a reason for so doing which is good for the company. For example, in *Sidebottom v Kershaw Leese & Co (1920)*, a change of articles allowing the board to require a shareholder in competition with the company to sell their shares, at a fair price, to nominees of the directors, was upheld as beneficial to the company.

It cannot be denied that there are *dicta* which would support the imposition of a fiduciary duty on shareholders in cases other than those where fraud on the minority (in the sense outlined above) is present. However, even those cases where the *dicta* are widest do not always find a fiduciary duty was owed by the majority. For example, decisions do not seem to support the view that a want of fair dealing, by itself, will impose a fiduciary duty on shareholders. In *Greenhalgh v Arderne Cinemas Ltd (1946)*, the directors of the company were desperate for new capital and persuaded G to invest in the company by purchasing ordinary shares. To protect G's position, his shares were subdivided into five shares, thereby quintupling his votes and giving him the power to block a special resolution. The company then proposed similarly to subdivide the rest of the ordinary shares, thereby affecting the efficacy of G's votes and depriving him of negative voting control. This proposal was approved by ordinary resolution (under what is now s 121 CA 1985) and G unsuccessfully challenged the subdivision. The Court of Appeal upheld the proposal despite the apparent unfairness to G. The result was to alter the voting equilibrium of the shareholders and deprive G of the negative voting control which had been a condition of his investment. In a later case between the same parties (*Greenhalgh v Arderne Cinemas Ltd (1951)*), the new majority sought to change the articles to remove the right of pre-emption conferred on G. He challenged this change again, alleging that, in voting in favour of the resolution, the majority had failed to vote '*bona fide* in the interests of the company'. Again G failed; the Court of Appeal was critical of the conduct of the majority but refused to strike down the alteration.

Dicta suggest that the shareholders were subject to a fiduciary duty, which they satisfied. If such is the case, the fiduciary might be thought to be so ephemeral as to be effectively non-existent. It could equally be argued that there was no fiduciary duty in that case. However, *Greenhalgh* can be contrasted with the case of *Clemens v Clemens Bros Ltd (1976)*, where Foster J felt able to distinguish the earlier decision and find a breach of fiduciary duty by the majority. In *Clemens*, the majority shareholder (55%), who was also the dominant director, authorised the allotment of shares to other directors, thereby depriving the minority shareholder (45%) of her negative voting control. The judge set the allotment aside; he felt able to classify the allotment as a breach of the fiduciary duty imposed on a majority shareholder, although he (wisely) did not attempt to explain why *Greenhalgh* did not apply. In two other cases, *Re Holders Investment Trust (1971)* and *Estmanco (Kilner House) Ltd v GLC (1982)*, the judges struck down votes by shareholders on the basis that they were not taken *bona fide* for the benefit of the company as a whole, although both could have been decided on other grounds. In *Estmanco*, Megarry VC took the view that no shareholder could vote in his own selfish interests or ignore the interests of the company, but these *dicta* are wider than anything contemplated by the Court of Appeal in *Greenhalgh* and should be confined to the (unusual) facts of the case. In fact, the Law Commission proposed that, unlike the position in *Estmanco*, a minority shareholder should not be allowed to bring a derivative claim against a majority shareholder, if the conduct complained of arises from the conduct of the majority shareholder rather than the directors (Law Commission,

Shareholder Remedies (1997)). This recommendation has been adopted by the Companies Act 2006 as part of a new two-stage procedure in allowing a member to bring a derivative claim. The Act also provides for a derivative claim to be brought in pursuance to a court order in proceedings under s 459 CA 1985.

A further problem encountered if the majority shareholder is under a general fiduciary duty to subjugate his own interests to those of the company is what is meant by 'the company' in this context (a hypothetical member, according to *Greenhalgh*). The court in *Greenhalgh* acknowledged another difficulty in imposing a general fiduciary duty on all shareholders whenever a vote is taken—should liability be imposed only on those who consciously fail to put the company's interests first, or should those who voted without giving the matter any thought also be liable?

Arguably, the existence or non-existence of a fiduciary duty cast upon members is irrelevant, given s 459 CA 1985. This section allows any shareholder to petition the court where the affairs of the company are being, have been, or will be conducted in a manner unfairly prejudiced against him. The section does not differentiate between acts, etc, which are initiated by the board and those initiated by the majority shareholder; the crucial issue is whether there is unfair prejudice to the interests of a member. An advantage of bringing an action against the majority at common law seems to be that it is treated as a derivative claim, thereby allowing the claimant to seek an immediate indemnity from the company rather than, as a petitioner, waiting for an order for costs if successful (*Wallersteiner v Moir (1974)*). Another advantage could be that the burden of proof in cases at common law *may* fall on those seeking to support a vote (see *Re Holders*) rather than on the petitioner, as with s 459 CA 1985. It is my view that any general common law fiduciary duty should be abolished and that shareholder actions should be judged by reference to unfair prejudice alone. It is also arguable that, even where a vote is authorised by statute, the resulting decision should be reviewable if it is unfairly prejudicial (note the case in evidence where judges have a discretion to exclude evidence where its admission would be unfair to the accused even if it is rendered admissible by statute).

Question 29

In 1995, Albert began a book selling business with two of his children, Ben and Connie. In 1998, a company, Bookit Ltd, was formed and the business was sold to the company in exchange for shares in the company. Albert, Ben and Connie had equal shareholdings and were directors of the company; most of the profits of the company were paid to the directors in salaries. In 2000, Albert died, leaving his shares to his wife, Anna, who was appointed to the board and draws a salary as a director although she takes no part in running the business and rarely attends meetings. On Albert's death, Ben took over as managing director and his wife, Diana, was appointed as a director.

In 2004, Ben proposed that the company specialise in books relating to sport and begin selling sporting memorabilia. Connie disagreed with this change of policy but Anna and Diana supported Ben and the plan went ahead. During the next financial year, the company made a loss. Consequently, Ben proposed to sell the company's premises to raise working capital. Connie objected to the sale but was voted off the board and the sale went ahead. The company is now beginning to prosper and Ben has suggested that the company should lend money to a company controlled by Diana which manufactures china models of sporting figures, to enable it to expand. Anna wishes to sell her shares to the company and emigrate to Spain but the company has refused to purchase them.

Advise Anna and Connie.

Answer plan

The main issues are:

- Anna—refusal to buy shares and consequent inability to realise value of shares;
- Connie as a director—removal from the board; and
- Connie as shareholder—lack of dividends, change of policy, sale of premises, loan to Diana's company.

Answer

Bookit (B) is a company which is beginning to prosper financially but is facing boardroom turmoil. Assuming that the parties cannot be reconciled with each other, what does the law provide? Anna, Ben and Connie have equal shareholdings, so that any one of them can block a special resolution and any two in combination can pass an ordinary resolution. The shares were allocated in exchange for non-cash consideration—the business, and as such can be treated as fully paid up (s 99 of the Companies Act (CA) 1985). There is no requirement that non-cash consideration be valued when it is used to purchase shares in a private company (s 103 CA 1985 imposes such a requirement in respect of public companies) and a court will treat shares paid for other than in cash as fully paid up unless the consideration is illusory or it is manifest that they are issued at a discount (*Re Wragg (1897)*). For example, shares allotted in return for the assignment of a statute-barred debt would be issued at a discount. Anna and Connie, two of the three shareholders, are unhappy with aspects of the company's operation, but unless they combine to form a majority they have a limited ability to influence the affairs of the company.

Anna, who plays little part in operating the company, would like to realise the value of the shares and emigrate. Since B is a private company, there is no ready market in the shares and an outsider is unlikely to be interested in purchasing a minority shareholding in a family company. This is a common problem for those holding shares in private companies and wishing to retire, and is indeed one of the reasons that the law was changed to allow a company to purchase its own shares (s 162 CA 1985). However, while a company may be empowered to purchase its own shares (the articles must allow it and there must be strict compliance with the statutory provisions), that does not mean that it is required to do so at the behest of a shareholder and the board can legitimately decline to purchase Anna's shares. On her own, Anna cannot change the board, nor can she issue instructions to the board as to how they are to operate the company; nor can she change the articles and take the power to run the company away from the board. However, in combination with Connie, she could pass a special resolution sacking Ben and Diana (s 303 CA 1985) and then run the company herself. Assuming that Anna does not have Connie's support, she could consider an action for unfair prejudice under s 459 CA 1985 or seek a just and equitable winding up under s 122(1)(g) of the Insolvency Act (IA) 1986. A successful application under s 122(1)(g) IA 1986 would result in an order to wind up the company, thus releasing its asset value to the shareholders. It is of little use to Anna if the company has no assets and it destroys what appears to be a viable business. There is an important statutory restriction on a court's ability to wind up a company on the basis that it is just and equitable so to do—s 125(2) IA 1986. This provides that, where the petitioner is a contributory (s 79 IA 1986), which Anna is, and it would be just and equitable to wind the company up, the court will *not* order winding up if there is some other remedy open to the petitioner *and* they are acting unreasonably in seeking winding up rather than pursuing that other remedy.

First, would it be just and equitable to wind this company up? The courts have used this provision where there is deadlock within a company so that it cannot operate (*Re Yenidje Tobacco (1916)*), or where the shareholders have justifiably lost confidence in the management, who appear to be lacking in probity (*Loch v John Blackwood Ltd (1924)*), neither of which appear to be applicable. The courts also use s 122(1)(g) when the company is a quasi-partnership company and relations within the company are such that, had the company been a partnership, it would have justified dissolution, that is, where there is a mutual justifiable loss of confidence in one's fellow shareholders. It is probable that B would be a quasi-partnership company, since it bears many of the hallmarks listed by Lord Wilberforce in the leading case of *Ebrahimi v Westbourne Galleries (1973)*. The fact that the company is small or private is not enough. In addition, the company should display all or some of the following factors: First, it will be an association formed or continued on the basis of a personal relationship involving mutual confidence—this may not apply, since Anna is not one of the founders of the company and has taken little part in its operation. Second, the company is one in which it has been agreed that all, or some, of the shareholders would participate in management—this seems to apply. Third, the shares of the company will not be freely marketable, thus locking a disappointed shareholder into the company. If B is within the ambit of the section, it is unlikely that simple failure to buy Anna's shares would be sufficient to justify winding up. Moreover, the change of direction and sale of the premises were supported by Anna and cannot form the basis of her complaint. The possible loan to Diana's company might be regarded as a breach of directors' duty by Ben (and Diana), but again seems unlikely by itself to justify just and equitable winding up. Arguably, Connie has a better case for winding up than Anna, in that she has been excluded from management. Even if winding up is possible, the court would not order it if Anna (or Connie) has an alternative remedy which she is rejecting unreasonably. Is there such a remedy?

Section 459 CA 1985 allows any member of a company to petition the court for an order that the affairs of the company are being, have been or will be conducted in a manner which is unfairly prejudicial to her interests. Extensive case law since 1980, when the section was introduced, has led to the formulation of several principles in determining applications under this section. First, a shareholder can be unfairly prejudiced, whether that was the intention of the company or not, that is, *mala fides* is not required although lack of *mala fides* may render prejudicial conduct 'fair' (*Re A Company (No 007623 of 1984) (1986)*). Second, misconduct on the part of the petitioner does not preclude a remedy (*Re RA Noble Ltd (1983)*). Third, a member must be unfairly prejudiced in their capacity as a member, for example, failure to buy goods from a shareholder would not affect a member in a shareholder capacity (*Re A Company (No 004475 of 1982) (1983)*). Fourth, what constitutes unfair prejudice depends on the facts, but inability to work together leading to the exclusion of a director is not necessarily unfair (*Re A Company (No 007623 of 1984) (1986)*). What is needed is a lack of fairness in the circumstances.

Fairness has been considered by the House of Lords in *O'Neill v Phillips (1999)*. In *O'Neill* a minority shareholder, O, had effectively run the business and the majority shareholder, P, had allowed O to keep 50% of the profits and had indicated that he might consider transferring some of his shares to O. Subsequently, P decided to return to management and not to transfer shares to O. P's conduct did not breach company law, the memorandum and articles or any concluded agreement between the parties. O argued that the disappointment of his legitimate expectation that he would continue in management and obtain more shares was unfairly prejudicial. The House of Lords rejected O's claim. Lord Hoffmann ruled that where there is no breach of company law or any agreement between the parties on the running of the company, there is no unfair prejudice unless equitable considerations make it unfair for those running the company to rely on their strict legal powers.

Failure by the management to pursue the course desired by the petitioner is unlikely by itself to be sufficient (*Re A Company (No 004475 of 1982) (1983)*) and this seems likely to apply to Anna. In *Re A Company (No 004475 of 1982) (1983)*, a shareholder alleged unfair prejudice on the basis that the company had failed to purchase the member's shares at the price he wanted and the company was expanding into new fields (a wine bar) which might prove unsuccessful. The court rejected both arguments: failure to buy the shares did not prejudice the petitioner as a member, and the court was reluctant to intervene in a commercial decision by the board to expand the company's business, even if there was no risk of loss to the company. Her final complaint, the proposed loan, might be sufficient for an action to proceed, in that any loan may be a breach of directors' duty, but an appropriate remedy is unlikely to include an order to buy her shares. Anna is unlikely to have any legal remedy for her complaint.

Connie could seek just and equitable winding up as well, with a greater chance of success. She was a founder member of the company and had been part of the business from its foundation, so that she might well argue that her exclusion from management, with its consequent loss of income, justified winding up the company. The facts of the case are similar to those in *Ebrahimi*, where a founder member who was legally excluded from the company which had taken over his business was able to obtain a winding up order. However, unlike Anna, Connie may be more concerned with regaining a place in the company and the court might regard such a remedy as a better alternative than winding up a profitable company. Has Connie a s 459 case?

There is no doubt that exclusion from management has been accepted as unfairly prejudicial to the interests of a *member*, where the member's interests included a legitimate expectation that she would be entitled to participate in management, in other words, equitable considerations limited the exercise of strict legal rights to dismiss a director. In such cases, to dismiss a director could found a successful petition (*Re A Company, ex p Holden (1991)* is an example). However, to dismiss a director, even a founder director, is not necessarily unfair prejudicial; each case turns on its facts. The lack of attention paid to the business by Anna might form part of an unfair prejudice claim (even if unlikely to be a breach of director's duty, given the modest level of attendance required of non-executive directors), as could any gross over-payments to the directors (*Re Cumana Ltd (1986)*), especially where the company pays only small, or no, dividends (*Re Sam Weller Ltd (1990)*). Allied to the exclusion from management, the lacklustre attendance record of Anna and the lack of dividends, Connie could also raise the proposed loan. Loans to directors, or persons connected to directors (Diana's company), are prohibited (s 330 CA 1985) and are voidable at the company's option (s 341 CA 1985). While the company is *prima facie* the proper claimant to pursue recovery of such a loan (unlikely here), so that Connie might not be able to succeed in an action for breach of director's duty, the loan could form part of the s 459 CA 1985 claim (breach of company law does not necessarily trigger s 459 CA 1985 but it is a factor—*O'Neill v Phillips (1999)*). There are exceptions to s 330 CA 1985 (for example, s 335 CA 1985—small loans in the course of business), but it is not obvious that any of these exceptions would apply to Diana. In addition, any loan authorised by the directors must be for a 'proper purpose' (breach is ratifiable) and, if such is not the case with this loan, the directors' conduct would strengthen Connie's unfair prejudice claim.

The change in the business and sale of the premises are not likely to be regarded as matters for the courts (as with the wine bar case *Re A Company (No 004475 of 1982) (1983)*) unless the directors have acted improperly, for example if the sale was to a director who failed to declare an interest. If Connie succeeds in claiming unfair prejudice on the part of the company, the court has an unfettered discretion as to the remedy (s 461 CA 1985). The court could order her to be bought out at a fair price, or that she be restored to the board, or it may even require the other shareholders to sell their shares to her (as in *Re A Company (No 00789 of 1987) ex p Shooter (1990)*), or award any other remedy it considers. It is likely that any loan would be declared invalid at the very least and, if she remained a shareholder but was not reinstated as a director, the court might order the payment of dividends to protect her income.

Perhaps Annie and Connie should combine their votes to become majority shareholders and achieve their aims without going to court.

▌NOTE

Other examples of cases on s 459 CA 1985 could be included but care must be taken in respect of cases decided before *O'Neill v Phillips (1999)*.

Question 30

In 2001, Tilda, Neil and Charles formed Parliament Ltd, a company providing advice to people lobbying Members of Parliament. Each of them became a director and was allotted one-third of the issued share capital. The articles of the company provide that any shareholder who wishes to sell his or her shares must first offer them to the other shareholders at a price calculated by the company's auditors, in accordance with a stated formula. The articles also provide that if any person ceases, for any reason, to be a director he or she must, if asked to do so, transfer his or her shares to a remaining director or directors at a price calculated in accordance with the same formula.

The company has generated a large income but, in order to develop the business, all profits, except for directors' remuneration, have been reinvested in the company. In 2006, Tilda died and her husband John inherited her shares; he now needs funds to develop his own business and wishes either to sell his shares to Fred, who runs a similar business in Brussels, or persuade the company to pay dividends. Charles, who is extremely short tempered, has fallen out with Neil and would like to remove him from the board, purchase his shares and replace him with his (Charles's) wife, Glenys. Neil is refusing to resign from the board and has said that he will not sell his shares if asked to do so because, he claims, the price-fixing formula for the shares is unfair.

Answer plan

Careful consideration must be given to the particular needs of the parties:

(a) John wants to sell his shares to an outsider. Can he do so? Alternatively, can he force the company to pay dividends?

(b) Neil does not wish to be forced out of the company or sell his shares.

Answer

The relations between the shareholders seem so unhappy that they might be best advised to wind up the company; if they cannot agree to a voluntary winding up, perhaps Neil should petition for a just and equitable winding up under s 122(1)(g) of the Insolvency Act (IA) 1986, since it seems plain that there is a mutual loss of confidence between the three shareholders. However, the difficulty with a business of this type (people and skills based) is that its break up value is not likely to be large. A company may be capable of generating large profits but have little in the way of assets, so that winding up is killing the (potential) golden goose, but there may be no other solution to the shareholder antipathy. Assuming that the shareholders do not seek voluntary winding up, what course of action is open to John and Neil?

(a) John (J)

J wishes to sell his shares to an outsider, so it can be assumed that Fred (F) is willing to pay a higher price than that generated by the price-fixing formula in the articles, perhaps because, being in the same line of business, he intends to try to merge the companies. However, J is not totally unhappy with Parliament Ltd (P), since he would be willing to remain a shareholder if the company paid dividends.

Obviously, J sees his shares as a means of generating revenue, so that he is neutral as to how this arises, but selling to F would produce a capital sum and would, it is assumed, be preferred by J. A shareholder, however he acquired his shares, is bound by the articles of the company and s 14 the Companies Act (CA) 1985 provides that the articles constitute a contract between the shareholder and the company (and, by implication, vice versa), and also between each and every shareholder *inter se*. It is not clear how a shareholder enforces this contractual right; *dicta* in the House of Lords suggested that it could only be enforced through the company (*Welton v Saffery (1897)*) but, in *Rayfield v Hands (1960)*, Vaisey J held that a shareholder could enforce relevant articles directly, without joining the company. Thus, in *Rayfield*, the directors were able, as members, to enforce a provision which required a shareholder wishing to sell shares to offer them first to the directors— similar to the provision in this case.

While criticism has been levelled at *Rayfield*, particularly in allowing *directors* to enforce the articles, it seems likely to be applicable here. Consequently, any attempt to sell shares without giving first refusal to the existing shareholders could be restrained by injunction and J should be so advised. However, J cannot force the existing shareholders to buy the shares: the articles require him to offer; he is not required to purchase. Should the other shareholders decide to purchase J's shares, s 14 CA 1985 would render the price-fixing formula enforceable against him. For a consideration of whether the price-fixing formula could be ignored, see (b) below.

J cannot require the company to pay dividends; the dividend policy is for the directors to determine, so he cannot guarantee an income from his shareholding. There are, however, a limited number of cases in which the courts have ruled that failure to pay an adequate dividend could constitute unfair prejudice to the interests of a member, that is, s 459 CA 1985, and have used their power under s 461 CA 1985 to instruct the directors to reconsider their dividend policy. A degree of caution should be exercised in advising J of these cases, since any application under s 459 CA 1985 necessarily turns on its own facts and simple non-payment of dividend may not be sufficient to constitute unfair prejudice. Moreover, these cases pre-date *O'Neill v Phillips (1999)*, in which the House of Lords stressed that where a company is complying with company law and the memorandum and articles (and failing to pay dividends is not a breach of the law or the memorandum and articles), it will find unfair prejudice only where equitable considerations require intervention.

In *Re Sam Weller Ltd (1990)*, the company had substantial net assets (including cash) and, in 1985, made net profits of £36,330. The sole director, W, who was a minority shareholder, proposed a dividend of 14 p per share absorbing £2,520, the same dividend as had been paid for the previous 37 years, and the petitioner alleged that the director was running the company for the exclusive benefit of himself and his two sons, who were employees of the company. In a preliminary action to strike out the petition, Peter Gibson J, in refusing to do so, held that it was arguable that failure to pay dividends at anything other than a very modest level, where profits were substantial, which decision was made by those who derived their income from the company, was unfairly prejudicial. He firmly rejected the idea that low dividends would be unfairly prejudicial in all cases and was influenced by the apparent use of company money by W to buy a holiday home for his sons and W's refusal to register the petitioners as holders of shares which they had inherited. While the directors of this company are not paying dividends and are taking directors' fees, the situation is different from *Weller*: the company is relatively new and unlikely to have substantial reserves; retaining funds to develop the business seems only prudent; and there is no allegation that the directors are effectively preferring themselves at the expense of shareholders in their use of profits. J's action for unfair prejudice is unlikely to succeed.

(b) Neil

Between them, Charles (C) and J could vote Neil (N) off the board (s 303 CA 1985, ordinary resolution), although if this also has the effect of terminating a service contract, substantial damages might be payable to N. If C is determined to sack N, J could use this as a bargaining chip to get what he wants in return for his votes. If N ceases to be a director, the articles provide that he may be required to transfer his shares to C (the only director left) and he is bound by this provision (see the argument above regarding J and the article on share transfer). If N is dismissed, can he complain, and is there any way he can evade either the requirement to sell shares or the price-fixing formula?

Section 459 CA 1985 permits a shareholder to petition the court, alleging that the affairs of the company are being, have been or will be conducted in such a way as to be unfairly prejudicial to his interests. Interests in this context have been held to be interests as a member only (see *Re JE Cade Ltd (1991)* for a reaffirmation), but interests extend beyond rights. Consequently, even where rights under the articles have not been infringed, an action for unfair prejudice may lie. Interests of a member can include a legitimate expectation that, where he has ventured capital on the understanding that he would participate in management, he would continue as a director (*Re A Company (No 00477 of 1986) (1987)*). The wider equitable considerations that the wording of the section has been held to permit would allow a court to rule that reliance by the company on its legal rights, for example use of s 303 CA 1985, could be unfairly prejudicial. However, where the articles accurately reflect the intentions of the members, a court would be unlikely to treat reliance on the articles as unfairly prejudicial.

N could argue that attempts to dismiss him, particularly where his conduct does not seem to justify it, would be unfairly prejudicial. If such is the case, a court could order any dismissal to be invalid, but the powers of the court under s 461 CA 1985 are not limited to any particular remedy. Since it seems unlikely that N and C can continue working together, a court might think it apt that one or other of them should be ordered to purchase the shares of the other (or perhaps s 122(1)(g) IA 1986 should be used). If such an order is made, the question arises as to how the shares should be valued. If C is allowed to exercise his right to purchase (contained in the articles), will the court simply adopt the formula in the articles? Early cases on s 459 CA 1985 held that, where the articles contained, as here, a price-fixing formula which the majority proposed to use, the court would not intervene, but this has been modified in later decisions. In *Re A Company (No 00330 of 1991) ex p Holden (1991)*, the majority shareholders (who were also the directors) argued that, since the articles provided for expert valuation by the auditor, Holden was assured of a fair price and, consequently, the court had no need to usurp the function of the articles in substituting its own price-fixing formula. Harman J accepted that, where the articles provided an adequate price-fixing formula for the compulsory purchase of the shares of the minority, the court would not usually intervene (see *Re A Company (No 006834 of 1988) ex p Kremer (1989)*), but that this issue must be adjudged in the light of the Court of Appeal decision in *Virdi v Abbey Leisure Ltd (1990)*.

In *Virdi*, the Court of Appeal accepted that a petitioner could reasonably refuse to accept a valuation conducted in accordance with the articles, and the court should not follow it if there was a risk that that method of valuation would depreciate the value of the interest. For example, in *Holden*, the judge found that such a risk arose, in that the auditor/valuer was not required to explain how he reached his valuation, leaving H no basis to attack it, and also in that there was no machinery for H to put relevant matters to the valuer, particularly those relating to any other legal claims against the company (the effect of which might considerably affect the value of shares), and the potential capital gains tax liability that the company's valuation procedure would impose on H. N could argue that any attempt to use the formula was itself unfairly prejudicial, and the court should not use it, if the price-fixing formula did not accurately reflect the value of his interest. Situations where a court has rejected the valuation machinery in the articles (apart from *Holden*) have included cases where the conduct of those prejudicing the petitioner has depressed the value of the shares (*Re A Company (No 006834 of 1988) (1989)*) or where the valuation machinery is arbitrary and unfair on its face (*Re A Company (No 00477 of 1986) (1987)*). Where a court substitutes its own valuation machinery for shares, it can also fix its own valuation date: for example the date of the judgment or petition or a date preceding the unfairly prejudicial conduct, whichever it thinks most appropriate (for some guidance see the Court of Appeal decision in *Profinance Trust SA v Gladstone (2001)*).

Since N has not yet been dismissed or requested to sell his shares, he should present an interim petition to the court, asking that the affairs of the company be frozen until a full hearing. It must be said that N might be well advised to try to buy J's shares (although J might challenge the price-fixing formula and he is not compelled to sell) and put himself in a majority, or sell his shares and go (if the price is right), or seek a just and equitable winding up, since it is plain that there is a loss of confidence between the remaining directors of what is plainly a quasi-partnership (noting as with J the probable lack of break up value).

Question 31

A limited company is more than a mere legal entity, with a personality in law of its own ... there is room in company law for recognition of the fact that behind it there are individuals, with rights, expectations and obligations *inter se* which are not necessarily submerged in the corporate structure [Lord Wilberforce in *Ebrahimi v Westbourne Galleries Ltd*].

To what extent does the interpretation placed upon s 459 of the Companies Act 1985 and s 122(1)(g) of the Insolvency Act 1986 'recognise the rights of individuals'?

Answer plan

This requires a brief exposition of the effects of the separate corporate personality of companies, then a consideration of the extent to which individual rights are still recognised despite their apparent submersion within the corporate form in judicial interpretation of s 459 of the Companies Act (CA) 1985 and s 122(1)(g) of the Insolvency Act (IA) 1986.

Answer

On incorporation, a registered company becomes a legal entity separate and distinct from its members. The internal management of the company is determined by company law and the constitution of the company. The individuals who are members of a company have to be consulted on various aspects of the operation of the company, but as members they are bound by decisions passed by an appropriate majority even if they did not vote in favour of the decision. In addition, shareholders have generally given up their right to run a company's day to day affairs and have bestowed this power on the directors of the company (for example by having Table A, Art 70). In return for the benefits of incorporation, particularly limited liability, shareholders have given up their individual rights and have agreed to be bound by acts of the company carried on in accordance with the law. Shareholders, particularly shareholders who have been engaged in business with their fellow shareholders prior to incorporation, may well incorporate the business with certain expectations as to how the company will operate. Similarly, individuals may join an existing company in some capacity on the basis of certain expectations as to their current or future roles within the entity. Prudent shareholders may choose to have their expectations embodied in a shareholder agreement or some other form of contract which gives enforceable rights and defined remedies in the event of internal disagreement and the disappointment of their expectations. Most shareholders, however, enter into the corporate adventure with high hopes and no thought of future disappointments. Having adopted corporate format, are the individuals who feel that their expectations are not being fulfilled able to pursue a remedy? The remedies open to unhappy shareholders who are unable to pass a special or ordinary resolution are limited. For example, breach of the articles not involving a membership right leaves a shareholder with no remedy and dealings in shares by the company (for example reduction or capital or an amendment of class rights) may be contrary to the wishes of a minority of shareholders, but there is nothing that a shareholder can do about these matters.

SECTION 459 OF THE COMPANIES ACT (CA) 1985

Section 459 CA 1985 may provide a remedy for disgruntled shareholders (the Secretary of State can also petition). The section provides that where the acts or omissions, current, past or proposed, of the company, the directors, or the majority shareholders are unfairly prejudicial to all or some of the shareholders, a shareholder can bring an action to complain. What constitutes unfair prejudice is a question of fact in each case but it is plain that in order to obtain a remedy, a member must be unfairly prejudiced in his capacity as a member. Thus, failure to buy goods from a shareholder would not affect a member in a shareholder capacity and could not found an action under s 459 CA 1985.

Can a shareholder who is unhappy with the way the company is being run (even if entirely compliant with the memorandum, articles and company law) complain that he or she is being unfairly prejudiced because it is not how he or she *expected* it to be operated? Useful guidance on the operation of s 459 CA 1985 has been provided by the House of Lords in *O'Neill v Phillips (1999)* and the Court of Appeal in *Re Saul Harrison & Sons plc (1995)*. In *Saul Harrison*, the holder of non-voting shares claimed that the directors of the company were keeping the company going purely to earn substantial salaries when a reasonable board would, given the company's prospects, have liquidated the company and distributed its assets. The court refused to find unfair prejudice. It ruled that, in deciding what is fair or unfair for the purposes of s 459 CA 1985, it was important to bear in mind that fairness was being used in the context of a commercial relationship. The court stressed that the relationship of shareholders is primarily governed by the memorandum and articles of the company, and commercial fairness can be seen as predominantly a question of complying with them. Even if conduct is not in accordance with the memorandum or articles, it is not necessarily unfair. For example, trivial and technical infringements of the articles will not attract the statutory remedy. However, the court accepted that sometimes the memorandum and articles do *not* represent the understandings on which the shareholders are associated, in which case it may be unfair to a shareholder for the company's controllers to exercise the powers in the memorandum and articles if doing so denies that shareholder's proper expectations. Such expectations may derive from a contract independent of the memorandum and articles but is not restricted to such cases; there is also a question of whether equitable considerations require express or implied promises not contained in the memorandum and articles to be honoured. Where such outside contracts or considerations exist, reliance on the memorandum and articles (and strict rights under company law) could be unfairly prejudicial.

The House of Lords in *O'Neill* affirmed this approach. In this case, P originally owned all the shares (100) in a construction company, but in 1985 he gave 25 shares to O, an employee; P also retired from the board, effectively leaving O as managing director. The profits of the company were legally divided between P (75%) and O (25%) but P voluntarily gave up 25% of the profits so that P and O received equal profit shares, and there were discussions about O's shareholding being increased to 50%. In 1991 there was a downturn in the construction industry and P returned to oversee management, giving O the choice of managing, under P's direction, either the English or the German branch of the business while remaining a director of the company; O went to Germany. Later that year, P claimed to be entitled to retain 75% of the company's profits and O left the company, claiming unfair prejudice. The House rejected O's claim. Lord Hoffmann approved *Re Saul Harrison* (in which he had given the leading judgment) and stressed that

> a member of a company will not ordinarily be entitled to complain of unfairness unless there has been some breach of the terms on which he agreed that the affairs of the company would be conducted. But there will be cases in which equitable considerations make it unfair for those conducting the affairs of the company to rely upon their strict legal powers. Thus unfairness may consist of a breach of the rules or in using the rules in a manner which equity would regard as contrary to good faith.

On the facts of this case, O had not been excluded from management, nor had P promised or agreed to transfer any shares to O (even if O had hopes of such a transfer), nor had O been promised that he would always receive 50% of the profits. Rather, he had been promised, at best, 50% while he was acting as managing director. P had done nothing in breach of the memorandum and articles and there were no promises by P which could give rise to equitable considerations which might have led the court to treat O as entitled to something other than that given in the company's constitution.

There are many illustrations of the operation of s 459 CA 1985. Exclusion of a shareholder from management may be unfairly prejudicial (*Re OC (Transport) Services*

Ltd (1984); *Re London School of Electronics (1985)*; *Re Distinct Services Ltd (2005)*), provided that he had a *legitimate* expectation that he would so participate; such an expectation may be based on an agreement not contained in the articles (it may even be contrary to the articles). However, where the company is a public company, or the articles were the product of considerable legal scrutiny before adoption (*Re A Company (No 005685 of 1988) ex p Schwarcz (1989)*), it is unlikely that the court will find a shareholder entitled to expect to participate in management if this is not provided for in the articles, since in such cases the agreement or articles must represent the totality of what the shareholder can expect.

Section 461 CA 1985 provides that the remedies available for breach of s 459 CA 1985 are at the discretion of the court and may not always be what the aggrieved shareholder would like. The most common remedy is a 'buy out' order, the court compelling the majority or the company to buy the shares of the petitioning shareholder (at a fair price).

SECTION 122(1)(G) OF THE INSOLVENCY ACT (IA) 1986

Section 122(1)(g) IA 1986 gives a court the power to wind up a company when it 'is of the opinion that it is just and equitable that the company should be wound up'. The courts have always held that the exercise of this provision is not restricted to particular circumstances or categories. However, there are certain factual situations where a case for just and equitable winding up is likely to be in issue. Examples are where members of a company cannot agree on how the company should be run so that it is effectively inoperable, or where a company, while operable and operating, is not being run in a manner which reflects the objectives upon which the shareholders agreed when the company was formed (*Loch v John Blackwood Ltd (1924)*). This section is now used less than s 459 CA 1985, which provides an alternative, more flexible remedy for disgruntled shareholders since the effect of s 122(1)(g) IA 1986 is to destroy the company. This is why s 459 CA 1985 is likely to prove a more popular remedy both for those shareholders who are unhappy, since they are likely to be bought out, and for those causing the unhappiness, since they still have a viable company.

The leading case on s 122(1)(g) IA 1986 is *Ebrahimi v Westbourne Galleries Ltd (1972)*. In *Ebrahimi*, E and N had traded in partnership as sellers of fine carpets from about 1945. In 1958 they incorporated the business, becoming the sole directors and shareholders. Shortly afterwards, N persuaded E to admit his son, G, into the business and G became a director and was given shares by both N and E; N and G held the majority of the shares. The company traded profitably and all profits were paid out as directors' fees. In 1969, disputes arose and N and G combined to vote E off the board using what is now s 303 CA 1985. Since no other remedy was then available,

E sought just and equitable winding up. In ordering the winding up of the company, Lord Wilberforce laid down general principles for the operation of the section. He stated that the words 'just and equitable' allowed a court to look behind the strict legalities and consider the rights and expectations of the shareholders. Justice and equity would not, he held, allow one party to disregard the obligations which he undertook on joining a company; the section allowed a court to subject the exercise of legal rights to equitable considerations. In other words, Lord Wilberforce accepted that, where people had combined to form a company, consideration must be given to their legal rights tempered by reference to their agreements and expectations in entering into the company. He accepted that this equitable overlay could not apply to all companies, only those which displayed specified characteristics. Traditionally, such companies are called quasi-partnerships. Lord Wilberforce held that the circumstances which permit the application of equitable considerations cannot be laid down conclusively. The fact that the company was small or private was not enough, but typically a company would display all or some of the following characteristics:

- it will be an association formed or continued on the basis of a personal relationship involving mutual confidence;
- in which it was agreed that all, or some, of the shareholders would participate in management; and
- the shares of the company will not be freely marketable, thus locking a disappointed shareholder into the company.

Where, as in *Ebrahimi*, the company is of the appropriate type, the conduct of the majority should be judged not purely by reference to their legal rights but by reference to the hopes and expectations of the parties. Plainly, E had anticipated remaining part of the company he had founded, and, since his hopes had been dashed, it was just and equitable to wind up the company.

▌CONCLUSION

While there is little doubt that in most cases company law and the constitution of the company prevail over any intentions or hopes possessed by all or some of the shareholders, it may be possible, particularly in small companies, that broader equitable considerations may allow a court to grant a statutory remedy to a disappointed shareholder.

Question 32

In 1995, Wisley, who had taken early retirement from his job as a teacher, began to develop his hobby of rose growing as a business. Five years later, he incorporated what was by then a thriving nursery as Rosejoy Ltd and he became 'director for life'.

The articles of the company create two classes of ordinary share: the 'A' shares and the 'B' shares. Each share carries one vote. The articles further provide that the holder of the 'A' shares has a right to veto a takeover and that, on a vote to dismiss a director, the 'A' shares carry 10 votes. On incorporation, Wisley was allotted all 100 of the 'A' shares and 200 of the 'B' shares; he gave 300 'B' shares to his son, Inverewe, who is also a director of the company, and the remaining 500 of the 'B' shares to his wife, who acted as company secretary. Wisley and his wife have always drawn a reasonable salary from the company, which has never paid dividends.

Wisley has continued to run the company as if it was still his own private business and, as he becomes older, enters into increasingly hazardous business ventures. Inverewe would like to be more involved in the business but his father refuses to allow him to take any significant part in management. Wisley's wife has recently died and has left her shares equally to their daughter, Malmaison, and Arnega, Inverewe's son, who would like to sell the company to a property developer who would use the land for building.

Malmaison, who is a highly successful accountant, is unhappy with the level of competence displayed by Wisley and has no great faith in her brother's business acumen. Arnega has suggested that she should join the board. All Malmaison's complaints, and Arnega's proposals, have been brushed aside by Wisley and Inverewe, who habitually refuse to hold company meetings.

Advise Malmaison and Arnega.

Answer plan

Another question involving many issues. The shareholders who are seeking your advice hold 500 of the 1,100 shares between them, which is sufficient to block a special resolution but insufficient to pass any type of resolution without the support of Inverewe (Inverewe's position is the same). They do not want the same thing but may form a tactical alliance. Issues which could arise include:

- the problems associated in attempting to dismiss W and I, noting in particular the weighted voting right;
- the effectiveness of the anti-takeover provision; and
- the level of management competence, the non-declaration of dividends and the absence of meetings, etc.

Answer

The shareholdings in this company give rise to several possible voting blocks. Malmaison (M) and Arnega (A) hold 500 of the 1,100 shares in the company, so that, without the support of another shareholder, they cannot pass an ordinary resolution, but they have (together) the power to block a special resolution. Wisley (W) and Inverewe (I) each hold 300 of the 1,100, so on their own they cannot pass an ordinary resolution (they can do so by acting in concert) but can, individually, block a special resolution. M or A acting with W or I would have 550 of 1,100 shares and could block a special resolution but could not pass an ordinary resolution (the votes are evenly split and no one has a majority). In addition, the 'A' shares have a weighted voting provision in respect of a vote to dismiss a director (not merely W but any director) which, if valid, gives the holder of the 'A' shares the ability to dismiss (or block the dismissal of) a director on his own if he also holds any 'B' shares (W has 1,200 votes on this basis and the remaining shareholders have 800). Can a combination of shareholders dismiss either W or I from the board?

(a) Dismissal of W

W is named in the articles of the company as 'director for life' and, to make extra sure, a provision has been included that on a vote to dismiss a director W's 'A' shares carry 10 votes. This entrenches W but not I, since he only holds 'B' shares. There is no age restriction on directors of private companies, so that W cannot be forced to step down because of increasing age or infirmity. The provision that W is to be a director for life is valid insofar as it applies to a non-executive role, but is ineffective as a basis for claiming that a lifetime service contract exists (s 319 of the Companies Act (CA) 1985). Section 319 CA 1985 provides that a contract providing for the employment of a director by a company cannot, without the prior approval of the general meeting, exceed five years. A contract which purports to exceed five years is invalid and the contract is terminable by reasonable notice. W alone could not approve his own service contract so that any service contract exceeding five years would be terminable by reasonable notice. One difficulty would be who gives the notice? Presumably, the board would be split on the issue, so that whoever has a casting vote (likely to be W) would prevail. If the power of dismissal was vested in the general meeting either by the articles or because of deadlock on the board (as, for example, in *Barron v Potter (1914)*), the question of dismissal, if put to the vote, would allow W to exercise his weighted voting power, assuming it to be valid (see below). Any attempt to terminate W's directorship (executive or non-executive) using s 303 CA 1985 would again fail, because W could muster 1,200 votes (opposition 800) if the weighted voting clause is valid.

In *Bushell v Faith (1970)*, the House of Lords upheld the validity of a weighted voting clause similar to this one. The clause conferred extra votes on a director threatened with dismissal, even though the effect was to make him unsackable and thus, it was argued, to render s 303 CA 1985 useless. The House of Lords did suggest that a weighted voting clause might not have been upheld had the company not been a small, private, family run company, but this would not help I since Rosejoy Ltd seems to fit this description. With the current voting structure, there seems no chance of removing W, even with the support of all other shareholders. Indeed, since W can, on his own, block a special resolution, M, I and A cannot band together to delete the clause. Further, any attempt to sack W might be unfairly prejudicial to his interests, allowing him to petition the courts using s 459 CA 1985.

(b) Dismissal of I

I is in a weaker position than W, in that the shareholders acting in concert can dismiss him, but M and A cannot dismiss him on their own. Indeed, if I retains the confidence of W, he is probably secure, in that W has a weighted voting clause which is applicable in respect of a vote to dismiss *any* director (not merely W). I should be cautious in trying to take more part in management if this is likely to prejudice W against him.

(c) The takeover bid

The mere fact that a shareholder wishes to sell the company to a takeover bidder does not mean that the company must be sold. However, if M and I were to act with A, they would command a majority of the votes and might seek to instruct the directors to sell. However, since this company has Art 70 of Table A, the directors need not comply with instructions given by ordinary resolution but only those given by a special resolution, which they cannot muster. Nor can this majority be changed other than by altering the articles—again, a special resolution is required. A company can create further shares (s 121 CA 1985, ordinary resolution required) and, if the share structure was altered, A (with M and I) might be able to outvote W. However, W seems to have a right to veto a takeover bid and attempts to ignore such a clause have been rejected by the courts (*Quin & Axtens v Salmon (1909)*). Attempts to delete such a clause would require a change of articles (special resolution required) and might be challenged by W as a variation of class rights, that is, he would have to approve the deletion of his right of veto at a separate class meeting. Ignoring a possibly lucrative takeover bid might be a factor which could be taken into account in determining whether s 459 CA 1985 applied, but disagreement about company policy is not usually regarded as unfairly prejudicial.

(d) Level of management competence

M and A are unhappy (as is I, albeit on different grounds) about the way the company is being run. They might well be successful in obtaining a remedy if they petitioned the court under s 459 CA 1985 (unfair prejudice) or s 122(1)(g) of the Insolvency Act (IA) 1986. It is unlikely that the shareholders would be able to sue for breach of duty by the directors because the obligations of the directors are owed to the company and not the shareholders (*Percival v Wright (1902)*), so that the company is the proper claimant to complain about any incompetence on their part (*Foss v Harbottle (1843)*). 'The company' in this context means those running the company, that is, the board, and while there are exceptional cases where the shareholders can sue to enforce the company's rights it is not certain that any exception operates in this case. The directors have the power to fix the dividends and the degree of competence required of directors is traditionally modest. At common law, directors are expected to carry out their duties with an appropriate degree of care and skill. The traditional formulation of the nature and extent of this duty is that given by Romer J in *Re City Equitable Fire Insurance Co Ltd (1925)*, in which he held that a director:

- need display only such skill as may reasonably be expected from a person of his knowledge and experience;

- need not give the affairs of the company continuous attention; and

- is entitled to leave the day to day running of the company to the officials of the company and is entitled to assume, in the absence of suspicious circumstances, that such officials are performing their duties honestly.

These propositions remain good law with regard to non-executive directors, but W (and perhaps I), as an executive director, would be constrained by his service contract and would have to comply with any greater obligation which it imposed. The most important aspect of a director's duty of care relates to the amount of skill he must exercise. Directors are not subject to the Supply of Goods and Services Act 1982, so they need not display reasonable care and skill. Therefore, W and I need only display such skill as may reasonably be expected of them, and perhaps little can be expected. If either of them holds professional qualifications, the degree of skill which can be expected is, of course, higher. It is plain that, if W and I are doing their honest best, they may be held to have exercised sufficient care and skill to evade liability for negligence—the test of liability is subjective, not objective. However, conduct which is not capable of litigation by the shareholders can be taken into account in determining applications under s 459 CA 1985 or s 122(1)(g) IA 1986. Failure to hold meetings might also be evidence in any application under these sections. In addition, failure to hold certain meetings is a breach of the CA 1985; a company must hold an annual general meeting (unless dispensed with by elective resolution, s 366A CA 1985) and failure to do so allows a shareholder to petition the DTI to order the calling of a meeting. Furthermore, shareholders holding at least 10% of the paid up share capital can requisition an extraordinary general meeting (s 368 CA 1985). However, breaches of the Act which are trivial or technical (failure to hold meetings would not be characterised as trivial) would not attract a statutory remedy (*Re Saul Harrison and Sons plc (1995)*, affirmed in *O'Neill v Phillips (1999)*).

If the shareholders simply wish to liquidate their investment in the company, they could apply for the company to be wound up on the basis that it is just and equitable to do so (s 122(1)(g) IA 1986). However, a court has to determine whether winding up would be just and equitable in this case. The company appears to be a quasi-partnership, albeit that W did give the shareholders their shares so that their investment may be locked in, but it is not their money which was hazarded. There may be a justifiable loss of confidence in the management, which could warrant winding up, but perhaps only if allied to a want of probity on the part of the board (there are parallels here with *Loch v John Blackwood Ltd (1924)*, where winding up was ordered). Even if just and equitable winding up would be permissible, s 125 IA 1986 provides that it should not be ordered if the petitioners have an alternative remedy which they are unreasonably failing to pursue. The possible alternative, and one which the shareholders might well prefer, is an action alleging unfair prejudice under s 459 CA 1985.

Section 459 CA 1985 allows any member of a company to petition the court for an order that the affairs of the company are being, have been or will be conducted in a manner which is unfairly prejudicial to her interests. Extensive case law since 1980, when the section was introduced, has led to the formulation of several principles in determining applications under this section. First, a shareholder can be unfairly prejudiced whether that was the intention of the company or not; that is, *mala fides* is not required, although lack of *mala fides* may render prejudicial conduct 'fair' (*Re A Company (No 007623 of 1984) (1986)*). Second, misconduct on the part of the petitioner does not preclude a remedy (*Re RA Noble Ltd (1983)*)— thus, W might be able to petition despite any shortcomings in his own conduct if he was dismissed as a director. Third, a member must be unfairly prejudiced in his capacity as a member; for example, failure to buy goods from a shareholder would not affect a member in a shareholder capacity (*Re A Company (No 004475 of 1982) (1983)*). Fourth, what constitutes unfair prejudice depends on the facts of each case, and conduct which is fair in one context might not be so in another. An example of unfair prejudice is denial of benefits legitimately anticipated by the member, even if not set out in the constitution of the company, including a right to participate in management (*Re Kenyon Swansea Ltd (1987)*)—relevant for W if sacked and perhaps for I. However, it must be noted that the House of Lords has narrowed the concept of legitimate expectations. In *O'Neill v Phillips (1999)*, the House held that a company acting in compliance with company law (and any specific agreement with a shareholder) cannot be regarded as unfairly prejudicing a shareholder unless there are equitable considerations which entitle him to rights over and above those conferred by the law.

The House of Lords in *O'Neill v Phillips (1999)* approved the Court of Appeal's view that, where the conduct complained of by the petitioner is in compliance with company law and the constitution of the company, there must be a good reason why the court should consider other expectations. Hence, the mere fact that A would prefer the land to be sold for building gives him no reasonable expectation that it would be sold (even if financially beneficial to the company) and would not found a s 459 action (see *Re Saul Harrison and Sons plc (1995)*). M and A could also point to W's eccentric conduct and his failure to recognise the fact that he is no longer a sole trader (this might preclude a successful s 459 action by W), drawing a comparison with *Re HR Harmer Ltd (1958)*, where conduct similar to that of W was held to justify an action under s 210 CA 1948, the precursor of s 459 CA 1985.

If, as seems possible, M and A are successful in their application under s 459 CA 1985 (I's case looks less strong), the court can award any remedy it sees fit (s 461 CA 1985). For example, in *Harmer*, the Court of Appeal allowed an elderly director who snooped on staff, ignored board decisions and insulted customers to remain as chairman with no executive role, and this might be applicable in the case of W. I could be brought more into management (or eased off the board) and the weighted voting clause could be deleted. Alternatively, the court might favour an order for W or I or the company to buy out M and A at a fair price, or, indeed, for them to buy out W and/or I. The court cannot make I competent if he is not so, nor can it order everyone to get on with each other. If relations have broken down irretrievably, the court might have no option but to order winding up.

CHAPTER 6

SHARE CAPITAL

INTRODUCTION

Questions about shares and share capital can cover a wide variety of issues, many of them dependent upon statutory provisions of immense complexity. Few questions are likely to be in the form of essays on the power to allot shares or reduce share capital, etc, but such issues could arise in the context of other questions, particularly ones involving directors, variation of class rights and shareholder remedies. This is one area where diagrams and/or sums may make an answer more comprehensible. The ability, where relevant, to explain the facts of *Brady v Brady (1989)* cannot fail to impress!

General questions arising in this area are on such matters as the power of the company and/or the board to issue or rearrange share capital (including schemes of arrangement under ss 425–27 of the Companies Act (CA) 1985) and the capital maintenance doctrine. This doctrine covers the issue of shares (including the nature of the consideration and valuation procedures), as well as dealings in respect of shares, such as the payment of dividends out of capital and the ability of the company to buy (or assist others to buy) its shares. In addition to questions on the issue of shares, this chapter includes questions on doing things with shares, for example, the transfer of shares, variation of class rights and issues relating to takeovers may arise in this context. When, for example, must a bid be made, and when can a takeover bidder acquire shares compulsorily (ss 428–30F CA 1985)? The Companies Act 2006 includes a number of amendments to the existing law, although, to date, these are not in force.

Some courses consider the Stock Exchange listing requirements, but this is more a matter for a course on financial services.

Question 33

Sandy, Laura and Mark are the directors of Bombay Ltd; each of them holds 15% of the company's shares. Of the remaining shares, 50% are split between a number of smaller shareholders, none of whom has more than 10%, and 5% remain unissued. The articles of the company depart from Table A, in that they include a provision which requires any shareholder who wishes to dispose of his shares to offer them first to existing shareholders who will buy them at a fair price. One shareholder has recently died and his widow is anxious to sell his shares. The directors would like to increase their total shareholding so that, between them, they hold at least 51% of the shares. A significant minority of shareholders are reluctant to allow the directors voting control of the company.

Advise the directors as to how they might achieve their aim, including, if relevant, how a scheme might be funded.

Answer plan

An open ended question which points you in no particular direction. There are two obvious ways of increasing a shareholding—buying issued shares from existing shareholders (or their representatives) or obtaining the allotment of unissued shares. Where this does not achieve the necessary majority, the creation and allotment of further share capital is a possibility. If the directors are seeking to obtain a voting majority, they could also seek to insert a weighted voting clause in the articles or to subdivide their shareholding whilst keeping one vote per share. You should consider these possibilities, and any other schemes, bearing in mind potential opposition.

Answer

The directors of Bombay Ltd wish to acquire at least 51% of the shares in the company. This may mean that they wish to obtain voting control rather than being concerned about the number of shares they own. If this is so, they could attempt to achieve their objective without altering the size of their shareholding or reorganising the company's share structure. For example, it is possible to alter voting rights of existing shares by the insertion in the articles of a weighted voting clause. Unfortunately for the directors, alteration of the articles requires a special resolution (s 9 of the Companies Act (CA) 1985) and obtaining a majority of three-quarters of the votes cast, given the likely opposition of existing shareholders, seems doubtful. Alternatively, the directors could seek to subdivide their shares into two or more shares, each of which carries a vote. Section 121 CA 1985 permits a company, whose articles so authorise (Art 32 of Table A provides authority), to subdivide shares into shares of smaller nominal value than that fixed in the memorandum. The decision to subdivide must be made by the company in general meeting, that is, an ordinary resolution is required. An ordinary resolution cannot be passed by the votes of the directors alone (unless some shareholders fail to vote), but they may be able to persuade holders of some shares to side with them and allow the subdivision. A subdivision will decrease the voting strength of the non-director shareholders, but, since their rights (one vote per share) remain unaltered, a subdivision is not treated as a variation of their class rights (*Greenhalgh v Arderne Cinemas Ltd (1950)*) and the requirements for the variation of class rights are not relevant.

The literal approach to class rights taken by the Court of Appeal in *Arderne*, where no regard was paid to the fact that A's shares, each carrying one vote per share, were rendered less valuable in voting terms when the shares of others were divided into five (thus quintupling their voting efficacy), was rejected by Foster J in *Clemens v Clemens Bros Ltd (1976)*. In *Clemens*, where the shares of the minority shareholder were reduced in voting value from 45% to less than 25%, the judge, for no very clear reason, struck down the scheme. This had the effect of diluting the voting strength of the minority shareholder. While the directors could be advised that *Clemens* may not be followed, they should note that an attempt to dilute the voting strength of the majority has been held to be unfairly prejudicial and subject to s 459 CA 1985 (see *Re OC Transport Ltd (1984)* for an example). If attempts to alter the weight of the two voting blocks are unlikely to succeed, the directors might wish to consider the acquisition of further shares.

The simplest solution open to the directors is to purchase shares from existing shareholders. In seeking to purchase shares, the directors do not owe a fiduciary duty to shareholders (*Percival v Wright (1902)*); nor are they at risk from the rules on insider dealing, which apply only to public companies. However, purchase of shares depends upon the existence of a willing seller and, fortunately, there is one available. Nevertheless, the articles of Bombay Ltd provide that shares must be offered to existing shareholders. Section 14 CA 1985 determines that the articles of the company create contractual rights between members and, while there is doubt about the precise effect of s 14 CA 1985, there is no doubt that this provision in the articles is enforceable by the members; see *Rayfield v Hands (1958)*. The difficulty is that the article merely requires the shares to be sold to existing members without specifying how to resolve a situation where more than one member wishes to purchase the shares. The attitude of the courts is to treat the articles as a business document and construe them so as to give them reasonable business efficacy (*Holmes v Keyes (1959)*), so that it would seem appropriate to regard this provision as offering shares to all shareholders. Whether the offer is accepted by the first person to reply is doubtful—it would be more appropriate to hold that the vendor offers the shares to existing shareholders in proportion to their existing holding. If the directors acquire further shares, they are required to report the addition to their existing holdings to the company in writing; this information would be entered in the register of directors' interests. Failure to disclose renders the directors liable to a fine and/or imprisonment. The price payable for any shares purchased from existing shareholders is fixed by the contracting parties, but in this case the articles require it to be a fair price.

If shares cannot be purchased to bring the directors up to their desired holding, they could seek to allot the unissued 5% to themselves (bringing their holding to 50%). In addition, or in substitution, they might try to increase the company's share capital and then allocate the new shares to themselves. To make their position impregnable, any new shares could have a weighted voting provision from the outset, since it is unlikely that the court will treat the articles of the company as unfair and contrary to s 459 CA 1985. Creation of further shares is authorised (for companies whose articles so permit; Art 32 of Table A does so permit) by s 121 CA 1985, provided that the increase in share capital is approved by ordinary resolution. The directors, again, need support from other shareholders to achieve a majority and may be well advised not to try to create shares with weighted voting rights, which may well arouse suspicion in the minds of the non-director shareholders.

If the directors propose to allot the existing unissued shares and/or any new shares to themselves, they face a number of legal difficulties. The power to allot relevant securities (defined in s 94 CA 1985 and including ordinary shares) is vested in the general meeting even when, as is usual, the power to run the company is vested in the board (s 80 CA 1985). However, s 80 CA 1985 provides that the shareholders can give the power to allot shares to the board either in the articles or by ordinary resolution. Originally, the shareholders had to vote to give the power to allot shares to the directors at least every five years, but s 80A CA 1985 allows a private company (by elective resolution in accordance with s 379A CA 1985) to give the authority for an indefinite period. It is unlikely that an elective resolution has been passed, since all shareholders must agree to it. Thus, the directors should consider whether they have the power to allot shares by consulting the articles of the company or any resolution already devolving the power to them.

The authority to allot may be general or limited (for example, only applying to some classes of share, or to a maximum number of shares at any one time). The directors can be advised that, if they breach s 80 CA 1985 and allot shares without authority, they are liable to a fine but the allotment is valid. Assuming that the directors are authorised to allot shares (or are willing to contravene s 80 CA 1985), they must still be wary of s 89 CA 1985, which provides a right of pre-emption for existing shareholders. Section 89 CA 1985 states that, where a company is proposing to allot equity securities (defined in s 94 CA 1985 and including ordinary shares) wholly for cash, the shares must first be offered to existing shareholders in proportion to their existing shareholding. Thus, s 89 CA 1985 allows the directors to offer only 45% of any increase in share capital (or of the unissued 5% of existing shares), which they are allotting, to themselves. A private company, such as Bombay Ltd, can exempt itself from s 89 CA 1985 under s 91 CA 1985 but appears not to have done so. However, if the directors breach s 89 CA 1985 and allot all the shares to themselves, the allotment remains valid, although the directors are liable to compensate shareholders to whom shares were not offered for any loss suffered thereby (under s 92 CA 1985, there is a two year limitation period). The directors can avoid any difficulties with s 89 CA 1985 by allotting the shares other than wholly for cash (see below).

The directors might think that, if they comply with (or avoid) all the statutory regulations, any allotment made by them would be unimpeachable. They would be wrong. The greatest hurdle to any scheme by the directors to allot shares (old or new) to themselves is the imposition on them of the fiduciary duty to exercise any power of allotment *bona fide* for the benefit of the company and for a proper purpose. The obligation to act *bona fide* is subjective, so that, provided that the directors honestly believe that they are acting properly in allotting themselves shares, they are not in breach of this limb of their fiduciary duty. However, the directors must exercise their powers not only honestly, but also for a purpose consistent with that for which the powers were conferred on them, that is, for a 'proper purpose'.

A leading case is the Privy Council decision in *Howard Smith Ltd v Ampol Petroleum Ltd (1974)*. In *Ampol*, the directors of HS, a company in need of further finance, issued shares to members who held a minority interest in the company but offered none to the majority shareholder (A), who had made an unwanted takeover bid. This allotment of shares reduced A's shareholding to below 50% and was challenged as an improper use of the directorial power to issue shares. The Privy Council ruled that, when a use of power is challenged, the court should first consider the nature of the power (that is, why was this power conferred on the directors whose exercise thereof is in question?) and then examine the substantial purpose for which it was exercised. If the power was not exercised for the proper purpose, the exercise of the power was void. The court stated that the decision as to whether the power was properly exercised is determined objectively. In this case, the court ruled that the power to allot shares is given to directors to raise funds for the company, and that, while the directors intended this allotment to raise capital, the primary purpose of the issue was to defeat A's bid and not to raise money. Consequently, this allotment was void.

Other cases on this area have held that an improper use of directorial power can be ratified by ordinary resolution (*Bamford v Bamford (1970)*; *Hogg v Cramphorn (1967)*), but the directors of Bombay Ltd cannot guarantee that they will be able, without shareholder support, to pass such a resolution. Whether the directors can convince the court that a proposal to increase their own shareholding is a proper use of directorial power depends upon why they were given the power to allot shares. Perhaps if the directors proposed to allot shares to themselves in return for an agreement to work for the company, this could be seen as beneficial to the company (even though no cash was raised, which is what the cases seem to say is the only proper purpose underlying an allotment) and, hence, an allotment for a proper purpose. Note that the power to raise the proper purpose point is technically a matter for the company (that is, *Foss v Harbottle (1843)* applies), but the courts have been prepared to allow a minority shareholder to raise the issue (*Hogg v Cramphorn (1967)*) unless and until the impropriety is ratified by the company in general meeting.

Finally, the directors should consider how they are going to pay for any shares they decide to allot to themselves. They could pay in cash. There is no requirement that the shares be issued at a price in excess of their nominal value (*Hilder v Dexter (1902)*), but the price which the directors agree to pay cannot be less than the nominal value (s 100 CA 1985). If shares are allotted at a discount, the allotment is valid but the allottee (and, in some cases, any subsequent holder) is liable to pay the amount of the discount, with interest, to the company (ss 100 and 112 CA 1985). The directors might prefer to pay other than in cash and s 99 CA 1985 provides that shares can be paid for in money or money's worth. This may be an attractive proposition, in that the directors do not have to pay cash and it evades the pre-emption rule. Since Bombay Ltd is a private company, there is no requirement that the non-cash consideration be professionally valued, and it is common practice in private companies for directors to pay for shares by agreeing to work for the company. Provided that the non-cash consideration is not wholly illusory (for example, when the agreement to work is given by a director who is incapable of work) and the company (manifested by the directors) honestly regards the consideration as approximating in value to the nominal value of the shares allotted, the court will not examine too closely the valuation of non-cash consideration (*Re Wragg Ltd (1897)*).

Undoubtedly, the simplest means of acquiring control of the company is to purchase shares from the existing shareholder, but, if this is not possible, then the directors should enlist the support of sufficient shareholders to be able to pass an ordinary resolution, create more shares and allot them to themselves, and then ratify any breach of directors' duty.

Question 34

The elaborate provisions of company law, designed to ensure that a company does not issue shares at a discount and maintains its share capital thereafter, are aimed at protecting the creditors of the company. Creditors would be better protected by a requirement that a company must have a minimum share capital which has been fully paid up in cash.

Comment on this assertion.

Answer plan

The question suggests that the rules relating to capital maintenance are ineffective in achieving their designated aim—the protection of creditors. Thus, three issues arise. First, what are the rules? Second, are the rules designed to protect creditors? Finally, having analysed the rules relating to capital maintenance, consider the minimum share capital requirements and comment on whether amendment of these rules would better protect creditors. On this latter point, you could also bring in the suggestions of the Company Law Review Steering Group (2001) aimed at amending the capital maintenance rules, some of which are implemented in the Companies Act 2006.

Answer

Shares in companies are not government issued bonds and directors are not trustees. Consequently, Parliament and the courts have always acknowledged that investors in, and creditors of, companies face some degree of risk. The directors cannot be expected to try to maximise profits without taking risks and their attempts may be unsuccessful because of bad luck, or incompetence, or general trading conditions, or changes in government policy, or for any number of other reasons. Parliament has sought to strike a balance between regulation of companies in pursuance of some perceived benefit (for example, minimising risk to investors) and allowing business people to conduct their affairs as they see fit with a view to maximising profit. In addition, Parliament has tried to ensure that company insiders (directors and shareholders) do not protect their own position at the expense of the company's creditors. Consequently, the current system is designed to be a balance—risk is not eliminated but is subject to management, and creditors, who have no control over how the company is run, have some protection from insiders. The way that the rules on capital maintenance operate may incidentally benefit shareholders (who arguably need less protection than creditors, since they have more control over the company) but the rules on capital maintenance are traditionally acknowledged as designed to protect creditors. In *Flitcroft's Case (1882)*, Jessel MR characterised a company creditor as person who gives credit to the company on the basis of a representation that the company would maintain its share capital, not misuse it and not return it to shareholders, albeit that his (a creditor's) right is enforceable ultimately only by winding up. Nowadays, the share capital (plus undistributable reserves) is often called the 'creditors' buffer'. This gives the impression that the funds subscribed by investors remain in a locked account available to be distributed to creditors if the company does not pay its debts. This is not the case. As the House of Lords readily accepted in *Trevor v Whitworth (1887)*, the money subscribed for shares can be used in the course of the business. All a creditor is entitled to expect is that the money subscribed for shares has been used in the legitimate course of business. Thus, capital maintenance can be seen as a means of creditor protection. The efficacy of this protection will now be examined.

There are two aspects of capital maintenance: first, the company must raise share capital; second, the company must not return it to the shareholders prior to winding up, except when authorised so to do.

RAISING SHARE CAPITAL

A private company limited by shares has no minimum share capital set out in the Companies Act (CA) 1985. All that is required is one subscriber (there can be more) to the company's memorandum and that subscriber must take at least one share. Shares must have a nominal value of a fixed amount (s 2 CA 1985), hence a private company must have a share capital of at least 1 p (1 x 1 p shares). A private company need not issue a minimum number of shares; all that is required is one for the (or each) subscriber to the memorandum (s 1 CA 1985). A private company need not issue shares fully paid, that is, with the full nominal value paid (in cash or otherwise) on issue, although most shares are issued fully paid. Where shares are not issued fully paid up, the company can make calls (demands for all or some of the nominal value not yet paid by the current or a former shareholder) upon the current holders of the shares for further sums, up to the full amount of a share's nominal value (and any agreed premium). If the nominal value of issued shares (plus any premium) has not been paid at the time of winding up, the shortfall is recoverable from the holders of those shares—but only if the company is unable to meet its liabilities. In practice, the majority of private companies have a total share capital of £1,000 or less and individual shares have a nominal value of 10 p or £1. Since most companies formed in the UK are private companies, the share capital subscribed at the outset (or claimable on an insolvent winding up) is not likely to be a large sum, so that it offers no real protection to creditors even if it the cash obtained remains unspent rather than simply forming an entry in the books of the company.

A persistent criticism of UK company law is that it allows grossly under-capitalised companies to be formed. It is true that most companies formed in the UK survive for less than 10 years, but, since companies can use money subscribed for shares (so long as they are used legitimately), it is not the lack of share capital which leaves companies vulnerable to cash flow problems but a lack of *cash*. Public companies are subject to a marginally more rigorous regime. A public company must have a minimum share capital of £50,000 (s 118 CA 1985), of which at least one-quarter must have been subscribed in cash (s 101 CA 1985) plus the whole of any premium, before the company can commence trading. In practice, most public companies (certainly quoted companies) have a share capital way in excess of this sum.

The CA 1985 lays down elaborate rules to ensure that shares are not issued at a discount (s 100 CA 1985), that is, at a price below the nominal value of the share. Note, however, that the full nominal value need not be paid on issue provided that the contract of sale provides that the price which the company may at some point demand (now or in the future) exceeds the specified nominal value (plus any premium provided for in the contract of issue). If shares are issued at a discount, the allotment is still valid, although the original allottee is liable to make good the discount (plus interest) and subsequent holders of the shares may also incur liability for any shortfall (ss 100 and 112 CA 1985). Where the discount is not recovered from a shareholder, the directors are liable to make good the shortfall.

In *Ooregum Gold Mining Co of India v Roper (1892)*, the company's existing £1 shares were trading on the market for less than their nominal value. The company wished to sell more shares and allowed people to subscribe for £1 nominal value shares for 25 p, which was specified in the contract of sale as the only sum payable. The House of Lords ruled that shareholders who had purchased these shares were liable to pay a further 75 p on the winding up of the company, despite the shares being described by the company as 'issued partly paid', since to issue a share partly paid is to issue at a discount. However, there is a major loophole in the 'no discount' rule: a company can accept payment for shares (other than those taken by the subscribers to the memorandum: s 106 CA 1985) in money or *money's worth* (s 99 CA 1985). Thus, non-cash consideration is acceptable and the courts make little inquiry into the value of non-cash consideration unless it is illusory or manifestly inadequate (*Re Wragg Ltd (1897)*).

The ability to outflank the no-discount rule by allotting shares other than for cash has been restricted in respect of public companies. Section 99 CA 1985 provides that an undertaking to work for a public company (or another) is not good consideration and the holder must pay the nominal value of the shares (plus interest). Section 102 CA 1985 prohibits the allotment of shares by a public company in consideration of an undertaking which is to be, or may be, performed more than five years after the date of allotment—an undertaking to be performed so far in advance is akin to being illusory. Section 103 CA 1985 provides that a public company shall not allot shares in return for the acquisition of a non-cash asset unless the asset has been professionally valued (there are exceptions, for example when there is a takeover and payment is by a share swap). The CA 1985 elaborates the valuation procedure at length. Breach of these provisions renders the allottee liable to pay the nominal value of the shares (plus any premium and interest). Subsequent holders of the shares are jointly and severally liable (s 112 CA 1985) unless they are purchasers for value without actual notice (or acquired the shares from such a holder). The courts can relieve a holder from liability where it is just and equitable to do so (s 113 CA 1985). Consequently, in *Re Ossory Estates plc (1988)*, a shareholder, who had partly paid for shares by means of non-cash consideration (land) which had not been properly valued, and was thus liable to pay the full nominal value of the shares, was relieved from liability when it emerged that the company had sold part of the land for a price far exceeding the notional value of all the land transferred to it. Relief was appropriate since there was manifestly no issue at a discount. The rules on the issue of shares have been called 'a pretty large sledgehammer to crack a fairly small nut'. However, they are largely reproduced in the Companies Act 2006.

MAINTAINING SHARE CAPITAL

Having obtained its share capital, the company must maintain it. This sounds as though the company must squirrel the money away, or at least deposit it in some extraordinarily safe investment. This is not the case. A company can use the money it has garnered provided that it is used legitimately. In particular, a company should not return this share capital to the shareholders, for to do so would illegitimately exhaust the funds available for creditors. To ensure the proper maintenance of share capital, a company cannot:

- pay dividends to shareholders other than out of distributable profits (ss 263–81 CA 1985);
- buy its own shares (s 143 CA 1985—no new capital and old capital used up improperly);
- provide financial assistance to others to buy its shares (s 151 CA 1985—again, the company's money is simply recycled); and
- reduce share capital without court approval (s 135 CA 1985).

The rules on what constitutes distributable profits which are available for payment as dividends (a company need not declare a dividend even if it has such profits) are now determined by statute and are a clarified version of those developed by the judges over 100 years. The statutory rules aim to ensure that unrealised profits, for example when land is revalued, are not used to justify dividends, and that profits made in one year cannot be paid out as dividends when the company has made substantial losses in previous years. Consequently, there is little opportunity for a company to pay a dividend unless it has generated a profit. However, there is nothing to stop a company paying directors or director-shareholders large fees or salaries for acting as a director of the company, whether the company has made such profits or not. Obviously, where director-shareholders have paid themselves large sums, despite the lack of profits, and the company has gone into insolvent liquidation, the directors may incur liability for fraudulent or wrongful trading under the Insolvency Act (IA) 1986 and may be required to contribute to the assets of the company.

There has been considerable concern expressed about the level of directors' salaries/fees in some companies, particularly when the company has not generated any or many profits. Part of the Combined Code, which is appended to the Listing Rules for public companies, suggests that the company's annual report should contain a remuneration policy and that a special remuneration committee, comprising non-executive directors only, should fix the rate of remuneration of executive directors. But no appreciable difference in salaries was noted and, in response, the government issued a consultative document setting out its views as to what should be best practice in relation to remuneration of directors of listed companies (*Directors' Remuneration* (DTI, 1999)). In 2002, the Directors Remuneration Report Regulations were passed, increasing the reporting requirements of directors' remuneration for all companies, although the amount of detail required for annual accounts and reports depends on whether the company is a quoted or unquoted company and small companies are allowed several exemptions from the requirements for unquoted companies. On the issue of very large payments to directors in lieu of notice, including payments made in respect of poor performance, consultation by the DTI in 2003 suggested that this was a matter best served by codes of practice (see, for example, the Combined Code).

The rules which prohibit a company from buying its own shares or providing financial assistance to another to purchase shares in the company were, until 1980, subject to few exceptions. Since 1980, the number of exceptions has increased. Underpinning the new exceptions are certain general principles—adequate publicity, shareholder approval and, where the funds used by the company are not distributable profits (which could have been paid to the shareholders as dividends anyway) but payments out of capital (only open to private companies), protection of creditors. These exceptions were part of a package of measures introduced to help companies, particularly private companies, raise money. Consider the purchase by a company of its own shares. Prior to 1980, a private company wishing to raise outside investment faced two difficulties: issuing new shares diluted existing shareholdings, thus affecting the control of the company (unattractive to current shareholders, particularly in a family company), and new investors would obtain a minority shareholding, which would be effectively unmarketable. The provisions allowing a company to issue redeemable shares or to buy back its own shares were designed to provide sufficient flexibility to permit existing shareholders to retain control whilst increasing the marketability of shares and continuing to protect creditors. Creditors are protected by the requirement that directors issue a statutory declaration that the company can, in their opinion, pay its debts (and will be able to do so for the following 12 months) before a resolution to allow self-purchase out of capital or financial assistance can proceed. The auditors of the company must then comment on the directors' opinion in a report and must confirm that, having looked at the company's state of affairs, they are not aware of anything which would render the directors' opinion unreasonable (ss 156 and 173 CA 1985). Section 176 CA 1985 allows a creditor to object to a purchase of shares by the company funded out of capital (five week time limit from date of resolution) and s 177 CA 1985 sets out the court's powers when an objection has been lodged; the court can, among other things, affirm, reject or modify the proposal and can order the objectors to be paid off. Where a company goes into liquidation within 12 months of a statutory declaration, the directors may be liable to contribute to the assets of the company (s 76 IA 1986). Apart from the excessively complicated nature of the provisions, these rules seem to provide adequate protection for creditors.

Section 135 CA 1985 permits a company to reduce share capital provided that the articles of the company permit a reduction, a reduction has been authorised by special resolution and the court has approved the reduction. Section 135 CA 1985 does not limit the circumstances in which a company may seek to reduce capital, but it does specify three possible grounds for doing so. Where one of these three grounds is the basis of an application, a court is likely to approve the reduction, provided that the position of the company's creditors is secured (ss 136 and 137 CA 1985 provide rules for dealing with creditors who are unhappy with the reduction). The Companies Act 2006 provides for an alternative method of reducing share capital in addition to the one outlined here.

CONCLUSION

Creditors, particularly unsecured creditors, are adversely affected when a company goes into insolvent liquidation—the current rules do not prevent such losses. However, it is by no means clear that requiring companies to have a larger share capital would prove an acceptable solution. Are the rules on non-cash consideration to be changed? Is there to be a minimum subscription for private companies? Would such changes stifle new businesses? Surely, an effective balance between encouraging business initiative and protecting creditors is to encourage efficient directors rather than further complicating the rules on capital maintenance. Interestingly, the difficulties faced by businesses in respect of such transactions was recognised by the DTI, as part of its wide ranging review of key aspects of company law. It suggested that the rules on financial assistance for the purchase of shares are causing unnecessary, substantial professional fees to be incurred by companies in their attempts to ensure that innocent and worthwhile transactions do not breach the rules (*Modern Company Law for a Competitive Economy* (DTI, 1998)). In a later consultation paper, the Company Law Review Steering Group proposed that the best way forward in dealing with this problem is for the financial assistance rule to be abolished completely in relation to private companies (see *Modern Company Law for a Competitive Economy: Developing the Framework* (DTI, 2000)), and this proposal is now contained in the Companies Act 2006 (although, to date, not in force).

NOTE

Further examples of the inadequacies of the current system and proposals for reform could be included.

Question 35

You have recently become company secretary of Glitz Ltd, a moderately successful company owned and run by various members of the Sparkle family. The board has decided to undertake a major acquisition of new machinery, which cannot be financed from the company's reserves. The machinery is likely to enhance production efficiency and capacity for a number of years. The directors do not wish to dilute their voting strength within the company and are uncertain whether the shareholders will support this major purchase. The board is keen to ensure that whatever means of financing is adopted will attract the necessary funds.

Outline the possible sources of finance and the extent to which these methods meet the requirements of the board.

Answer plan

First, analyse the requirements of the board, then consider possible sources of finance—particularly loans and shares (ordinary and preference)—in light of them. Draw a conclusion on suitability.

Answer

The board wishes to raise finance for a long term project designed to increase the profitability of the company. It wishes to ensure that the money is raised, so the proposed source of funding must be sufficiently attractive to potential investors. However, the directors do not wish their voting strength to be diluted and, given the possible disquiet among existing shareholders, the board will need to ensure that its shareholdings and benefits are not diminished. Possible sources of finance will be examined bearing in mind these constraints. It may be noted in passing that the unease of the shareholders does not preclude this project from proceeding. By virtue of Art 70 of Table A, the directors run the company (subject to the giving of directions by special resolution) and need not bow to the wishes of the shareholders, although the risk of being dismissed if too many shareholders are upset cannot be ignored (s 303 of the Companies Act (CA) 1985, ordinary resolution required).

Possibly, the unease of the shareholders could be quietened by the circulation of some explanation for the new scheme, pointing to the possibility of enhanced profits, even if there is a temporary reduction in distributable profits.

What are the relative merits of shares and loans in this context?

(a) Shares and loans

The issue of further shares may be attractive to a company from a financial point of view, in that dividends must be paid only if the company has made a distributable profit and the directors have declared a dividend (s 263 CA 1985; Art 102 of Table A). Thus, shares provide a means of raising capital without any continuing payment obligation on the part of the company. Nor is a company required to repay the capital acquired by means of an allotment of shares (unless they are redeemable shares), so the funds raised for the machinery need not be repaid by the company. Consequently, to an investor, the purchase of shares can be seen as a risky investment. There is no guarantee of income and the capital invested is, at best, recoverable on winding up. Indeed, on winding up, a shareholder has claims on the assets of the company only when the creditors have been paid in full. While the company is a going concern, and particularly if the machinery is as useful as suggested, there is the possibility of capital growth within the shares, but in a private company this growth is hard to realise, the shares are not freely marketable and the attitude of the Sparkle family to new shareholders may not be accommodating if the allottee wishes to sell out subsequently. Hence, seeking new shareholders (even if the practical problems of issue can be overcome—see below) from outside the company may not be successful. Of course, the board can always offer shares to existing shareholders to raise further funds. Indeed, a further issue of shares to outside investors may be unattractive to existing shareholders who see the pool of money available for the payment of dividends being available to a greater number of participants than previously. Further, extra shareholders would diminish the proportion of shares held by existing shareholders, including the directors, which the board wishes to avoid if this dilutes its voting strength. Of course the pre-emption rules, if applicable, could prevent dilution of the voting strength of a shareholder or group of shareholders.

Loans, on the other hand, do not dilute existing shareholdings but do carry a continuing financial commitment. The interest payable on the loan must be paid even if the company has not made any profits, although interest payments can be deducted from income to determine the company's net profits. In addition, the loan will have to be repaid in accordance with the loan particulars and failure to meet repayments could lead to the lender initiating action against the company. A loan may be secured or unsecured. The latter will carry a higher rate of interest, and for a potential investor the secured loan is more attractive. A lender may have power to intervene in the affairs of the company if the loan contract so authorises, but a secured lender has statutory and common law powers to seize the charged asset or appoint a receiver to act on his behalf if his security is at risk. The obvious lenders whom the company should consider approaching if this is the preferred route are the existing shareholders, especially in a family owned company, and the company's bankers.

One way of reconciling some of the advantages of shares and those of loans could be to attract investment into a new class of shares which do not have voting rights and, thus, do not affect the current voting position within the company. However, non-voting ordinary shares would not be very appealing to an investor and it might be necessary to consider the creation and allotment of preference shares.

(b) Preference shares and loans

Preference shares (voting or non-voting) have the attraction from the company's point of view that the financial commitment to pay the preference dividend is, like interest on a loan, a predetermined sum—assuming that the company has profits to sustain any dividend. As with ordinary shares, there is no obligation to repay capital while the company is a going concern, although many preference shares are created as redeemable shares and the company will have to redeem them at some future date. Unlike loans, preference shares cannot be issued at a discount (s 100 CA 1985) so that the contracted purchase price cannot be below the nominal value of the shares; thus, there can be no question of investors buying preference shares of £100 nominal value for £70 and obtaining £100 on redemption. However, Glitz Ltd could sell loan notes with a face value of £100 for £70 with the contract providing that, when the loan is discharged, the loan notes would be redeemed in full so that the holder would receive back £100. Glitz Ltd should be told that it is possible to redeem shares at a premium if the articles so permit and a person buying a share from an existing shareholder may be able to pay a price below the nominal value of the shares, although this is hardly a hopeful sign.

Preference shares might be unattractive to Glitz Ltd for several reasons. First, the shares may be issued at a time of high interest rates, thus requiring the company to issue them with a relatively high fixed dividend which remains a continuing commitment even when interest rates fall; this problem is obviated by the use of redeemable shares. Second, a preference shareholder is a member of the company and has, unless the articles provide otherwise, the right to vote and otherwise participate in the running of the company; this is easily overcome by issuing the shares without any or with limited voting rights, but, unless this is done, the directors may find their voting strength diminished. Third, extra classes of shares complicate the share structure of the company and can give rise to problems if the company wishes to vary class rights. Again, in common with ordinary shares, preference dividends are paid out of taxable profit and cannot be set against profits. While a lender is not a member of the company and has no direct influence over its affairs, which might be attractive to the company, Glitz Ltd might still feel the necessity to listen to a major creditor and the documents creating the loan might confer rights on a lender, for example to appoint a director. A lender who seeks to influence the company from outside runs the risk of being classified as a 'shadow director' with consequent directors' duties, but the same could apply to an influential shareholder. However, the courts have been very cautious about treating shareholders as shadow directors, and even more cautious about non-shareholders (see, for example, *Secretary of State for Trade and Industry v Laing (1996)*).

(c) Practical issues

The board might be able to retain voting control, even if further shares are issued, without using non-voting shares. For example, it is possible to alter voting rights of existing shares by the insertion into the articles of a weighted voting clause. Unfortunately for the directors, alteration of the articles requires a special resolution (s 9 CA 1985) and obtaining a majority of three-quarters of those present and voting, given the likely opposition of existing shareholders, seems doubtful. Alternatively, the directors could seek to subdivide their shares into two or more shares, each of which carries a vote. Section 121 CA 1985 permits a company, whose articles so authorise (Art 32 of Table A provides authority), to subdivide shares into shares of smaller nominal value than that fixed in the memorandum. The decision to subdivide must be made by the company in general meeting; that is, an ordinary resolution is required. If the directors decide to raise the necessary capital by allotting shares, they can allot any existing unissued shares, but, if there are no such shares, they would have to create a new class and then allot them. Creation of further shares is authorised (for companies whose articles so permit, and Art 32 of Table A does so permit) by s 121 CA 1985, provided that the increase in share capital is approved by ordinary resolution. The directors may need support from other members of the Sparkle family to achieve a majority.

If the directors propose to allot any existing unissued shares and/or any new shares, they face a number of legal difficulties. The power to allot relevant securities (defined in s 94 CA 1985 and including ordinary but not preference shares) is vested in the general meeting even when, as is usual, the power to run the company is vested in the board (s 80 CA 1985). However, s 80 CA 1985 provides that the shareholders can give the power to allot shares to the board either in the articles or by ordinary resolution. Originally, the shareholders had to vote to give the power to allot shares to the directors at least every five years, but s 80A CA 1985 allows a private company (by elective resolution in accordance with s 379A CA 1985) to give the authority for an indefinite period. As company secretary, you should be able to discover whether such a resolution has been passed. The authority to allot may be general or limited (for example, only applying to some classes of share, or to a maximum number of shares at any one time). The directors can be advised that, if they breach s 80 and allot shares without authority, they are liable to a fine but the allotment is valid.

Assuming that the directors are authorised to allot shares (or are willing to contravene s 80 CA 1985), they must still be wary of s 89 CA 1985, which provides a right of pre-emption for existing shareholders. Section 89 CA 1985 states that, where a company is proposing to allot equity securities (defined in s 94 CA 1985 and including ordinary but not preference shares) wholly for cash, the shares must first be offered to existing shareholders in proportion to their existing shareholding. Thus, s 89 would require the directors to offer any new issue of shares to members of the Sparkle family before seeking outside investment, but the section also provides that breach of it does not invalidate the allotment. Breach does, however, expose the directors to liability. The power to organise loans falls within the remit of the board and there is no need to involve the shareholders in any way, so there are practical advantages for a board with sceptical shareholders using loans to raise funds for expansion. Further, the allotment of shares, but probably not the raising of loans, is subject to the fiduciary duty to exercise any power of allotment *bona fide* for the benefit of the company and for a proper purpose. The obligation to act *bona fide* (and for the benefit of the company— probably) is subjective, so, provided that the directors honestly believe that they are acting properly in allotting shares to raise funds for the machinery, they are not in breach of this limb of their fiduciary duty.

CONCLUSION

You might inform the board that, from the potential investor's viewpoint, both preference shares and loans offer a fixed rate of return, but, while loan interest must be paid, a dividend is not always covered or declared; so, if the company wishes to be sure of success a loan looks more promising. Also, the degree of security that a loan can offer may attract investors. The right to influence the company by attending general meetings and voting is open only to shareholders and not (directly) to creditors, but preference shareholders often find their rights curtailed by the articles, so an outside investor might not be influenced by this factor, even if the board is. To an investor, the benefits of loans appear to outweigh those of shares and the same is probably true for Glitz Ltd.

Question 36

Krisp Ltd was incorporated in 1997. Its share capital is divided into 5,000 £1 shares—2,000 6% preference shares and 3,000 ordinary shares. The articles provide that the preference shares confer on the holders thereof:

(a) the right to a dividend of 6% on the paid up value of the shares held; and

(b) the right on winding up to secure the paid up value of the shares in priority to any payment to the ordinary shareholders.

On incorporation, Crunch became the sole director of the company, the shares of which were all allotted, fully paid, as follows:

- 2,999 ordinary shares to Crunch in consideration of his transferring to the company his existing business;
- one ordinary share to Mrs Crunch for cash; and
- the preference shares to Mrs Crunch's elderly mother, Mrs Brittle, for cash.

Crunch is paid a generous salary by the company and Mrs Crunch is also paid handsomely for acting as company secretary. The company has made modest profits every year since it commenced trading but has never declared a dividend on either the ordinary or preference shares. Mr and Mrs Crunch have recently separated and there are rumours that Mr Crunch will appoint as company secretary Ms Toffee, his new partner. Mrs Crunch would like to bring an action in Krisp Ltd's name to restrain alleged transfers of assets from Krisp Ltd to a new company founded by Mr Crunch and Ms Toffee.

Advise Mrs Crunch and Mrs Brittle as to their entitlements as shareholders while the company is a going concern and on winding up, and the likelihood of being able to bring an action on behalf of Krisp Ltd against Mr Crunch.

Answer plan

You are asked to deal with two main issues. First, the entitlements of ordinary and preference shareholders while the company is a going concern and the rights of these shareholders if the company is wound up. Second, whether Mr Crunch could incur liability to the company for his actions and, if this is the case, who could bring such an action.

Answer

Before considering the position of the shareholders (other than Crunch), it may be noted that the allotment of shares to Crunch in return for the transfer of his existing business to the company is valid. Section 99 of the Companies Act (CA) 1985 permits shares to be paid for in money or money's worth and there is no requirement that the non-cash consideration be professionally valued (as would be the case if Krisp Ltd was a public company). A court has the power to treat shares issued for non-cash consideration as shares issued at a discount (allotment still valid but shares must be paid for), but it is exercised very rarely and only when the alleged consideration is manifestly illusory—that is not the case here. Even if the shares had been issued at a discount, the allotment would be valid and Crunch would be liable to make good the shortfall. Thus, there is no doubt that Crunch is the majority shareholder in the company. The extent of his majority depends upon whether the preference shares carry the right to vote at general meetings of the company. Let us consider the position of the minority shareholders.

SHAREHOLDER RIGHTS

(a) Mrs Crunch

While the company is a going concern, Mrs Crunch has the usual rights of a member, for example, in relation to Table A, she can attend meetings (Art 38) and vote (Art 54) and she is entitled to a dividend, if one is declared (Arts 102–08). As a minority shareholder with only one share, she has no influence within the company, although she would be entitled (subject to the discretion of the court) to bring a derivative action on behalf of the company if Crunch was in breach of directors' duty and his actions were a fraud on the minority (on which see below). However, even with one share, she could petition under s 459 CA 1985 if the affairs of the company were being conducted in a way that was unfairly prejudicial to her interests as a member. Unfortunately, even if that is the case, the remedy most likely to be awarded is that the company should buy her share at a fair price, which is unlikely to yield a large return. Has she a s 459 claim? While Mrs Crunch might object to the absence of dividends, she has been paid 'handsomely' for acting as company secretary. Exclusion from the post of company secretary (should it arise) would not by itself be unfairly prejudicial, but, if she had a legitimate expectation based upon a legal agreement or equitable considerations that she would participate in some way in the corporate governance of the enterprise, albeit not as a director, she might have a remedy, but this seems improbable. Further, if the allegations about the asset-stripping are proved, this breach of duty by Crunch would be grounds in itself for a s 459 action. In addition, she could seek just and equitable winding up (s 122(1)(g) of the Insolvency Act (IA) 1986) but she would have to establish some basis for the winding up, which seems unlikely on the facts given. Even if just and equitable winding up was a possibility, the court could deny her this remedy if she had an alternative remedy (s 459 CA 1985 is the obvious one) which it is unreasonable to refuse. Arguably, to destroy a viable company when her likely entitlement on winding up is small (£1, being the nominal value of her share plus a percentage of any surplus assets after the claims of the company creditors and her mother have been satisfied) if she can be adequately compensated for any wrongs in some other way is unreasonable and is unlikely to be awarded by a court.

Crunch may be equally keen to disengage himself from any business connection with his estranged wife. He could achieve this by offering to buy her out, which preserves the company as a going concern, or he could choose to initiate a voluntary winding up of the company. A voluntary winding up requires the passing of a special resolution s 84 IA 1986 and his ability to achieve such a resolution depends upon whether Mrs Brittle can vote.

(b) Mrs Brittle

Mrs Brittle's position is very different. In determining her rights, the courts have regard to two canons of construction (presumptions drawn in the absence of evidence to the contrary). First, the House of Lords in *Birch v Cropper (1889)*, in which the issue was whether the ordinary and preference shareholders had equal rights to the surplus assets of a company on winding up, ruled that all shares of whatever class are presumed to carry equal rights unless this presumption is rebutted by words indicating an inequality. Thus, where the articles are silent, all shareholders have the right to attend all company meetings and vote on all resolutions. The courts have tended to find words sufficient to rebut the presumption of equality with relative ease. However, on the facts of this case, there seems no reason why Mrs Brittle should not be entitled to vote; she (with Mrs Crunch) controls two-fifths of the votes at a general meeting and has the power to block a special resolution, but not an ordinary resolution. The second presumption applied by the courts is that, where the articles (or other relevant documents) specify that preference shares carry particular rights, that is, a statement of maximum entitlement, this presumption is extremely difficult to rebut. Consequently, where, as here, the articles of the company provide that the preference shares carry a right to a preferential dividend (6% in this case), the preference shareholder must be paid her dividend (if the company has made profits and declares a dividend) in full before the ordinary shareholders are entitled to a penny. However, having received her 6% (£120 per annum), that exhausts her right to dividend and she has no further entitlement to dividend on those shares.

Does this mean that where, as in this case, a company has declared no dividends for some years, the company continues to roll up profits and at some point in the future decides to pay a dividend of 6% to Mrs Brittle for that year and then distribute the balance to the ordinary shareholders (this sounds very tax inefficient)? In other words, is a preference dividend, once missed, lost for ever, or does the unpaid dividend roll up year on year so that the accumulated sum must be paid before the ordinary shareholders can receive anything? In *Webb v Earle (1875)*, the court held that preference dividend is presumed to be cumulative (that is, unpaid dividend rolls up) unless there is evidence to rebut the presumption—the articles of Krisp Ltd do not appear to render preference shares non-cumulative (but note the position if the company is wound up—see below). Non-payment of dividend, particularly if Crunch could be said to be using the company's profits unfairly to enhance his own position (generous salary), might justify a finding of unfair prejudice (s 459 CA 1985, *Re Sam Weller Ltd (1989)*), which would allow the court, if it wished, to order that the dividend be paid or to amend the articles to strengthen Mrs Brittle's rights (s 461 CA 1985).

Mrs Brittle appears to have the power to block a voluntary winding up of the company (Crunch cannot pass a special resolution if she votes against it), but she could not prevent an unpaid creditor petitioning. It might be argued that Mrs Brittle should seek a just and equitable winding up of the company (s 122(1)(g) IA 1986) on the ground that this company was a family company, that she invested in the company to support her son-in-law and that, if the Crunches divorce, the relationship of the members is such that, had they been partners, a dissolution of the partnership would have been ordered (*Ebrahimi v Westbourne Galleries Ltd (1973)*).

If there is a voluntary winding up (on whatever basis) and, after payment of the liquidator and the creditors, there are surplus assets, what are Mrs Brittle's rights? The articles plainly displace the presumption of equality—she is entitled to £1 per share (£2,000) if the assets are sufficient, but to no more (*Scottish Insurance Corp v Wilson & Clyde Coal Co Ltd (1949)*), whatever the size of the surplus. Thus, if Krisp Ltd has surplus assets of £2,000, it all goes to Mrs Brittle; if £5,000, then each shareholder receives £1 per share; but if £11,000 then Mrs Brittle gets £2,000 and the ordinary shareholders share the remainder (£3 per share). One further point—suppose that, at the date of any winding up, Mrs Brittle is owed arrears of preference dividend, are these arrears a debt which must be paid off before the shareholders receive anything, or are arrears not paid off prior to winding up lost? It appears that, unless the presumption can be rebutted, arrears of preference dividend are lost once winding up commences. This would allow an unscrupulous board to miss dividends for many years, build up surplus funds from profits which could have been paid as dividends, put the company into liquidation and pay the accumulated surplus (less any prior claim to return of capital vested in the preference shareholders) to the ordinary shareholders alone. Not surprisingly, the courts have tended to find words to rebut the presumption that the unpaid dividend is lost on winding up if at all possible (*Re Wharfedale Brewery Co Ltd (1952)*). In this case, the wording of the articles might, surprisingly, suffice— 'in priority to any payment to the ordinary shareholders' could be the straw to which a court would cling to avoid the unfairness of denying arrears to Mrs Brittle.

Mrs Crunch and Mrs Brittle would be well advised to pursue the statutory remedies (ss 459 CA 1985 and 122(1)(g) of the IA 1986) open to them as members, rather than rely on their contractual rights as shareholders. Alternatively, they might seek to sell their shares to Crunch, but cannot force him to buy them. It is too late to do anything in this case but, should Mrs Crunch remarry and Mrs Brittle wish to invest in her new son-in-law's business, they should avoid irredeemable preference shares. Indeed, one could argue that all private investors should avoid all types of preference share!

ACTION AGAINST CRUNCH

As the director of the company, Crunch owes a fiduciary duty to the company (not to the shareholders, *Percival v Wright (1902)*; *Peskin v Anderson (2001)*) and his obligations include a duty not to allow his personal interests and his duty to conflict. Simply receiving a large salary is not breach of fiduciary duty, although there are certain requirements which must be complied with if a director is to contract with his company (essentially duties of disclosure). Failure to meet these requirements may make certain contracts voidable at the company's option but do not confer any right to sue on Mrs Crunch or Mrs Brittle in their own right or on behalf of the company. However, if Crunch is stripping assets from Krisp Ltd and transferring them to a new company, he may be also be in breach of the duty cast on all directors not to misuse corporate assets. If he is so engaged, he is unlikely to wish to initiate litigation against himself on behalf of Krisp Ltd, Krisp Ltd being the proper claimant in an action since it is the company's assets which are being removed (*Foss v Harbottle (1843)*). However, while shareholders are not normally permitted to act on behalf of the company in respect of wrongs done to the company, an action is permitted where the wrongdoers control the company. Crunch controls Krisp Ltd and he, allegedly, is a wrongdoer, and it would seem that Mrs Crunch or Mrs Brittle could sue on behalf of the company. However, the right of a shareholder to act for the company is limited by the courts to those cases where the shareholder is acting for the company (and not in pursuance of some private agenda) and the action is likely to benefit the company.

An illustration of the operation of these principles is contained in *Barrett v Duckett (1995)*. In that case, a shareholder, B, owned 50% of the shares of T Ltd and was the mother-in-law of the other shareholder, D, who was the director of the company. D and B's daughter had divorced. The Court of Appeal ruled that a shareholder who sought to sue on behalf of a company must establish 'to the satisfaction of the court' that he should be allowed to sue on behalf of the company and that 'the shareholder will be allowed to sue on behalf of the company if he is bringing the action *bona fide* for the benefit of the company for wrongs to the company for which no other remedy is available. Conversely, if the action is brought for an ulterior purpose or if another adequate remedy is available, the court will not allow the derivative action to proceed.' In this case, as in *Barrett*, there may well be an ulterior motive in seeking to bring an action on behalf of Krisp Ltd. There is probably an alternative action (liquidation or s 459 CA 1985) open to the minority shareholders. Liquidation would certainly deprive the alleged wrongdoer of his control of the company and allow an independent liquidator to pursue such remedies against him as he thought appropriate. A s 459 action would also involve exposing Crunch's dealings to the courts and, if he has been asset-stripping, the court could order him to reimburse the company, be bought out by another shareholder or compensate the minority shareholders for any losses attributable to his misdealing (s 461 CA 1985).

Question 37

Surplus plc was once a large trading concern and has substantial cash assets. Over recent years it has hived off the majority of its activities into new companies, over which it retains control, leaving itself with little in the way of direct trading operations, but it continues to generate substantial profits.

The articles of the company provide that rights attaching to any class of shares can be varied, provided that holders of three-quarters of the nominal value of the issued shares of that class approve, in writing or at a meeting, the proposed variation. The preference shareholders have no right to vote at general meetings of the company.

The company proposes the following:

(a) To reduce share capital by paying off at par the 'A' preference shares which carry a right to a 10% preference dividend, are preferential as to return of capital and have a right further to participate on winding up to a maximum of £1 per share.

(b) To redeem immediately at £2 over par the 'B' preference shares which carry a right to a 15% dividend and which are redeemable at par next year.

(c) To reduce the preference dividend payable on the 'C' preference shares (which carry rights of equal participation on winding up) from 12% to 10%.

(d) To issue bonus shares to the ordinary shareholders on a one-for-one basis.

Amy, who owns 'A', 'B' and 'C' preference shares, objects to these proposals. She believes that the majority of the A and B preference shareholders would accept the proposals. Advise her on the legitimacy of these proposals.

Answer plan

The first two proposals involve a reduction of share capital, and Amy may also allege that they are a variation of her class rights. The third proposal is not a reduction but may be a variation. The final proposal is not a reduction but indirectly affects the preference shareholders. Finally, s 459 of the Companies Act (CA) 1985 may be relevant.

Answer

Amy is faced with proposals for massive restructuring of the share capital of the company. She is unhappy with the scheme put forward by the management, but believes that she will be in a minority in objecting to it. Two or more classes of shareholder may be unpopular with the management of the company, who may prefer a simpler share structure, and multiple classes can lead to disputes between classes of shareholder over the rights which each class possesses. The Companies Act (CA) 1985 allows a company to alter its share capital by ordinary resolution (s 121 CA 1985) but provides special rules for the reduction of capital and the variation of rights attaching to any class of shares. Can Amy avail herself of any of these provisions? At present, a reduction of capital requires the consent of the court. However, there are recommendations by the Company Law Review Steering Group that court permission should no longer be a requirement for a reduction of capital. It is suggested, instead, that the directors of a company proposing a reduction of capital should be required to make a declaration of insolvency and that this should be accompanied, if appropriate, by an auditor's report. For the protection of the interests of creditors of public companies, it is further suggested that, in order to comply with the EC Second Directive, such creditors should be given the right to ask the court for an order granting adequate security for their debts, or for some other appropriate relief to be granted (*Modern Company Law for a Competitive Economy: Company Formation and Capital Maintenance* (DTI, 1999)). Some of these proposals are implemented in the Companies Act 2006, but, to date, are not in force.

REDUCTION OF CAPITAL

The proposals concerning the A and B preference shares both involve a reduction of share capital. Reduction of share capital has an adverse effect on the creditors' buffer and may also, as here, be opposed by shareholders whose shares will be abolished. Reduction is possible if it is done in compliance with the CA 1985. Section 135 CA 1985 states that a company can reduce share capital provided that:

- it has the power to do so in its articles (Art 34 of Table A gives such a power);
- it passes a special resolution to do so; and
- the court confirms the reduction.

The creditors of Surplus plc are given *locus* to object to any reduction, but it seems that none is doing so. It is assumed that the proposed reduction will not reduce the share capital of the company below the minimum specified in the Act (s 117 CA 1985). There are no specific provisions in the CA 1985 dealing with the rights of shareholders when a reduction is proposed, but the House of Lords determined in the nineteenth century that the courts have a discretion to confirm or reject a proposed reduction of capital. The definitive view of when the discretion should be exercised was given in *Scottish Insurance Corp Ltd v Wilsons & Clyde Coal Co (1949)*, in which the House of Lords held that the jurisdiction of the courts was not limited to ensuring the technical accuracy of a petition to reduce but was extended to ensuring that the reduction was fair and reasonable. However, despite the existence of a broad jurisdiction to reject an application to reduce, the courts have exercised that power very infrequently. In *Re Ratners Group plc (1988)*, Harman J ruled that, assuming that the reduction was not a 'hollow and pointless act', the court would confirm a reduction where three principles had been satisfied. First, all shareholders should be treated equitably (which generally, but not necessarily, means equally, unless some shareholders have agreed to being treated differently). Second, the proposals should have been properly explained to the shareholders so that they could exercise an informed judgment on them. Third, creditors must be adequately protected. As a gloss on Harman's view, it must be added that, where a scheme is supported by the company, creditors and the majority of shareholders, it is unlikely to be rejected by the court. Consequently, Amy should be advised that the procedures for reduction of capital may be satisfied. What may cause a court to pause before confirming the proposals for the A and B shares is the fact that the preference and ordinary shareholders are being treated differently *and* there is perhaps a variation of class rights.

REDUCTION AND VARIATION OF CLASS RIGHTS

In determining whether to confirm the reduction of share capital, the courts will decide whether the proposal treats the preference shareholders equitably. Where the reduction involves a variation of the class rights of the relevant shareholders, the court will not treat the proposal as fair and equitable unless the relevant class have consented to the proposal. The court will ascertain whether there is a variation of class rights by comparing the rights of the preference shareholders on winding up (or redemption in the case of the redeemable shares) with their rights under the proposed reduction. This literal approach has been much criticised but remains the norm for variation of class rights cases. An extreme example of the literal approach is *Re Mackenzie (1916)*, discussed below.

In this case, Surplus plc is seeking to repay the preference shareholders the par value of their shares with, in the case of the B shares, a £2 bonus. The B shareholders are being deprived of their income (the dividend) but are receiving that which they would get on redemption plus a bonus. The A shareholders are obtaining a preferential right to return of capital but are losing their right to dividend and the right to participate on winding up to the extent of a further £1 per share. What will the courts do in such cases? Amy should be advised that the courts have generally been reluctant to treat the abolition of preference shareholders (with consequent loss of an assured income) as a variation of class rights. In *Re Saltdean Estate Co Ltd (1968)*, Buckley J said that, where a company wished to pay off capital as surplus to its requirements, *prima facie*, it should repay first those shareholders who would be repaid first on winding up. The A and B shareholders would appear to have rights which would require them to be repaid before the ordinary shareholders, and thus to pay them off would not be regarded as unfair. In the same case, Buckley J said that no doubt the preference shareholders hope to retain their interest in the company, but this expectation is always vulnerable to a future winding up or reduction of capital: '...this vulnerability has always been a characteristic of the preferred shares. Now that the event has occurred [reduction], none of the preferred shareholders can assert that the resulting state of affairs is unfair to him.' The decision in *Saltdean* was approved by the House of Lords in *House of Fraser v ACGE Investments Ltd (1987)*, but these cases left open the problem of the preference shareholder whose rights on winding up extended beyond a preferential right to return of capital.

The A shares have a limited participatory right on winding up (£1 per share over par—assuming sufficient surplus assets), which abolition will destroy. In *Re William Jones & Sons Ltd (1969)*, the court confirmed a reduction by which the preference shareholders with such a participatory right were abolished. However, the preference shareholders made no objection to the scheme, which involved them being paid off at par when the market value of the shares was below par. The judge, Buckley J again, treated the right of participation as ephemeral given that there was no prospect of the company being wound up. Whether the lack of an immediate prospect of winding up justifies the refusal to treat the abolition of the preference shareholders' rights as unfair seems doubtful. Clearly, when winding up is imminent, an attempt to implement a reduction of capital which abolishes preference shareholders with participatory rights is a variation which could lead to a rejection of a capital reduction proposal (*Re Old Silkstone Collieries Ltd (1954)*).

It seems probable that these proposals will be confirmed by the court. However, if the reduction of the A shares is a variation of class rights, it is likely that the company would be required to comply with its own variation clause in order to obtain confirmation of the reduction. It is possible that the articles of the company provide that *any* reduction of share capital is a variation of the rights of a class of shares which is subject to the reduction. If this is so, then the usual rules for variation apply (see *Re Northern Engineering Industries plc (1994)*, where the articles were so construed). Where the company has to consult its shareholders about a proposal because it is a variation, s 127 CA 1985 provides an unhappy shareholder with a further line of attack.

VARIATION WITHOUT REDUCTION

Is the proposal to reduce the C preference dividend a variation of the class rights of holders of those shares? The courts adopt a narrow view of variation, in that a comparison is drawn between the right which would attach to a share before and after the proposed amendment of the class right and the right which would arise—if the right is literally the same, there is no variation. Hence, in *Re Mackenzie & Co Ltd (1916)*, the company had 4% preference shares with a nominal value of £20, thus paying a dividend of 80 p per share. The company amended its articles to reduce the nominal value of the preference shares to £12, thus reducing the preference dividend to 48 p per share. The court held that, since the preference shareholders had the same right both before and after the amendment (4% dividend), their class rights had not been varied. However, in this case, the proposed amendment is a variation (reduction of dividend from 12% to 10%). That being the case, the company must comply with the appropriate procedures for the variation of class rights.

It is not clear whether Amy's class rights are conferred by the memorandum or the articles—the latter is more usual. Class rights contained in the articles can be varied if the company has a class rights variation clause (whenever included in the articles) and complies with it. There is no such clause in Table A but Surplus plc has a clause. Consequently, the C shareholders should be consulted to see if they support the proposal and, if they do not approve by the necessary majority (consent seems improbable), the variation cannot take effect. Even if the relevant shareholders do approve the variation, s 127 CA 1985 allows a dissentient shareholder(s) who holds 15% of the relevant class of shares and who did not vote for the variation to apply to the court to have the variation set aside. The application must be within 21 days of the vote unless and until the court confirms that the variation has no effect. The court can refuse to confirm a variation if it would unfairly prejudice the shareholders of the class represented by the applicant. There are very few cases on this provision, so it is difficult to advise Amy as to what might constitute unfair prejudice. If the class rights are contained in the memorandum, s 125(3) CA 1985 provides that they can be varied if the company has a class rights variation clause in the articles *which was included in the articles at the time of incorporation* and the company complies with its own rules. Hence, Surplus plc could seek to amend the dividend rights, but the proposal is subject to approval by the C shareholders. If the C shareholders agree, Amy, provided that she has the requisite number of shares, can apply under s 127 CA 1985. If the variation clause did not form part of the original articles, then s 125(5) CA 1985 applies. Section 125(5) CA 1985 provides that, in such a case, class rights can be varied only if all shareholders in the company (not just of the relevant class) agree to it. Where the company proposes to hold a class meeting to vote on the variation, the CA 1985 lays down rules for the amount of notice, etc, required.

The proposed allotment of bonus shares to the ordinary shareholders will not, it seems, be treated as a variation of the rights of the preference shareholders, even if, as here, the preference shareholders (at least the A shares until abolished and the C shares) have a right to participate in the assets of the company. Thus, any increase in the number of shares potentially reduces the amount of surplus assets payable in respect of each share (*Dimbula Valley (Ceylon) Tea Co v Laurie (1961)*).

Given that Amy believes that the majority of preference shareholders will support these proposals, she is unlikely to be successful in her applications to court, even where she has *locus*. Perhaps she is best advised to bring an action under s 459 CA 1985 alleging unfair prejudice—however, the likely remedy would be to be bought out at a fair price, that is, she would not be able to retain her stake in the company. It might be argued that since many public companies provide that, on a reduction of capital in circumstances such as these, the company will pay the former shareholders the market value of their shares, for Surplus plc to seek to do otherwise is inherently prejudicial. If the reduction in dividend was seen as unfairly prejudicial, the court could order the dividend to be restored (s 461 CA 1985) or grant such other remedy as it saw fit. The issue of bonus shares is unlikely to be unfairly prejudicial without some other element of impropriety.

Question 38

Teddy has recently taken over as company secretary of Bear plc, an unlisted public company, and has been investigating the administration of the company. He has discovered the following and seeks your advice:

(a) Six months ago, Rupert purchased shares in the company and applied to be registered as a shareholder. The directors have just decided to refuse to register Rupert but have given no reasons. The articles of the company provide that 'The directors may choose to refuse to register as a member any person to whom shares have been transferred.'

(b) Paddington, the registered holder of 1,000 shares, claims that his share certificate was stolen and that a forged transfer of shares was made in favour of Bungle. Bungle is seeking registration as a shareholder.

(c) Bear plc has recently paid a dividend and it has come to light that payment was made to six members who had sold their shares in the previous year. This occurred because the names of these members had not been removed from the register.

(d) It has just emerged that the previous company secretary, X, forged a share transfer from a member, Yogi, and issued a share certificate in respect of the shares so 'transferred' to his wife. Winnie innocently purchased shares from X's wife, was registered as a shareholder and was issued with a share certificate by X. Yogi wishes to be reinstated on the register of members.

All the shares in Bear plc are fully paid up.

Answer plan

The question, on various aspects of share transfer, is broken down into four single issue parts. The issues raised are: the right (if any) of the directors to refuse to register a transferee of shares; the effect of a forged share transfer; the effect of non-removal from the register of members; and whether the company is bound by an act of forgery committed internally.

Answer

Currently, all companies are required to have a company secretary (s 283 of the Companies Act (CA) 1985), who may be a natural legal person or a company and who may also be a director of the company, but not the sole director (s 283 CA 1985). Public companies like Bear plc are encouraged to appoint as company secretary a person of appropriate qualification and experience (s 286 CA 1985). Teddy, as company secretary, is likely to carry out many of the administrative tasks imposed on companies by the CA 1985 and supervise the general administration of the company, including the maintenance of the company's registers. One register which is required to be kept is a register of members (s 352 CA 1985), which must be kept at the company's registered office (s 353 CA 1985). In this case, Teddy appears to have discovered some problems in respect of the register of members and seeks your advice about four particular cases.

(a) Rupert

Shares in a company are freely transferable (s 182 CA 1985). The basic transfer procedure is that the registered holder completes and signs an instrument of transfer and delivers it with his share certificate to the transferee (Rupert), who completes the instrument of transfer, has it stamped, and then delivers it with the share certificate to the company. However, agreeing to a transfer does not make Rupert a member of the company. He must be registered as a shareholder if he is to be a member of Bear plc and, until registration, the company will not issue a share certificate in his name. Article 24 of Table A entitles the directors to refuse to register *partly* paid shares, but no discretion to refuse to register fully paid shares unless the articles so provide. The articles of this company do so provide. If Bear was a *quoted* public company, the Stock Exchange listing requirements (which require shares in quoted companies to be freely transferable other than in exceptional cases) would preclude the articles from empowering its directors to refuse transfers. However, an unquoted company can have such a provision. The courts will construe the power to refuse to register narrowly, since the shareholder has a *prima facie* right to be registered. If the directors, as in this case, are given an absolute discretion to refuse to register, they need not give reasons for the refusal, even if legal proceedings are brought (*Berry and Stewart v Tottenham Hotspur FC Ltd (1935)*). However, a refusal to register can be challenged if the directors were not acting *bona fide* for the benefit of the company and in the interests of the company (*Re Smith & Fawcett Ltd (1942)*). The burden of proving a lack of *bona fides* falls on those challenging the refusal to register, which, given that no reason may be given, is a heavy burden. In this case, the directors' decision to refuse to register Rupert appears to be unchallengeable. However, when directors decline to register a shareholder, they must notify the shareholder of their decision within two months of an application to be registered and failure so to do renders the company liable to a fine and the directors liable to a fine and/or imprisonment (s 183 CA 1985). More importantly for Rupert, the courts have determined that a refusal to register must be taken within a reasonable time and treat the two month period as a reasonable period (*Re Swaledale Cleaners Ltd (1968)*; the period can be extended if there are special circumstances), so Bear plc seems to have exceeded the time limit. Thus, Rupert can apply to the court for rectification of the register (s 359 CA 1985) and the issue of a share certificate.

(b) Paddington

Shares in a company are transferable (s 182 CA 1985), but in this case it is alleged that the share transfer was forged—who is entitled to be registered as a member of Bear plc: Paddington or Bungle? A share certificate is *prima facie* evidence that the named member has title to the shares (s 186 CA 1985), so that Paddington should be regarded as having title unless the shares have been validly transferred to another person. Thus, Bungle bears the burden of proving his entitlement to be registered as a shareholder. Section 183 CA 1985 requires a transfer of shares to be made in writing by a proper instrument of transfer. The Stock Transfer Act 1963 sets out forms of transfer document for fully paid shares and it is assumed that an appropriate form was used. If the signature of the holder is forged on an instrument of transfer of those shares, then the instrument is void (*Dixon v Kennaway & Co (1900)*). Consequently, the shares are not transferred and Paddington remains the holder of the shares. Bungle's remedy is against the person who purported to transfer the shares to him—if he can be found. Indeed, even if Bungle succeeded in being registered, the company could remove him from the register because the only basis for registration is the forged transfer (*Sheffield Corp v Barclay (1905)*).

(c) The six members

Section 361 CA 1985 states that the register of members is *prima facie* evidence of its contents. Thus, the six members to whom dividends were paid were *prima facie* members and entitled to the payment. However, the register is not conclusive evidence and s 359 CA 1985 provides that it can be rectified and s 359(1) CA 1985 states that, if there is any unnecessary delay in entering on the register the fact that a person has ceased to be a member, the person aggrieved or any member of the company can apply for rectification. While rectification of the register would correct the register for the future, it does not determine the fate of the past dividend payment. It is assumed that the transferees of the shares were also paid a dividend and, if they were not, they are entitled to a payment from the company, whether the company can recover the money from the former shareholders or not. Section 359(3) CA 1985 authorises the court to decide any question necessary or expedient to be decided for rectification of the register. The ability of the company to recover dividends wrongly paid is arguably not a question 'necessary or expedient to be decided for rectification of the register', so the court would not have the power to order the return of the money under this section. It is assumed that the quasi-contractual (restitutionary) rules on money paid by mistake operate and the dividends may be recoverable by reference to the general law.

Whether rectification can be arranged by agreement between all relevant parties, that is, the company and transferors and transferees, is as yet unsettled, with cases both supporting and denying the efficacy of informal rectification.

(d) Winnie

Winnie has been issued with a share certificate. A share certificate is *prima facie* evidence of title (s 186 CA 1985). However, the presumption raised by the share certificate, that Winnie owns the shares, can be rebutted. Where there is evidence in rebuttal, the presumption will still prevail if the company is estopped from relying on that evidence. Thus, in Winnie's case, there are three issues. First, can the company disclaim the share certificate altogether? Second, can it produce evidence to rebut the presumption that the person in possession of the share certificate is the rightful owner of the shares? Finally, is the company estopped from relying on that evidence?

The company might seek to disclaim all liability for the share certificate on the basis that the person who had issued it on behalf of the company, X, was not authorised so to do. For example, in *Ruben v Great Fingall Consolidated (1906)*, the company secretary forged a share transfer and issued to Ruben a share certificate, which was signed by the secretary and bore the names of two other directors of the company. The signatures of the directors had been forged by the company secretary. The issue for the House of Lords was whether the company could deny the validity of the certificate. The House of Lords stated that the forged certificate was a complete nullity and could not bind the company. It was held that a company secretary had no authority to guarantee on the company's behalf the genuineness or validity of a document. While this decision may have been appropriate in 1906, it is surely the case nowadays that the company secretary does have authority (actual or ostensible) to guarantee the validity of a document such as a share certificate. However, if X was not so authorised, the company can deny the validity of the share certificate issued to X's wife. That being so, it could be argued that the wife had nothing to transfer and the subsequent transfer to Winnie was a nullity. It seems very odd that Bear plc should be able to deny liability or the acts of its employee, and it can be hazarded that *Ruben* would not now be followed, particularly since the role and authority of a company secretary has been greatly enhanced since 1906 (see, for example, *Panorama Development Ltd v Fidelis Furnishing Fabrics Ltd (1971)*).

The evidence that the transfer to X's wife was forged is evidence on which the company could rely to rebut the presumption of title raised by the share certificate. However, it appears that, since Winnie has paid for the shares on the faith of a share certificate, albeit one issued as the result of a forged transfer (to the wife), the company is estopped from denying the genuineness of its own issued certificate (subject to the previous paragraph). Winnie is entitled to say: you issued a certificate, I believed what it said (that X's wife was the owner), so I am entitled to rely on it (*Re Bahia and San Francisco Rly Co Ltd (1868)*). If the company is estopped from denying Winnie's right to be a member and has to reinstate Fred, it can seek compensation from X's wife, even if she was not party to the fraud (*Royal Bank of Scotland plc v Sandstone Properties Ltd (1998)*). Should X's wife be found liable, she can seek a contribution from the company if it was negligent in registering the transfer, although this seems unlikely unless it should have spotted and curtailed X's fraudulent activities earlier. Estoppel allows Winnie to assert her rights against the company, but it does not affect the validity of Fred's title, unless perhaps he knew of the original forged transfer and failed to denounce it with reasonable speed. If Fred was tardy once he discovered the truth in asserting his rights, he would be estopped from raising the forgery and might not be able to demand reinstatement on the register of members.

Public companies generally insure themselves against the consequences of acting on a forged transfer. If Bear plc was a listed company, it could have uncertificated shares and use the computer-based system which records title to shares and enables title to be transferred.

Question 39

Answer *both* parts:

(A) Section 143(1) of the Companies Act 1985 provides that 'A company limited by shares shall not acquire its own shares, whether by purchase, subscription or otherwise.'

Why might a company wish to (or have to) acquire its own shares?

(B) Prof Ltd was formed as a subsidiary of a large computer conglomerate. Subsequently, it was the subject of a management buyout by Brain and Drain. Brain now wishes to reduce his involvement in the company and it has been suggested that Prof Ltd acquires 100,000 of its own £1 shares at par from Brain. The proposal is that the purchase will not be accompanied by a fresh issue of shares but will involve the transfer of all the company's distributable profits (£58,000) to a capital redemption reserve and a permissible capital payment to make up the shortfall.

Student plc, a creditor of the company, has just warned the company that unless all outstanding invoices (totalling some £25,000) are paid it will consider putting Prof Ltd into liquidation.

Comment on any legal issues arising from the above facts.

Answer plan

As with all two part questions, time management is important and, unless there is a mark allocation to the parts of a question, try to allow equal time for each part. Part (A) does not require an essay on the rule but rather a consideration of cases when (and why) it does not apply—do not answer unless you know what you are talking about: guessing is difficult in this area, although the statute (s 143 of the Companies Act (CA) 1985) gives some help. Part (B) requires consideration of whether the proposed payment to Brain is valid and, if not, what could be alternatives open to the company and/or Drain. Also note the consequences where there is an insolvent liquidation within 12 months of a permissible capital payment (PCP).

Answer

(A) Acquiring shares

The rule contained in s 143 of the Companies Act (CA) 1985, that a company may not acquire its own shares, restates the common law decision in *Trevor v Whitworth (1887)*. The House of Lords in that case showed the courts' concern for the interests of creditors and held that, since a creditor effectively 'lent' money to the company (by allowing credit), he has a right to expect that the company will retain its capital and not use it improperly (including not returning it to the shareholders). The share capital (plus undistributable reserves) can be called the 'creditors' buffer'. Consequently, s 143 CA 1985 provides that a company cannot reduce its share capital (nominal value of shares subscribed by shareholders) by buying its own shares (no new capital provided and existing capital used). This does not mean that the money subscribed for shares cannot be used and must be locked away in the bank—the money can be used in the course of the business. All that a creditor is entitled to expect is that the money subscribed for shares has been used in the legitimate course of business. There are, however, a number of exceptions to s 143 CA 1985.

Section 143(3) CA 1985 provides that a company can acquire its own shares where:

(a) the redemption or purchase of shares is made in accordance with ss 159–81 CA 1985; or

(b) the acquisition is part of an authorised reduction of capital; or

(c) the acquisition of shares is ordered by the court pursuant to its powers under s 5 CA 1985 (alteration of objects), or s 54 CA 1985 (re-registration of public company as private), or s 461 CA 1985 (remedy for unfair prejudice); or

(d) the shares are forfeited by the company because the acquirer has not paid for them.

Exceptions (b), (c) and (d) have existed for a number of years and the reasons for such exceptions are generally obvious (less so in the case of reduction of capital). Moreover, (b) and (c) are subject to judicial control, in that a reduction of capital must be confirmed by a court (s 135 CA 1985) and the CA 1985 provides for the protection of creditor interests, and the exceptions in (c) arise only when the court orders the acquisition. The exception in (a) is of recent origin and its use and operation are more controversial. Why, then, might a company wish to (or be required to) purchase its own shares?

(a) Redemption or purchase of shares

Both public and private companies may redeem or purchase their own shares, provided that the company maintains the creditors' buffer. Indeed, private companies can reduce the creditors' buffer and make a permissible capital payment (PCP) provided that they comply with the strict procedures laid down in the CA 1985. This exception was part of a package of measures introduced in the early 1980s to help companies, particularly private companies, raise money. Prior to 1980, a private company wishing to raise outside investment faced two difficulties—issuing new shares diluted existing shareholdings, thus affecting the control of the company (unattractive to current shareholders, particularly in a family company), and new investors would obtain a minority shareholding which would be, effectively, unmarketable. The provisions allowing a company to issue redeemable shares or to buy back its own shares were designed to provide sufficient flexibility to permit existing shareholders to retain control whilst increasing the marketability of shares and continuing to protect creditors. The ability to issue redeemable shares means that a company increases its capital and the investor knows that he will be locked in only for a determinable period. The ability to re-purchase shares allows a company to reorganise its share structure as and when (and if) required and gives an investor some possibility of releasing his investment even if the company does not go public. The facility to re-purchase allows a company to buy out a founder-shareholder when he wishes to retire (assuming that other shareholders lack the funds or the desire to purchase the shares), or to buy out a troublesome shareholder. Alternatively, re-purchase may have financial benefits, for example to enhance the earnings value of the remaining shares (this has been the principal reason why public companies have used the re-purchase provisions) or reduce future dividend payments (by abolishing preference shares, for example).

A public company might also seek to purchase its own shares to preclude a takeover bid (but this might involve a breach of directors' duty—breach of the proper purpose doctrine—and should be carefully scrutinised before proceeding).

When a company wishes to redeem redeemable shares or purchase its own shares, there are extremely onerous procedural requirements designed to ensure that only certain funds are used for these purposes and that an appropriate amount of publicity for the proposed scheme is provided. However, a court order is not required. Any attempt to redeem or re-purchase other than in compliance with the CA 1985 leaves the company open to a fine and every officer of the company in default liable to a fine and/or imprisonment. Further, the acquisition will be void (s 143(2) CA 1985).

(b) Reduction of capital

Section 135 CA 1985 permits a company to reduce share capital, provided that the articles of the company permit a reduction, a reduction has been authorised by special resolution and the court has approved the reduction. Section 135 CA 1985 does not limit the circumstances in which a company may seek to reduce capital, but it does specify three possible grounds for so doing. Where one of these three grounds is the basis of an application, a court is likely to approve the reduction, provided that the position of the company's creditors is secured. Section 135 CA 1985 lists as possible grounds for reduction:

- the extinction or reduction of unpaid share capital (no self-acquisition by company);
- cancellation of paid up share capital which is lost or unrepresented by available assets; and
- payment off of any paid up share capital in excess of the company's wants.

Cancellation of paid up share capital is designed to reflect reality. There is little point in a company having a high nominal capital when trading losses have reduced its net assets to a lower figure. Reduction of capital here would allow a company to resume dividend payments; this might be regarded as a sensible basis for reduction. Paying off unneeded share capital involves returning money to the shareholders and is most often encountered when a company is scaling down its trading activities (commonly encountered in the past following nationalisation). In all cases of reduction, the court has to be satisfied that the creditors of the company are adequately protected before confirming the reduction. A recommendation of the Company Law Review Steering Group, if implemented, would do away with the need for court permission to be required for a reduction of capital. In its place, directors of a company proposing a reduction of capital should be required to make a declaration of insolvency and this should be accompanied, if appropriate, by an auditor's report. But, to ensure that the interests of creditors (of public companies) are nonetheless protected, it is further suggested that such creditors should be given the right to seek a court order providing for adequate security for their debts or for some other appropriate relief to be granted (*Modern Company Law for a Competitive Economy: Company Formation and Capital Maintenance* (DTI, 1999)). These proposals have been implemented in the Companies Act 2006, although, to date, are not in force.

(B) Paying for shares

There are two matters of concern to Prof Ltd. The threat of liquidation (probably designed to get the debt paid) is also a useful reminder of some of the issues involved in a share acquisition by a company.

(a) Liquidation

Student plc is threatening to put Prof Ltd into liquidation. S 122(1) of the Insolvency Act (IA) 1986 provides that a company may be put into liquidation if it is unable to pay its debts, and s 123 IA 1986 provides that a company is deemed unable to pay its debts if, *inter alia*, it has failed, within three weeks of receiving a written demand in prescribed form, to pay a debt in excess of £750. Thus, in this case, it seems likely that Student plc has the ability to seek compulsory liquidation of Prof Ltd. Compulsory winding up is both lengthy and expensive and, if liquidation is really likely, it would be better if Student plc could persuade the directors of Prof Ltd to initiate a creditors' voluntary winding up if the company really is insolvent. This would require Prof Ltd to pass an extraordinary resolution (three-quarters majority of those present or votes cast required) in favour; the winding up would be subject to close supervision by the creditors.

A liquidator, who must be a licensed insolvency practitioner, has to swell the assets of the company and pay such money as the company has to the creditors in order of priority. In seeking to swell the assets, a liquidator can try to recover funds from directors who have broken any of their duties and can, where apposite, pursue actions for fraudulent trading (s 213 IA 1986) or wrongful trading (s 214 IA 1986). In addition, the liquidator should seek to have set aside or re-opened certain transactions entered into within the periods specified in the IA 1986. For example, floating charges granted within 12 months of the winding up are *prima facie* invalid (s 245 IA 1986, two years for a charge in favour of a connected person). If Prof Ltd were to pay them, and then go into insolvent liquidation within six months of the payment, a liquidator might seek to have the payment set aside as a 'preference' (s 239 IA 1986), although there are strict requirements for the operation of this provision. However, the threat by Student plc may be just a means of galvanising Prof Ltd into paying its debts and may have no effect on the proposed acquisition of shares. Of course, if the proposed acquisition goes ahead and liquidation (whether initiated by Student plc or another) does ensue within 12 months, there are consequences for Prof Ltd and its directors.

(b) Share acquisition

The proposed share acquisition must be approved by the board of Prof Ltd, which must exercise its decision whether or not to purchase Brain's shares *bona fide* for the benefit of the company. Breach of duty would render the directors liable to reimburse the company for any loss and the recipient of corporate funds (Brain) might also be liable to refund the money under the principles of constructive trusteeship. If the scheme is acceptable, the shares must be paid for. Obviously, existing shareholders may be prevailed upon to buy the shares, but this does not seem likely in this case. Perhaps the shareholders have no funds and no desire or ability to borrow the necessary sums. However, the company is willing to buy the shares. How can it pay Brain? A new share issue has been rejected; perhaps because it would dilute the ownership of the company, and it is proposed to fund the acquisition partly by a payment out of income (£58,000 from distributable profits) and partly from capital (£42,000). Private companies (Prof Ltd is private) are permitted to purchase their own shares, provided that certain conditions are complied with, and may use the funds proposed in appropriate cases. Does the purchase by Prof Ltd comply with the statutory provisions?

These provisions are complex but are designed to ensure that the shareholders approve the purchase, that only appropriate funds are used for the purchase and that there is adequate publicity for the purchase. First, the company must have authority to purchase its own shares—Prof Ltd is authorised (Art 35 of Table A). Section 162 CA 1985 then sets out conditions for payments for shares made out of corporate 'income'. The conditions are that the contract to purchase was approved in advance by special resolution (s 164 CA 1985, a written resolution would suffice and Brain must not have voted) and that the purchase so authorised was paid for out of the company's distributable profits (s 168 CA 1985, or a fresh issue of shares made for the purpose, ss 160, 162 CA 1985—which does not apply here). Thus the payment of £58,000 would appear to be acceptable (made out of distributable profits, defined in s 263 CA 1985). Further, s 170 CA 1985 requires a transfer of a sum representing the share purchase price from distributable profits to the capital redemption reserve (CRR). These sections appear to be satisfied. However, a purchase made in compliance with s 164 CA 1985 must also be given appropriate publicity for the purchase (s 169 CA 1985, notice to Registrar, copy of contract at registered office, etc).

Turning to the balance of the payment, s 171 CA 1985, which applies only to private companies, allows companies to purchase their own shares out of capital—such a payment (which may represent all or part of the purchase price) is a PCP. Needless to say, there are strict rules for the use of a PCP. Section 173 CA 1985 provides that the payment must have been approved by special resolution (at a meeting or unanimously by written resolution) obtained *after* the directors of Prof Ltd had made a statutory declaration. This statutory declaration by the directors must specify

- the amount of the PCP; and
- that the directors, having made full inquiries into the affairs and prospects of the company, are of the opinion that the company will be able to meet its debts immediately after the PCP and will continue as a going concern for the next 12 months after the PCP, and be able to pay its debts as they fall due.

The auditors must have commented on the statutory declaration to the effect that, having inquired into the company's affairs, they were not aware of anything which would render the directors' opinion unreasonable (s 173 CA 1985). After a special resolution approving a PCP has been passed, the decision must be publicised (s 175 CA 1985). The publicity must mention the power of members and creditors to object. If Prof Ltd complies with all of these rules, the payment of £42,000 will also be valid. However, even if a PCP is valid at the time that it is made, the directors and Brain can incur liability to any subsequent liquidator of Prof Ltd. Section 76 IA 1986 provides that, where a company goes into insolvent liquidation within 12 months of the payment out of capital being made, the directors who signed the statutory declaration are liable to contribute to the company's assets. The directors can escape liability if they can establish that they had reasonable grounds for their opinions; it seems probable that the auditors' approval would be a 'reasonable ground', provided that the directors had not concealed any information from the auditors. Section 76 IA 1986 would also render Brain liable to contribute to the assets of the company to the extent of the PCP.

Question 40

In 1998, A and B formed a company, Shark Ltd. The shares in Shark Ltd were allotted to A and B equally in return for the transfer to the company of the business which they have been operating as a partnership. A and B were the sole directors of the company. In 2001, A and B agreed to purchase from C, for £10,000, all the shares in an existing company, Lamb Ltd, which C controlled. A and B became the directors of Lamb Ltd and paid C £5,000 in cash and the balance by the issue of a redeemable, interest-bearing debenture secured by a floating charge on Lamb Ltd's stock. Both companies traded successfully but A and B found that they had different views on how to expand their business enterprises. Thus, they formulated a scheme to split the companies. The scheme required A to transfer his 50% shareholding in Shark to Wolf Ltd (a company controlled by B) in return for B transferring his shares in Lamb to A and agreeing to pay A £50,000 over the next five years. This debt was to be secured by a charge over the assets of Shark. Subsequently, B refused to transfer his Lamb shares, claiming that he overestimated the value of the Shark shares and that he is not prepared to proceed without an amendment of the agreement. A is seeking specific performance of the agreement as originally drawn.

Comment on any legal issues which arise from these facts.

Answer plan

It is not clear who, if anyone, is seeking advice on the affairs of these companies, so the legal issues cannot be tailored to any particular client. The principal matters that arise appear to relate to the initial purchase of Lamb shares from C and the proposed scheme to divide the companies between A and B. Other issues include the allotment of Shark shares and other possible ways of splitting the businesses between the protagonists. In some ways, it is a narrow question, but it does demand familiarity with the complicated provisions on financial assistance.

Answer

There are a number of legal issues which arise from the facts outlined in the question. First, it should be noted that the allotment of shares in Shark Ltd to A and B is not contrary to the Companies Act (CA) 1985. In common with many traders who incorporate their business, they have transferred that business to the company in return for an allotment of shares. Section 99 CA 1985 provides that the consideration for shares may be provided in money or, as here, in money's worth. Section 100 CA 1985 states that shares must not be issued at a discount, but, where the consideration for shares is not in the form of cash, it is unlikely that the shares would be treated as anything other than fully paid. There is no statutory requirement that the consideration for shares in a private company be valued and the courts will not treat consideration such as this as other than full payment unless it is manifestly inadequate or illusory (*Re Wragg (1897)*). Indeed, in the classic case of *Salomon v Salomon & Co Ltd (1895)*, where the promoter transferred his boot business to the company, the House of Lords refused to investigate too closely the value of the business transferred by S in return for shares and a secured loan, even though the value appeared to have been, at best, a wildly optimistic figure. Indeed, who suffers if the business is overvalued? A and B, who are the shareholders anyway.

A and B subsequently agree to purchase from C his shares in Lamb Ltd. There can be no objection to a shareholder selling his shares in a company, since shares are supposed to be transferable (s 182 CA 1985). However, the method of payment may cause problems. A and B paid C partly in cash and partly by means of redeemable, interest-bearing debenture, that is, by means of a loan secured on the stock of Lamb Ltd, the very company whose shares are being purchased. Section 151 CA 1985 provides that, where a person is acquiring shares in a company, it is not lawful for that company to give financial assistance directly or indirectly for the purposes of the acquisition before, during or after the acquisition. The arrangement whereby A and B, once they become directors of Lamb Ltd, authorised Lamb to grant a debenture (a secured loan) over its stock is plainly such assistance (see *Carney v Herbert (1985)*). This is so despite the fact that courts have bound themselves to look at the commercial realities of a situation; that is, is there really financial assistance? There are exceptions to s 151 CA 1985.

Two of the exceptions to s 151 CA 1985 are clearly irrelevant. These are when the company lends money in the ordinary course of business, for example where a bank customer borrows money to buy shares in the bank, and where the financial assistance is authorised by some other provision of company law. Section 153 CA 1985 also lists various circumstances which do not seem to be within the ambit of s 151 CA 1985 simply to avoid argument on the point. The remaining group of exceptions, ss 153(1), (2) and 155 CA 1985, is designed to ensure that the broad scope of the prohibition does not unintentionally ensnare genuine commercial transactions which are of benefit to the company. Section 155 CA 1985 does not apply to A and B, but they might seek to argue that s 153(1) or (2) CA 1985 does. Section 153 CA 1985 states that a company can give assistance if its principal purpose in doing so is not to give financial assistance to facilitate the acquisition or to reduce or discharge any liability incurred by a person (A and B here) for the purpose of the acquisition of the shares but is an incidental part of some larger purpose of the company *and* it is given in good faith in the interests of the company. The ambit of this exception is uncertain.

In *Brady v Brady (1989)*, the House of Lords expressed the view that this provision required those responsible for authorising the financial assistance to have acted in the genuine belief that it was being done in the company's interests. Could A and B argue that C's management is so poor that the scheme represented the only way in which the company could be saved (the larger purpose), so that their intervention was beneficial to present and future creditors (whom these sections are designed to protect by ensuring the company does not squander its share capital) and present employees? The difficulty is that A and B appear to have benefited to a greater degree than anyone else, so that one might query their *bona fides* in authorising the financial assistance and thereby cast doubt on the reality of any larger purpose. The meaning of 'larger purpose' is discussed below when considering the break-up scheme.

The civil consequences of breach of s 151 CA 1985 are dependent on the common law, but the section provides that any company which breaks this provision is liable to a fine and the officers of the company who authorised the financial assistance, A and B in this case, are liable to a fine and/or imprisonment. A and B, as the directors who authorised the breach of s 151 CA 1985, are in breach, thereby, of their duties to the company and must compensate the company for any loss it has suffered in consequence. In this case, the interest on the debenture would be recoverable, as would any capital payments which have been made. An action against A and B could be initiated by Lamb Ltd but, in the circumstances, this is most unlikely since A and B control Lamb and are hardly likely to authorise it to sue them. Once the relationship of A and B deteriorates, B may seek to bring a derivative action on behalf of Lamb in respect of the breach. However, B may find himself precluded from bringing an action on behalf of Lamb, since he was party to the illegality of which he later seeks to complain (*Nurcombe v Nurcombe (1985)* was prevented a shareholder from bringing a derivative action when she had knowingly benefited from the conduct of the director of which she later sought to complain on behalf of the company). Indeed, C, the recipient of the debenture, may find that he is a constructive trustee of the benefits received as a consequence of the unlawful financial assistance, since he was well aware of the breach of duty, having benefited from it. Alternatively, C may discover that the purchase of shares (or at least the method of payment) by A and B is void, owing to the breach of s 151 CA 1985.

The issue of the effect of breach on the transaction for which the assistance was given arose in a number of cases concerning the forerunners of s 151 CA 1985. In *Victor Battery Co Ltd v Curry's Ltd (1946)*, the facts of which resemble the present case, Roxburgh J said that the granting of a debenture could not, in law, be financial assistance unless the debenture was valid, and consequently concluded that breach of s 151 CA 1985 did not invalidate the financial assistance. Later cases, while not overruling *Victor Battery*, have looked at the commercial realities and concluded that, where the financial assistance has the effect in fact of underpinning the acquisition, it is financial assistance (whether it is legal or not) and is void (*Heald v O'Connor (1971)* and *Carney v Herbert (1985)* are two examples). However, this leaves open the question of whether the debenture is void or the purchase is void. In *Carney v Herbert* (1985), the Privy Council determined that where the unlawful assistance was ancillary to the overall transaction *and* its elimination would leave unchanged the subject matter of the transaction, it could be severed, leaving the remainder of the transaction enforceable. In *Carney*, the court felt able to sever from a contract for the sale of shares a guarantee of the purchaser's debt given by the company whose shares were being sold. In this case, severance seems less likely, since part of the consideration for the contract of sale is unlawful and the courts will not rewrite contracts under the guise of severance.

We now turn to the scheme formulated to split the existing businesses between A and B. In passing, it should be noted that A and B might have been wise to enter into a scheme of arrangement under s 425 CA 1985, which allows a court to sanction a proposal which might otherwise be breach of s 151 CA 1985. Alternatively, the procedure whereby a private company can give financial assistance by complying with s 155 CA 1985 could have been contemplated. Section 155 CA 1985 provides that a private company, for example Lamb, can give financial assistance for the acquisition of its own shares if it has net assets (ss 154, 155 CA 1985) which are not reduced by the assistance or, if reduced, the assistance is provided out of net profits. In effect, a company can make a loan, etc, if it gets its money back (no reduction of net assets) or if the loan comes out of money payable to shareholders (net profits) so that the creditors of the company are not adversely affected by the scheme. Unfortunately, neither of these was adopted and it is probable that the proposed scheme is in breach of s 151 CA 1985.

First, A agrees to transfer his Shark shares to Wolf Ltd—nothing objectionable in that. This leaves Wolf indebted to A for the value of the Shark shares. A third party, B, discharges Wolf's liability by agreeing to pay A—again, nothing objectionable so far. B discharges Wolf's debt by transferring the Lamb shares to A (a share swap) and agreeing to pay A £50,000. If the scheme stopped there, the transaction would be unimpeachable. Unfortunately, B's agreed payment of £50,000 was to be secured and the security provided was to be a charge over the assets of Shark, the very company whose shares were being acquired by Wolf. Thus, there is an apparent breach of s 151 CA 1985 and a court would not order specific performance of the contract unless the financial assistance provided indirectly by Shark is within an exception to s 151 CA 1985 or this part of the agreement can be severed. Does the exception in s 153(2) CA 1985 apply? As mentioned above, this requires the assistance to be an incidental part of a larger purpose of the company and the assistance must be given in good faith in the interests of the company. The good faith and interests of the company part is satisfied here—the scheme is needed to break the deadlock between the parties. What constitutes a larger purpose was discussed by the House of Lords in *Brady v Brady (1989)*.

In *Brady*, the facts of which are rightly characterised by Farrar as 'labyrinthine', two brothers, who had fallen out, sought to split a family business, which operated through a series of interlinked companies, into two main spheres (haulage and soft drinks). A plan was evolved which was designed to leave one brother with the haulage-based business and the other brother with the soft drinks-based business. The plan (in simplified form!) required M to purchase all the shares in Brady (the holding company) from O, leaving M with a debt due to O. This debt was partly paid by the transfer to O of assets belonging to Brady. Clearly, Brady was contributing financial assistance to the purchase of its own shares. It was argued that the assistance was simply incidental to a larger purpose—the reorganisation of the family business—and that it was in the interests of Brady, since the only alternative, given the rancour between the brothers, was to wind up Brady. The House of Lords accepted that the plan was in the best interests of the company (as in this case). However, the Lords, reversing the Court of Appeal, found no larger purpose to which the financial assistance was merely incidental. It ruled that the financial assistance in this case was driven by a more important reason than the provision of the assistance—the reorganisation plan—but said that purpose and reason were different. Simply because there was an important reason underpinning the scheme did not make it incidental to a larger purpose. On the facts, the scheme was designed to facilitate the purchase of shares in Brady, even if the reason was to split the family businesses, and there was no larger purpose to which it was incidental.

This narrow interpretation of s 153 CA 1985, ignoring the commercial context and focusing on the disputed transaction, seems likely to apply to this case, so that A would not obtain his order for specific performance. It should be noted in passing that, in *Brady*, it was ultimately accepted that s 155 CA 1985 could apply and the plan (and the one here) could be implemented by use of that section. As Gower remarks, it would have been a great deal cheaper for everyone if the s 155 route had been explored earlier. Indeed, the difficulties faced by businesses in respect of the financial assistance rules has been recognised by the Department of Trade and Industry (DTI) as part of its review of modern company law. The DTI suggests that the rules on financial assistance for the purchase of shares are causing unnecessary, substantial professional fees to be incurred by companies in their attempts to ensure that innocent and worthwhile transactions do not breach the rules (*Modern Company Law for a Competitive Economy* (DTI, 1998)) and, in a later consultation document, the Company Law Review Steering Group proposed that the best way forward in dealing with this problem is for the financial assistance rule to be abolished completely in relation to private companies (*Modern Company Law for a Competitive Economy: Developing the Framework* (DTI, 2000)). This proposal has found its way into the Companies Act 2006, although, to date, it is not in force.

Question 41

Christie, James, Rendell and Sayers hold all the issued share capital of Detective Ltd, of which they are the executive directors. Christie has indicated that she would like to retire from the business and sell her shareholding. James, Rendell and Sayers would like the company, which is highly profitable, to pay Christie £100,000 for her past services (she has received a salary and has a company pension). The memorandum and articles of the company permit the company to make gratuitous payments.

Christie is willing to sell her shares in the company when she retires; the remaining directors would prefer these shares to be retained within the company.

None of the remaining shareholders has sufficient funds of their own to purchase all of Christie's shareholding.

Advise the directors how to proceed in order to achieve their aims.

Answer plan

Two issues arise: the payment to Christie—is it legal, and if so, how can it be achieved? Second, keeping the shares in the company. In respect of the purchase, can it be by the company or existing shareholders and how is it to be funded?

Answer

PAYMENT TO CHRISTIE

The proposed payment on retirement does not appear to be *ultra vires* (the company has power to make gratuitous payments) and the board, it can be assumed, is authorised to make such payments since the board has the power to run the company. Indeed, since the directors are also the shareholders, there is no one to object to the proposal. Thus, the payment would seem to be valid provided that the directors were not in breach of their fiduciary duty in authorising it and s 312 of the Companies Act (CA) 1985 (payment to directors on retirement) has been complied with. There should be no difficulty in complying with s 312 CA 1985, since all that is required is approval in advance by the shareholders, and the remaining directors are also the shareholders of Detective Ltd. There is still some doubt as to the ability of the directors to give away the company's money, even where the company is authorised to make gratuitous payments, but where some benefit, however elusive, to the company can be discerned such payments are valid (*Re Horsely & Weight Ltd (1982)* took a more generous view and did not require any benefit to the company). Certainly, a gratuitous transaction decided on by the directors other than *bona fide* for the benefit of the company would presumably be invalid as well as being a breach of duty by the directors (see *Aveling Barford Ltd v Perion Ltd (1989)*, sale of asset to company controlled by a director at gross undervalue was breach of director's duty— an attempt to defraud the company). If Detective remained solvent, this transaction is unlikely to be challenged, since all the shareholders were party to the decision. However, if the company went into insolvent liquidation, the liquidator might wish to challenge its validity. If the company failed to make the payment, it is unlikely that Christie would have a contractual claim to the money, since she has not provided any consideration for the agreement. Perhaps she should suggest that the price of the shares is augmented by £100,000 and she forgoes the retirement gift.

SALE OF SHARES

Although the remaining directors do not wish Christie's shares to be sold to an outsider, Christie is not debarred from selling her shares to anyone who wants to buy them, unless the articles of the company limit their transferability. Table A contains no such restriction, so it can be assumed that this company has no such provision, although an attempt could be made to insert such a clause since the remaining shareholders could change the articles (s 9 CA 1985) by special resolution (they control three-quarters of the votes). Any attempt by the majority to change the articles in this way might be challenged by Christie as being an abuse of majority power, in that it was not *bona fide* for the benefit of the company (*Allen v Gold Reefs of West Africa Ltd (1900)*), although this not an area where the courts have proved very interventionist. Alternatively, Christie could seek to challenge any proposed amendment by a petition alleging unfair prejudice (s 459 CA 1985). On the facts, it appears that the remaining shareholders and Christie are on good terms, so that the insertion of such an article is unlikely to be sought. The board of Detective Ltd does not have a power to refuse to register a new fully paid up shareholder, so indirect pressure cannot be put on Christie by a threat to refuse to register any transferee. However, an outsider who purchased the shares would not be a director, unless appointed by the board (to fill a casual vacancy) or the shareholders. Consequently, an outsider would be unlikely to wish to purchase a minority shareholding unless this was a scheme acceptable to the remaining shareholders. Christie might prefer, as the remainder of the board would, to sell her shares to the company or to the existing shareholders.

Section 143 CA 1985 appears to preclude the simple solution that the company purchase the shares. The inability of a director-shareholder to retire and sell his shares to the company was one of the reasons put forward to permit, in prescribed cases, a company buying its own shares. There are two ways of approaching the issue: Detective Ltd could seek to buy the shares either out of income or out of capital (only private companies can purchase shares out of capital). The statutory provisions are complex but are designed to ensure that the shareholders approve the purchase, that only appropriate funds are used for the purchase and that there is adequate publicity for the purchase. On any vote to approve a purchase, the shareholder who is intending to sell to the company cannot vote. If Detective Ltd does purchase the shares, they are cancelled thereby, reducing the issued share capital (and reducing capital if the purchase is made out of capital). The resolutions that must be passed to approve the purchase (sometimes ordinary, sometimes special) may be obtained by holding a meeting or, since Detective Ltd is a private company, by means of a written resolution (s 381A CA 1985, unanimous support of those entitled to vote required). Consider first purchase with payment out of income. Section 162 CA 1985 allows a company to buy its own shares if authorised to do so by its articles (Art 35 of Table A applies here) and the conditions set out in the CA 1985 are complied with. The conditions are that the contract to purchase is approved in advance by special resolution (s 164 CA 1985) and any purchase so authorised to be made must be paid for out of the company's distributable profits (s 168 CA 1985) or a fresh issue of shares made for the purpose (ss 160, 162 CA 1985). The distributable profits of a company are determined by reference to s 263 CA 1985 and are, in essence, the company's accumulated, realised profits (not previously distributed or capitalised) less its accumulated, realised losses (not previously written off in an authorised reduction or reorganisation of capital). Effectively, the fund used to pay for the shares must be money which could have been paid to the shareholders or constitute new capital. Since Detective Ltd is 'highly profitable', it seems likely that the directors could decide to pursue this method of purchase and have the funds to do so. If a purchase is made in compliance with s 164 CA 1985, s 169 CA 1985 requires appropriate publicity for the purchase (notice to Registrar, copy of contract at registered office, etc) and s 170 CA 1985 requires a transfer of a sum representing the share purchase price from distributable profits to the capital redemption reserve. The capital redemption reserve forms part of the share capital of the company and can be reduced only by compliance with the usual rules (s 135 CA 1985) for the reduction of share capital. There is one exception to the rules on reduction in respect of the capital redemption reserve—it can be used to pay up unissued shares to be allotted to members as fully paid up bonus shares.

The board of Detective Ltd could be advised that, if the company has insufficient distributable profits to apply for the purchase of Christie's shares, the company might still be able to buy the shares. Section 171 CA 1985, which applies only to private companies, allows companies to purchase their own shares out of capital—such a payment (which may represent all or part of the purchase price) is a PCP. Needless to say, there are rules for the use of a PCP. Section 173 CA 1985 requires the payment out of capital to be approved by special resolution after the directors of Detective Ltd have made a statutory declaration. This statutory declaration must specify:

- the amount of the PCP;
- that they have inquired into the financial situation of the company; and
- that, in their opinion, after the company has purchased the shares, it will be able to pay its debts and the company will continue business as a going concern for a full year.

The auditors must comment on the statutory declaration to the effect that, having inquired into the company's affairs, they are not aware of anything which would render the directors' opinion unreasonable (s 173 CA 1985). After the special resolution approving the PCP has been passed, the decision must be duly publicised (s 175 CA 1985), and this notification must inform the creditors of their right to object to the payment. Section 176 CA 1985 allows a member or creditor to object to a PCP (five week time limit from date of resolution) and s 177 CA 1985 sets out the court's powers when an objection has been lodged; the court can, among other things, affirm, reject or modify the special resolution and can order the objectors to be paid off. In this case, all three shareholders would have to vote for the proposal, so only creditors would be able to object. The directors might prefer not to use a PCP because, if the company goes into insolvent liquidation within 12 months of the payment out of capital being made, s 76 of the Insolvency Act (IA) 1986 provides that the directors who signed the statutory declaration are liable to contribute to the company's assets unless they can establish that they had reasonable grounds for their opinions. Christie would also incur liability to the extent of the PCP.

If the company seeks to purchase Christie's shares other than in accordance with the CA 1985, the purchase is unlawful and the directors are in breach of duty (there are also criminal penalties).

While no single shareholder may be able to afford Christie's shares, the shareholders might be able to afford a block each or purchase the total block jointly. Either scheme could preserve the existing share balance between the remaining shareholders and not allow any one of them to obtain a dominant position within the company. However, even if one shareholder purchased all of Christie's shares, she would still have only 50% of the votes, and this amount is insufficient on its own to pass a resolution. Alternatively, all or some of the directors could seek to borrow money from the company to allow them to purchase Christie's shares. This gives rise to two problems. First, the loan by a company to a person to enable him to purchase shares in the company is prohibited by s 151 CA 1985 and, second, a company cannot make loans to a director (s 330 CA 1985). While s 151 CA 1985 provides that a company cannot provide financial assistance (loans are included, s 152 CA 1985) to a person for the purchase of its own shares (there are criminal penalties for so doing and the assistance is void), private companies can do so provided that they are solvent and adhere to the statutory procedure provided. Section 155 CA 1985 provides that Detective Ltd could give financial assistance for the acquisition of its own shares if it has net assets (ss 154, 155 CA 1985) which are not reduced by the assistance or, if reduced, the assistance is provided out of net profits. In effect, Detective Ltd can make a loan if it gets its money back (no reduction of net assets) or if the loan comes out of money payable to shareholders (net profits) so that the creditors of the company are not affected by the self-dealing.

The procedural hurdles which must be surmounted to allow financial assistance are similar to those applicable to a purchase of shares by the company—approval by special resolution (a written resolution can be used) and a statutory declaration by the directors which is supported by the auditors. The statutory declaration is not identical to that required for a PCP but requires the directors to declare that, in their opinion, following any proposed financial assistance, the company can pay its debts and will be able to do so in the next year following the assistance (or, if the company is to be wound up in that period, that it will be able to pay all debts). The auditor's report must confirm that, having looked at the company's state of affairs, they are not aware of anything which would render the director's opinion unreasonable (s 156 CA 1985). There are provisions for shareholders to object which would be inapplicable here, given that all the remaining shareholders would have to approve the assistance (assuming that all vote or a written resolution is used). A director who makes a statutory declaration without reasonable grounds for his opinion is liable to a fine or imprisonment (but there is no civil liability under the CA 1985). There are onerous publicity requirements. If financial assistance is provided other than in accordance with the CA 1985, a director who authorised the assistance is in breach of duty—in this case the directors, being the recipients of the loan, would have to return the money. Assuming that the provisions for the granting of financial assistance are complied with, there is still the difficulty that the proposed loan is to the directors.

Section 330 CA 1985 provides that a company cannot make a loan to a director and that any loan made is voidable at the company's option (s 341 CA 1985). However, since the directors are the shareholders, they are unlikely to seek to void the loan. Consequently, the loan would not be challenged unless the company went into liquidation and the liquidator sought to recover the loan on behalf of the company. Presumably, the shareholders can approve the loan and thus render the loan unimpeachable, even if liquidation ensues (it is not clear whether simple inaction is approval). A liquidator might then argue that the breach of duty by the directors in authorising the loan in the first place enabled him to sue the directors (unless breach ratified by shareholders?). There are exceptions to s 330 CA 1985 where loans to directors are valid and, if one of these applies, there is no wrongdoing of which the company can complain. For example, s 334 CA 1985 allows small loans (up to £5,000).

There seems little doubt that, one way or another, the remaining shareholders will be able to purchase Christie's shares if she is willing to sell them either to them or to the company.

NOTE

In line with the recommendations of the Law Commissions (1999) and the Company Law Review Steering Group (2001), a number of changes are made to ss 330–42 CA 1985 by the Companies Act 2006. There will no longer be a prohibition on company loans, etc. Loans will be permitted, subject to member approval, and the criminal penalties will be abolished. The new requirements will apply to all companies and there will be an extended meaning of 'connected person'. The changes, when in force, will also consolidate, simplify and extend the exceptions that apply in this area.

CHAPTER 7

LOAN CAPITAL

▌INTRODUCTION

Loan capital is the rather grand name attached to a company's borrowings (so remember that your overdraft is your loan capital); borrowing is an important method of financing for many companies. Loan capital can be divided into two categories. First, sums owed by the company as a specific debt, for example a loan from X, the most common example of which is the company's overdraft; and, second, marketable loans. Marketable loans are in essence potential debts which may be issued (sold) to investors. These loans will be issued on strict terms and conditions relating to date when the interest is due, date of redemption and other rights attaching. A company could create £1 million of marketable debt divided into £1 units bearing interest at X%, which it can sell as and when required and for whatever price it will fetch (there is no prohibition on issuing a loan at a discounted price unless it is convertible into shares). If £1 of redeemable debt is sold at a discount, the owner at redemption, who receives the face value of the debt and not the issue price, will make a capital profit. Marketable loans are frequently known as bonds. Individual loans or marketable loans may be secured by a charge or unsecured; much of the law in this area concerns company charges. Fashions in marketable loans vary. The highly specialised rules relating to international or euro bonds fall outside the scope of a company law syllabus.

Any document which states the terms on which a company has borrowed money may be called a debenture (s 744 of the Companies Act (CA) 1985) whether or not it carries security, but in the business world an unsecured loan is likely to be called an unsecured loan note rather than a debenture. Charges have to be registered to be valid against other creditors of the company, but the position on registration is presently something of a mess. The registration of company charges is subject to the 1985 Act. The 1985 provisions were prospectively replaced by the 1989 Act but these 1989 changes will not be implemented. The Law Commission Working Paper on Company Charges, *Registration of Security Interests: Company Charges and Property other than Land* (2002), proposed a fundamental change in this area of the law.

Loan capital raises general issues—the ability of the company to borrow, the powers of the directors to borrow and the issue of marketable loans—and specific provisions relating to company charges. Questions on loan capital often involve a company which has gone into insolvent liquidation and requires the liquidator to be advised on the validity and priority of certain debts. In all questions of this type, two issues arise: how can the liquidator maximise the company's assets (for example, sue the directors for wrongful trading, or have some charges set aside); and how should the liquidator determine priorities between competing creditors?

Question 42

Answer both parts:

(a) What is the distinction between a fixed and floating charge? Why is the distinction important?

(b) In 1997, Lo Cost Loans plc lent £600,000 to Finger Foods Ltd. The loan was secured by a charge, which was termed 'fixed', over book debts. As customers paid Finger Foods, the amount was paid into a special account. Finger Foods was able to draw on this special account unless and until Lo Cost Loans told it to stop, but was not able to assign its book debts to a third party.

Lo Cost Loans has become uneasy about the loan to Finger Foods and seeks your advice on the nature of the charge and its position should Finger Foods become insolvent.

Answer plan

As with all two part questions, effective time management is critical, since roughly equal time should be devoted to both parts of the question (unless it is clear that the mark allocation is not equal).

The first part is relatively straightforward. What is needed is a comparison of fixed and floating charges and a clear explanation of why the distinction matters.

In the second part, give an analysis of the nature of the charge and why it is important in the event of Finger Foods' insolvency.

Answer

(a) Distinguishing fixed and floating charges

If a company decides to borrow to expand its business, any creditor is likely to require security. Companies can deploy two forms of security—fixed charges, that is, a charge over a specific, identifiable asset or property, or floating charges, that is, a charge over a class of asset. Shareholders are largely unaffected by the type preferred. Both types of charge are subject to registration and if not registered are void (s 395 of the Companies Act (CA) 1985), although the underlying debt is unaffected by non-registration. Both ss 238 and 239 of the Insolvency Act (IA) 1986 allow a liquidator (or administrator if the company is in administration) to apply to the court to have certain transactions, entered into by a company within the statutory period prior to the commencement of the winding up (or administration), set aside and the position of the company restored to what it would have been but for the disputed transaction. These transactions could include the granting of a charge. Neither section operates if at the time of the disputed transaction the company could pay its debts, and this position was not affected by the disputed transaction. There is no distinction for the purposes of these sections between fixed and floating charges. How, then, do fixed and floating charges differ?

Fixed charge

A fixed charge may be legal or equitable. For example, if a company charges its real property to its bank by means of a mortgage, the bank has a fixed legal charge over that property. The bank will obtain the title deeds to the property, which effectively precludes the company from dealing with the property without the knowledge and consent of the bank. A fixed equitable charge is less formal and can be achieved by the deposit of title deeds. The holder of a fixed charge can, on winding up or if the security is at risk, seize the charged property and sell it to discharge the indebtedness, thereafter accounting for any surplus to the company. A fixed chargeholder does not claim against the general assets of the company on winding up, he simply claims against 'his' asset, and provided he has ensured that it is of adequate value he is not in competition with the other creditors for the assets of the company unless the same asset has been used as security for a further loan—when a question of priority will arise. A fixed charge generally prevents the company from dealing with the charged asset without the consent of the chargeholder and is, it would seem, an inappropriate form of security for assets which are constantly changing, for example stock or book debts.

Floating charge

There is no statutory definition of a floating charge, and what the parties call the charge is not conclusive evidence of its status (*Re New Bullas Trading Ltd (1994)*).

While the decision in *Bullas* was doubted by the Privy Council in *Re Brumark Investments Ltd (2001)* and overruled by the House of Lords in *National Westminster Bank plc v Spectrum Plus Ltd (2005)*, it was approved on this point. Judicial pronouncements have isolated certain factors which are likely to be present if a charge is to be classified as floating. These factors, derived from *Re Yorkshire Woolcombers' Association Ltd (1903)*, are:

• that the charge is over a class of assets both present and future;
• which assets are constantly changing, for example book debts; and
• that the charge leaves the company free to use and deal with those assets.

While it is tempting to see fixed charges as relating to permanent assets and floating charges as attaching to changing assets, this is not the case. In the decision of *Siebe Gorman & Co Ltd v Barclays Bank Ltd (1979)*, where it was held that the company had created a fixed charge over book debts, the judge stressed that the courts will not regard any single factor as crucial in seeking to classify a charge as fixed or floating. However, as authority, *Siebe Gorman* was doubted by the Privy Council in *Re Brumark* and was overruled by the House of Lords in *Spectrum Plus*, and freedom to deal with the assets without consulting the chargee has generally been regarded as close to conclusive evidence that the charge is floating, irrespective of the wording adopted by the parties to the charge (*Re Cimex Tissues Ltd (1995)*; *Re Cosslett (Contractors) Ltd (1998)*). Thus, in *Re Brumark*, where a company had created a charge over uncollected book debts which left it free to collect and use the proceeds in the ordinary course of business (subject to certain conditions imposed by the lender), the Privy Council held that the company had not created a fixed charge, whatever the contract of charge provided *Re Brumark* was approved by the House of Lords in *Spectrum Plus*.

Differences between fixed and floating charges

Since a floating charge is over a class of assets, the chargeholder is uncertain as to the value of his security at any moment before the charge crystallises (transmutes into a fixed charge on the happening of certain events, for example receivership, liquidation or the giving of notice by the chargeholder). If there is a fixed and floating charge over the same asset, the fixed charge (being fixed and legal) will generally have priority over the floating charge, even if created later than the floating charge. Floating chargeholders, to protect themselves, may include in their charge notification that they take priority over later chargeholders (even if fixed), that is, a negative pledge clause, but such a clause is effective only if the later chargeholder has actual notice of the clause. It can be argued that this restriction on the company's ability to deal with its asset—by double charging—is contrary to the whole nature of a floating charge, which supposedly allows a company freedom to deal with the charged asset. Floating chargees are also experimenting with automatic crystallisation clauses, which seek to provide that if a company attempts to charge an asset subject to a floating charge, the charge automatically crystallises (without any intervention on the part of the chargeholder) and becomes fixed, thus retaining its priority over the new charge. The efficacy of such clauses is not yet settled.

There are three further drawbacks of a floating charge as compared to a fixed charge. First, a floating charge ranks behind preferential debts on winding up. Second, it attaches only to assets of the relevant class which belong to the company. Consequently, where a floating chargee has a charge over raw materials to be used in production, he may find that the supplier of the goods has retained title to them until he is paid (a retention of title clause), thus allowing him to remove them, if not paid, from the company's premises and out of the grasp of the floating charge (*Aluminium Industries BV v Romalpa Aluminium Ltd* (1976); *Clough Mill Ltd v Martin* (1985); *Hendy Lennox Industrial Engines Ltd v Grahame Pullick Ltd* (1984)). Similarly, goods are not company assets susceptible to the clutch of a floating charge if they are subject to a lien or a trust or have been leased. Third, a floating charge created within 12 months of winding up (or two years if the chargeholder is a connected person) is invalid (s 245 IA 1986) unless the company was solvent at the time the charge was granted. If a charge is *prima facie* invalidated by s 245 IA 1986, it will remain valid to the extent of any consideration provided for the charge. Hence, if a company negotiates a loan facility of £100,000 secured by floating charge six months before liquidation and at liquidation the company has used £30,000 of the facility, then the charge is valid to the extent of £30,000. In contrast, if the company owed X £100,000 and six months before liquidation granted a floating charge to secure that loan, all the security would be invalid—no new consideration would have been provided by X.

(b) Lo Cost Loans (LL) and Finger Foods (FF)

Assuming that LL's charge is properly registered, LL has a charge, which is expressed to be fixed, over the book debts of FF which provides security for the loan. If the charge is indeed fixed, LL could require FF's creditors to pay it directly and would not suffer any of the disadvantages of floating charges outlined above, for example, lack of priority over preferential creditors and any expenses incurred by a liquidator if FF was to go into insolvent liquidation. Hence, LL hopes that its charge is fixed so that if FF went into liquidation it could instruct debtors to pay it directly, thus ensuring that these funds did not pass into the hands of FF's liquidator. The critical issue is whether it is possible to create a fixed charge over book debts and, if it is, whether LL has successfully created a fixed charge.

In *Siebe Gorman & Co Ltd v Barclays Bank Ltd* (1979), it was accepted that it was possible to create a fixed charge over book debts. However, as indicated above, the fact that the parties have called the charge 'fixed' is not conclusive of the status of the charge. Thus, both in this case and in *Re Brightlife Ltd* (1987) it was held that if the company granting the charge was free to collect the debts and use the proceeds without restriction, then the charge was floating. In *Re New Bullas Trading Ltd* (1994), the court had been willing to distinguish between the book debts prior to collection (which could be subject to a fixed charge) and the debts once collected, at which point the sums received were subject only to a floating charge. *Bullas* was disapproved in *Re Brumark Investments Ltd (2000)* and overruled by the House of Lords in *National Westminster Bank plc v Spectrum plus Ltd (2005)*. The current view is that the courts must seek to determine what the parties intended but not necessarily give effect to that intention; ultimately it is a question of categorisation by reference to the law. The courts should apply the 'tests' set out in *Re Yorkshire Woolcombers Association Ltd (1907)*. Hence, it seems that where the contract of charge contemplates that the company will be able to deal with the assets covered by the charge without reference to the chargee, then the charge is likely to be floating. In contrast, where the assets can be dealt with only after being released from the charge by the chargee, then it is probably a fixed charge. In *Re Brumark* the charge purported to be fixed in respect of uncollected book debts and floating once the sums were collected. The Privy Council was not willing to treat uncollected book debts as subject to a fixed charge unless the party having the benefit of the security had placed one of two possible restrictions on the chargor. To be fixed, either:

• the chargor must be prohibited from collecting the book debt itself or realising it by assignment without the consent of the secured party; or

• the chargor must pay the proceeds of book debts it collects into a blocked account that is controlled by the secured party and actually operated as a blocked account.

It was argued in *Re Brumark* and *Spectrum Plus* that (as in *Bullas*) it was possible to split the book debts into uncollected debts and proceeds and have different charges over the two. However, the Privy Council in *Re Brumark* and the House of Lords in *Spectrum Plus* held that a restriction on sale or transfer of the book debt would not be sufficient to create a fixed charge if the chargor remained free to collect the book debts and use the proceeds without any restriction.

Given these cases, has LL done sufficient to ensure that the charge is indeed fixed? The money collected when book debts were paid was to be paid into a special account and FF was not able to assign the proceeds of book debts—this would tend to support the view that the charge was fixed. However, FF had freedom to deal with the sums collected until given instructions to the contrary by LL. Given the weight placed upon freedom to deal with the charged asset expressed in *Re Brumark* and *Spectrum Plus*, it may well be that this freedom is fatal to LL's case and the charge would be treated as floating, with all the disadvantages which follow if FF were to become insolvent.

Question 43

Conservative Ltd had been experiencing severe financial difficulties since early 2002 but its directors, John and Kenneth, continued to trade, hoping that the company's trading position would improve, although they thought it unlikely that the company would be able to pay its debts unless there was a massive upturn in business. They gave up the struggle and called a meeting on 1 June 2003 to wind up the company.

Conservative Ltd has assets of £34,000. Additionally, its plant and machinery has an estimated value of £22,000. The company's liabilities are:

(a) £25,000 loan owed to Big Bank plc secured by a fixed charge, created in March 2001 and duly registered, over plant and machinery;

(b) £15,000 overdraft owed to Small Bank Ltd secured by a floating charge over the company's assets and undertaking, created in August 2001 and duly registered;

(c) £20,000 owing to employees (one month's salary for 20 workers); and

(d) £21,000 owed to sundry trade creditors.

In November 2002, Kenneth negotiated the sale of property to the company, for which he was paid a commission by the vendor, thereby making a profit of £8,000; he has not, so far, disclosed this profit to John or the shareholders.

Liquidation costs are likely to be around £5,000.

Advise the liquidator on any relevant issues of company law and indicate which creditors will be paid.

Answer plan

The usual issues arise—how can the assets of the company be augmented (actions against directors, etc) and how should the assets be distributed? Consider each debt in turn to determine its validity and conclude with a rank order for payment.

Answer

On the appointment of a liquidator, the powers of the directors of a company cease, except insofar as they are permitted to act either by the company in general meeting or the liquidator. The liquidator has to comply with a complex web of procedures, but his principal obligation can be summarised by reference to s 143 of the Insolvency Act (IA) 1986 (albeit that this section only applies to companies being wound up by the court), which is 'to secure that the assets of the company are got in, realised and distributed to the company's creditors and, if there is a surplus, to the persons entitled to it'. In carrying out this duty, the liquidator must maximise the assets before determining who receives any money.

▌SWELLING THE ASSETS

In addition to seeking contributions from shareholders who hold partly paid shares and pursuing legal actions against third parties, the liquidator of Conservative Ltd might wish to consider whether he can recover any sums from the directors of the company. Consider first the contract negotiated by Kenneth. The House of Lords in *Aberdeen Rly Co v Blaikie Bros (1854)* ruled that a director could not benefit directly or indirectly from a contract made by his company. This has been modified to provide that a director cannot benefit from a contract between himself and his company or between his company and a third party without making *adequate disclosure* of his own interest. Disclosure in this company could have been achieved by disclosure to the board (because the company has Art 85 of Table A), but the consequences of failing to disclose to the shareholders or, where permissible, the board are the same. If there has been inadequate disclosure, the company is allowed to rescind the contract (where the director has received a direct benefit and rescission is still possible) or make the director liable to account for any indirect benefits (as in this case). In this case, the liquidator should seek to recover the £8,000 from Kenneth.

Another possibility which the liquidator might pursue is an action against the directors for wrongful trading. The concept of wrongful trading was introduced by s 214 IA 1986 and it allows a court to declare a director liable to contribute to the assets of the company if the director knew, or ought to have concluded, that there was no reasonable prospect of the company avoiding insolvent liquidation and he did not take every step he ought to have taken to minimise the potential loss to the company's creditors. Thus, if this is an insolvent liquidation, the liquidator can seek a court order for one or more directors of the company to contribute to the assets of the company. Section 214 IA 1986 does not authorise an order requiring a director to contribute towards the costs of liquidation or post-liquidation debts. An order is to contribute to the assets of the company and the section does not authorise an order that a particular creditor be paid, nor only those creditors whose debts were incurred after the director should have known that the company would go into insolvent liquidation (*Re Purpoint Ltd (1991)*). John and/or Kenneth cannot be liable under s 214 IA 1986 unless they knew or ought to have concluded that insolvency could not be avoided *and* they failed to take every step to minimise loss to creditors which they ought to have taken. The section only envisages the imposition of liability on a director who has both not realised what he should have done and has not done what he should have done.

In determining whether a director has met the standard expected of him, s 214 IA 1986 provides guidance. Sub-section (4) says that a director is to be judged by what a reasonably diligent person with the 'general knowledge, skill and experience that may reasonably be expected of a person carrying out the same functions as are carried out by that director' (that is, the director potentially subject to an order) and the 'general knowledge, skill and experience' of the director whom it is sought to make liable. This somewhat obscure provision seems to mean that what a director should have known or done is to be judged by reference to a theoretical director who possesses those skills that may 'reasonably be expected' of a director, unless the director is better qualified than this theoretical director, when he is to be judged by reference to his own qualifications. Assuming that John and Kenneth have no special skills, they are to be judged by reference to the theoretical director who possesses those qualifications which can reasonably be expected from a director; the IA 1986 is silent as to what qualifications one can reasonably expect a director to possess and the courts have been reluctant to list what can be expected. It could be argued that cases suggest that one cannot reasonably expect a great deal: certainly, in *Re Elgindata Ltd (1991)*, the judge concluded that poor management was one of the risks which an investor had to bear, although in some cases on s 459 of the Companies Act (CA) 1985, mismanagement has been deemed to be unfair prejudice (see *Re Macro (Ipswich) Ltd (1994)*, for example).

In determining whether John and Kenneth did all that could be expected of them, consider the case of *Re Produce Marketing Consortium Ltd (1989)*. In *Re produce*, the company had traded successfully for some nine to 10 years and remained profitable until 1980. Thereafter, between 1980 and 1984, the company built up an overdraft, and in 1984 had an excess of liabilities over assets and a trading loss. Between 1984 and 1987, when insolvent liquidation ensued, the trading loss continued, as did the excess of liabilities over assets, but the overdraft approximately halved due to an increase in indebtedness to the company's principal supplier. By February 1987, one of the directors realised that liquidation was inevitable but the company was allowed to trade until October, the decision being justified as allowing disposal of the company's supplies of perishable goods which were held in cold store. Knox J found that the directors should have concluded by July 1986 that liquidation was inevitable because, although accounts were not available until January 1987, their knowledge of the business was such that they must have realised that turnover was down and that the gap between assets and liabilities must have increased. Since the IA 1986 provides that the directors are to be judged by reference to what they know and what they ought to know, Knox J held that they ought to have known the financial results for the year ending 1985 in July 1986 at the latest, so that the fact that these results were not known until 1987 was no excuse. Moreover, the directors had failed to take all steps to minimise loss—the directors had not limited their dealings to running down the company's stocks in cold store, even if this was a justified step. Knox J held that both directors must contribute £75,000 to the assets of the company, this being the loss which could have been averted by speedy liquidation. It could be argued that John and Kenneth were even more reprehensible, since they seemed to be aware that the company was unable to meet its obligations and seem to have done nothing to minimise the company's debts. The loans taken out in 2001 were presumably to prop up the business and there seems to have been no rational business plan operated by the directors to improve the company's position. Assuming that John and Kenneth have funds, an action for wrongful trading seems appropriate. Under s 10 of the Company Directors Disqualification Act 1986, the court can make a disqualification order against a director who has been subject to an order under s 214 IA 1986.

PAYING THE CREDITORS

Let us assume that some money has been recovered from the directors. To whom should it, and the other corporate funds, be paid? Consider the four competing claims. Note that if any of them should have been registered and were not, then they become unsecured debts (s 395 CA 1985), that transactions at undervalue or constituting a preference may not be enforceable (ss 238–41 IA 1986) and that a floating charge created within a specified period of winding up may be void (s 245 IA 1986). In practice, secured creditors dispose of the asset to which their charge relates and account for any surplus to the liquidator, but, in theory, the realisation of a charged asset can be left to the liquidator.

Big Bank plc lent the company £25,000 secured by a fixed charge, duly registered, some 14 or 15 months before liquidation commenced. If this charge is valid, the proceeds of the sale of plant and machinery will be paid to Big Bank, leaving them with a projected shortfall of £3,000 in respect of which they are an unsecured creditor. There seems to be no evidence that this charge was a preference and, even if it was, the IA 1986 only permits the setting aside of preferential transactions entered into in the six months prior to liquidation (unless the bank was a connected person, which it is not). Big Bank drop out of the liquidator's sums except to the extent of £3,000.

Small Bank Ltd lent the company £15,000 (the overdraft), secured by a floating charge, duly registered, some 9 or 10 months prior to the liquidation. Section 245 IA 1986 provides that a floating charge created within 12 months of insolvent liquidation (the bank is not a connected person; if it were, the period would be two years) is invalid (the debt remains valid but unsecured) *except* to the extent of any money paid to the company after the creation of the charge and in consideration for the charge. Since Small Bank Ltd lent money to the company, it seems likely that they fall within the exception and that the charge is valid. Thus, the only issue for the liquidator to determine is whether the overdraft arose after the charge and is thus secured or whether all or part of it arose prior to the charge, in which case that part would be unsecured. It seems unlikely that the overdraft arose prior to August 2001. Even if the company had an overdraft at that date of £15,000 or more, the case of Re Yeovil Glove (1965) would probably protect the bank. In Yeovil Glove, the company had an overdraft of around £66,000 and the company's bank sought security, which the company granted by creating a floating charge over its assets. Within a year, the company went into insolvent liquidation, having at that time an overdraft of around £66,000. The issue for the court was whether the overdraft at liquidation and at the time that the charge was created should be treated as the same overdraft—if they were, then the charge was invalid (created within 12 months of winding up and no new money provided to the company). The Court of Appeal held that, since the company had been allowed to operate its bank account during the period between the granting of the charge and the liquidation (some £110,000 had been paid in and drawn out), the overdraft existing at the time of liquidation was not to be regarded as the same debt as the overdraft in existence at the granting of the charge. The money paid in after the charge was granted and before liquidation paid off the original overdraft even if the company then drew out an equal amount of money from its account—those drawings created a new debt. Hence, the liquidation overdraft was a post-charge debt which provided new money to the company and was secured. Thus in this case, if the overdraft existed prior to the charge and the company was allowed to continue using its account after the charge was granted, *Re Yeovil Glove* would apply so that, as money flowed through the account, the old (unsecured) loan would be discharged to be replaced by a new (secured) loan. Thus, Small Bank Ltd has a claim over the assets of the company to the extent of any consideration provided for the charge—probably the full sum.

Small Bank Ltd would, however, be paid after any preferential creditors (s 175 IA 1986). The employees of the company are preferential creditors in respect of unpaid wages up to a maximum of £800 per employee (s 386 and Sched 6 IA 1986). Thus, each employee must be paid £800 (£16,000 total) before any other creditors are paid by the liquidator. The balance of their unpaid wages is an unsecured debt.

Thus, the liquidator should pay the costs of the liquidation (£5,000) (the priority of recoverable expenses is contained in the Insolvency Rules 1986), then the employees (£16,000), making a total of £21,000. This leaves assets of £13,000, which must be paid to Small Bank Ltd (owed £15,000), leaving Small Bank Ltd £2,000 out of pocket. If the liquidator obtains any money from John and Kenneth, this is used first to pay Small Bank Ltd its £2,000 and the remainder is divided between Big Bank Ltd (£3,000), the employees (£4,000) and the unsecured creditors, namely, trade creditors. The unsecured creditors rank equally and each will receive the same percentage of their debt, according to the funds available.

▌NOTE

The facts of the question are set prior to the changes introduced by the Enterprise Act (2002) which took effect in respect of any 'new' Insolvency from 15 September 2003.

Question 44

In May 1999, Funfood Ltd, a company engaged in the manufacture of snack foods, borrowed £20,000 from D, the brother of one of the directors. This loan was expressed to be repayable on demand. In August 2001, the company created a floating charge over its assets and made an undertaking in favour of ABC Bank to secure the company's overdraft (then standing at £48,000) up to a maximum of £100,000. The floating charge, which was duly registered, prohibited the company from granting a further floating charge over all or any part of its assets or undertaking without first giving notice to ABC Bank, and further provided that the granting of any such floating charge entitled the bank to give notice to Funfood, which notice would crystallise the bank's charge. In December 2001, the company borrowed £60,000 from E. This loan was secured by a fixed charge over the company's factory; the charge was duly registered. In January 2002, D threatened to recall his loan unless it was secured. The company repaid the loan and D then lent the same amount of money to the company; the loan was secured by a floating charge which was duly registered.

On 1 June 2002, the Inland Revenue, who are owed £16,000 in unpaid PAYE contributions, presented a petition to wind up the company. At that date, the company's overdraft stood at £104,000, the extra £4,000 over the agreed limit having been borrowed to pay staff wages. The company's factory is worth £85,000 and the other assets of the company are likely to realise about £42,000. Liquidation costs are estimated at £6,000.

Advise the liquidator.

Answer plan

In any question of this type, the possible issues are how the assets of the company can be augmented (actions against directors, etc) and how the assets should be distributed. Primarily, this question addresses the second issue. When considering the payment of creditors, the liquidator must check the validity of each claim and, where two creditors claim a charge over the same asset, which is insufficient to satisfy both debts, determine which has the prior claim.

Answer

While the obligations of a liquidator are twofold—to gather in the assets of the company and, where possible, augment them, and to pay out the assets to the appropriate claimants—this question does not appear to raise any particular issues relating to the acquisition or augmentation of the company's assets. It may be that the directors were reckless in trading in a parlous state for so long, so that an action for wrongful trading (s 214 of the Insolvency Act (IA) 1986) might be apposite, but the main thrust of the question is towards distribution of such assets as there are. In practice, secured creditors dispose of the asset to which their charge relates and account for any surplus to the liquidator, but, in theory, the realisation of a charged asset can be left to the liquidator and, if the liquidator disputes the validity of a charge, the chargee cannot simply seize the asset and sell it.

VALIDITY OF CLAIM OR CHARGE

Before considering any question of payment, the liquidator must check that all the claims lodged, and any charge relied upon, are valid. Consider each claim in turn. It can be assumed that, since the company is a trading company, it has an implied power to borrow (*General Auction Estate & Monetary Co v Smith (1891)*) so that, even if the company has no express power to borrow, the borrowings are not *ultra vires*. It can be assumed that the board has the power to initiate borrowings and there seems no question of unauthorised loans being entered into. If the loans were *ultra vires* or negotiated by a person lacking authority, the creditor would probably be protected by ss 35 and 35A of the Companies Act (CA) 1985.

First in time (May 1999) is D's loan, which appears to be valid but is unsecured. D is, provisionally, an unsecured creditor and ranks at the bottom of any list of creditors when the assets are being distributed. D reappears later.

Second is the floating charge granted by the company to ABC Bank to secure the overdraft facility (August 2001). The charge was registered so that the loan and the charge appear to be valid. However, s 245 IA 1986 provides that a floating charge created within the relevant period is invalid unless the company could pay its debts at the time the charge was granted (that is, was solvent) or s 245(2) IA 1986 applies. The relevant period is within 12 months of the winding up (s 245(3) IA 1986), so that the charge of August 2001 falls within it and, unless the company was solvent at that date, the charge is invalid except to the extent that s 245(2) IA 1986 applies. This section says that a charge granted within the relevant period is valid to the extent that money was paid to the company in consideration for the creation of the charge. Consequently, £56,000 is secured by the charge (£104,000 − £48,000), which gives the bank a claim on the assets of the company in priority to an unsecured creditor. Indeed, since the £4,000 over the agreed overdraft limit is used to pay wages, it is a preferential debt insofar as it was used to pay employees who could have claimed any unpaid wages as a preferential debt, that is, the bank is subrogated to the position of the employees (para 11 of Sched 6 IA 1986).

The remaining £48,000 may also fall within s 245(2) IA 1986 even though the company's overdraft stood at that sum when the charge was granted, if the principle enunciated in *Re Yeovil Glove Ltd (1965)* applies. In *Re Yeovil Glove*, the company had an overdraft of around £66,000 and the company's bank sought security, which the company granted by creating a floating charge over its assets. Within a year, the company went into insolvent liquidation, having at that time an overdraft of around £66,000; the facts resemble the current case. The issue for the court was whether the overdraft at liquidation and at the time the charge was created should be treated as the same overdraft—if they were, then the charge was invalid (created within 12 months of winding up and no new money provided to the company). The Court of Appeal held that, since the company had been allowed to operate its bank account during the period between the granting of the charge and the liquidation (some £110,000 had been paid in and drawn out), the liquidation overdraft was not to be regarded as the same debt as the overdraft in existence at the granting of the charge. The money paid in after the charge was granted and before liquidation paid off the original overdraft. This was the case even if the company had then drawn out of its account a sum equal to that it had paid in—those drawings created a new debt. Hence, the liquidation overdraft provided new money to the company and the charge was valid.

Thus, in this case, if the company has paid at least £48,000 into its account after the charge was granted and was then allowed to draw that sum out before liquidation commenced, *Re Yeovil Glove* would apply. Consequently, as money flowed through the account, the old (unsecured) loan would be discharged, to be replaced by a new (secured) loan. It seems that £100,000 is secured by the floating charge.

The bank's floating charge contained a restriction on the company's freedom to deal with the assets subject to the charge. This restriction, if broken, entitled the bank to serve notice and thereby crystallise the floating charge, that is, turn it into a fixed charge. However, this restriction applies only to future floating charges, so that it is unaffected by the fixed charge in favour of E. Moreover, the ability of the bank to crystallise its charge on the creation of future floating charges is not an *automatic* crystallisation clause—it merely gives the bank power to serve notice and thus crystallise its charge. ABC Bank appears not to have exercised this power in respect of D's floating charge. The effect of having two floating charges over the same property (if D's charge is valid) is discussed below.

Third in time is the charge in favour of E. This charge was registered and, being fixed, it does not fall within s 245 IA 1986 and therefore appears to be valid. The only doubt about the validity of E's security is raised by s 239 IA 1986. This section provides that, where a company has, within the relevant period, given a preference to a person, the liquidator can apply to the court challenging the alleged preference. The court, if its finds that a preference has been given, can make such order as it sees fit for restoring the position which would be operative but for the preference. Thus, if this is a preference, the liquidator could seek to have the security set aside. The charge is within the relevant period—six months prior to the onset of winding up (s 240 IA 1986)—but is it a preference? There is scant case law on this provision but it seems that the liquidator must establish that the company desired to prefer E, that is, wished him to be treated more favourably than other creditors. Since E would no doubt have refused to make the loan but for the charge, he is not being preferred over other existing creditors—it simply is a condition of the loan (see the parallel case of *Re MC Bacon Ltd (1990)*). Thus, E can sell the factory to discharge his loan and give any surplus to the liquidator, where it will form part of the assets of the company. E can be ignored by the liquidator in determining priorities, since he has been paid in full.

In January 2002, D threatened to recall his loan, which the company duly repaid but replaced it with an identical loan secured by a floating charge. The loan, like the 2001 loan, is a valid debt, but is the charge valid? If it is a floating charge created within 12 months of winding up, it is invalid unless the company was solvent, which is doubtful, except to the extent of any consideration provided for the creation of the charge. While, technically, D has lent the company money, he has simply recycled the existing loan and not provided any new funds. In such a case, the court has the power to disregard the alleged consideration as not being *bona fide* (*Re Destone Fabrics Ltd (1941)* is similar to this case) and invalidate the charge. Thus, D remains an unsecured creditor. Had the floating charge been validated by s 245(2) IA 1986, it might anyway have been regarded as a preference contrary to s 239 IA 1986. If D's charge had been valid, he would have been in competition with ABC Bank, which also has a floating charge over the assets and undertaking of the company. As the company's assets are insufficient to satisfy both claims, then, in such cases, the first charge has priority (floating charges rank on creation).

The final sums to be considered are the unpaid PAYE contributions and the liquidation costs—both are valid.

PRIORITY OF PAYMENT

Having determined which claims are valid, the liquidator must determine whom he should pay and in what order. E has dropped out of the picture, leaving the liquidator with £67,000 at his disposal and claims of £140,000, so that those at the bottom of the rank order will receive nothing unless all claims are required to abate equally. Funfood Ltd, in collecting PAYE contributions from its employees, was acting as a tax collector for the government. Withholding taxes of this type are treated as preferential debts and preferential debts are payable in priority to all other debts (s 175 IA 1986)—thus, £16,000 is payable to the revenue, leaving £51,000, of which £4,000 is payable to ABC Bank as a subrogated creditor; which leaves £47,000. The liquidator can then deduct his costs, in accordance with s 175(2) IA 1986 and the Insolvency Rules 1986, which leaves £41,000. *Re Barleycorn Enterprises Ltd (1970)* established that liquidation costs take priority over floating charges which is payable to ABC Bank in respect of its floating charge over the assets of the company. However, the House of Lords in *Buchler v Talbot, Re Leyland Daf Ltd (2004)* overruled the Court of Appeal decision in *Re Barleycorn Enterprises Ltd* (1970) and ruled that liquidation expenses were not payable out of the floating charge realisations in the hands of the receiver. However, the general effect of the decision in *Leyland Daf* is likely to be reversed on the coming into force of an proposed amendment to the IA 1986 by the Companies Act 2006. Assuming the previous position, that leaves ABC Bank £59,000 out of pocket and D with nothing at all. Had there been any surplus after payment of all the creditors, that sum would have been repaid to the shareholders.

NOTE

The Enterprise Act 2002, by amending the IA 1986, has abolished the category of preferential creditor except for employees. However, the amendment only takes effect in respect of any insolvency after 15 September 2003.

Question 45

You have been appointed liquidator of an insolvent company, Reindeer Ltd, which was founded by Rudolf and which has been engaged in the manufacture of novelties for festivals. The majority of the issued share capital of Reindeer Ltd is owned by Rudolf, who was the sole director of the company, with the remainder being owned by his brother, Gandalf.

What, if anything, should be done about the following, which the liquidation has revealed:

(a) A year prior to the commencement of liquidation, Reindeer Ltd sold its factory to Elk Ltd for £110,000 (which was its book value) and then leased the premises back from Elk Ltd. Elk Ltd, which is controlled and run by Gandalf, has recently contracted to sell the property for £0.75 million.

(b) Shortly before your appointment, the company redeemed a floating charge which had been granted to Christmas Bank plc six months earlier as security for the company's overdraft, which was guaranteed by Gandalf.

(c) The company collected a substantial amount of income tax from the employees which should have been remitted to the Inland Revenue; at Gandalf's suggestion, the money was used to pay off other creditors of the company who were pressing for payment.

Answer plan

A number of issues for the liquidator to consider, which, as is usual, includes swelling the assets of the company (sale of property, redemption of floating charge) and determining the distribution of the assets (preferential debts). In addition, appraise the conduct of Rudolf and Gandalf and consider whether an action for disqualification should be commenced, and its impact if successful.

Answer

As liquidator, you have been asked to consider a number of issues which have emerged in the course of the liquidation of Reindeer Ltd. The substantive issues can be treated separately.

(a) Sale of property

One duty cast upon a liquidator is to augment the company's assets available for distribution to creditors. In this case, the company has sold an asset at a price which appears to be an undervalue. A number of possibilities arise. Can this transaction be set aside, can the profit on the resale be recovered from Rudolf, Gandalf or Elk Ltd, or can damages be recovered for a foolish commercial decision or for any other reason?

First, it must be seen whether the rise in value of the property sold is attributable to some external factors; if this is the case, the company was unlucky but the transaction is not actionable. If, however, the difference between the sale price and the new price is not so attributable, you may wish to pursue the issue of the sale further. A sale by a company to a third party cannot generally be rescinded merely because the company could have got a better price for the asset, but, if the sale falls within s 238 of the Insolvency Act (IA) 1986, a court can make an order to restore the company to the position it would have been in had it not entered into the transaction. Section 238 IA 1986 covers the situation where the company sells an asset at an undervalue, but the section is applicable only if the transaction falls within the relevant period defined in s 240 IA 1986. The relevant period for a transferee who is a connected person is two years, whereas in other cases it is six months. Thus, the critical issue is whether the purchaser, Elk Ltd, is a connected person. Section 249 IA 1986, which defines 'connected person', treats directors and shadow directors and associates as connected to the company. Elk Ltd is neither a director nor a shadow director of Reindeer Ltd, although Gandalf may well be a shadow director (a person in accordance with whose directions the directors of the company are accustomed to act, s 741 of the Companies Act (CA) 1985), since he seems to play a large role in the affairs of the company. If Gandalf is a shadow director, it might be that the court would lift the veil of incorporation and treat Elk Ltd and Gandalf as one and the same for the purposes of s 238 IA 1986 (a similar approach was manifested in *Aveling Barford v Perion Ltd (1989)*). Alternatively, if Elk Ltd is an associate of Reindeer Ltd, the two year statutory period will also operate. Section 435 IA 1986 defines 'associate' in some detail, but the upshot is that, if Rudolf controls one company and Gandalf another, then Elk Ltd is an associate of Reindeer Ltd either because they are brothers or because Gandalf is a shadow director of Reindeer Ltd. Thus, the sale at the undervalue can be set aside unless Reindeer Ltd could pay its debts at the time of the sale. This seems the simplest way of dealing with the sale of property, but if, for some reason, s 238 IA 1986 is inapplicable, other routes may be open to you.

A liquidator may sue a director if he has broken the duties cast upon him (there is no *locus* problem since the power to run the company passes to the liquidator on winding up), although it will not be worth doing so if Rudolf has no money. Is selling an asset at an undervalue a breach of duty? Rudolf, in authorising the sale, may have been negligent, but it is unlikely that simple negligence from which he has not benefited would render him liable for breach of the common law duty of care and skill. The conventional formulation of the nature and extent of this duty is that given by Romer J in *Re City Equitable Fire Insurance Co Ltd (1925)*, in which he held, *inter alia*, that a director need display only such skill as may reasonably be expected from a person of his knowledge and experience. It is plain that, if Rudolf has made a misguided but foolish decision, he will not be negligent. Arguably, trying to raise funds by selling an asset is perfectly sensible, although failure to have the property revalued seems very misguided. The sale is not to a director, and so the sale itself cannot be a breach of fiduciary duty by Rudolf (it is not clear whether shadow directors owe a fiduciary duty) if he acted *bona fide*. However, directors are supposed to exercise an independent judgment and, if it can be shown that Rudolf simply implemented Gandalf's instructions without paying proper regard to the interests of the company, that might be a breach of duty.

Whether Gandalf can incur liability if s 238 IA 1986 does not apply is uncertain. He may well be a shadow director. There are no cases discussing whether the common law rules on company contracts benefiting directors apply to shadow directors, but if they do apply, there can be no question of approving this sale if it is a misappropriation of a corporate asset. If a director does so appropriate, he is liable as a constructive trustee and must return the property; constructive trusteeship could also be imposed on Elk Ltd if it had knowingly received misappropriated property. While the common law position is uncertain, there is no doubt that the statutory provisions on substantial property transactions are applicable to such persons. Thus, if, as seems possible, he is a shadow director, s 320 CA 1985 will apply to any sale of property to Elk Ltd if that company is 'connected' with Gandalf, since the asset is a non-cash asset of requisite value (over £100,000). Section 346 CA 1985 defines a connected person (the definition differs from the provision in the IA 1986); it includes a company with which a shadow director is associated, so there is no doubt that, since he controls Elk Ltd, Gandalf and Elk Ltd are connected for the purposes of s 320 CA 1985. Section 320 CA 1985 does not prevent Gandalf (via Elk Ltd) from buying a corporate asset from Reindeer Ltd but does require the transaction to be approved by the shareholders in general meeting, and the apparent lack of such a resolution in this case *prima facie* renders the sale voidable (s 322 CA 1985).

While all the shareholders in Reindeer Ltd knew about the transaction, this is probably not a case where knowledge would be regarded as approval. While there are bars to the operation of s 320 CA 1985, there is no statutory time limit on the ability of the company to rescind an improper transaction (a possible advantage over s 238 IA 1986). Further, s 317 CA 1985 requires a director or shadow director to make adequate disclosure of his interest in any contract between himself and his company. Failure to disclose his interest in Elk Ltd, even though known to Rudolf, appears to be a breach of s 317 CA 1985, which gives rise to a criminal penalty.

It should also be noted that, in the case of *Aveling Barford v Perion Ltd (1989)*, the facts of which resemble this case, the sale of an asset by the claimant company to the defendant company, which was controlled by the majority shareholder of the claimant company, at a gross undervalue was held to be an unauthorised return of capital and incapable of ratification. The defendant company was held liable to account as a constructive trustee.

(b) Redemption of the floating charge

A floating charge granted within 12 months of the commencement of a winding up is invalid, unless the company was solvent at the time, except to the extent of any consideration provided for the charge (s 245 IA 1986). Consequently, the floating charge in favour of the bank was potentially invalid. However, by the time of winding up, the debt which the charge was designed to secure had been repaid. While the charge would have been invalid, the underlying debt would not have been affected by s 245 IA 1986, so that where, as here, the debt has been repaid, the potential invalidity of the charge is irrelevant (*Mace Builders Ltd v Lunn (1987)*). However, a debt paid within six months of winding up may be challenged as being a preference contrary to s 239 IA 1986. This section provides that, where a company has, within the relevant time, given a preference to a person, the liquidator can apply to the court, which can make such order as it sees fit for restoring the position which would be operative but for the preference. Thus, if this repayment is a preference, the liquidator could seek to have the security set aside.

Is this a preference? There is scant case law on this provision, but it seems that the liquidator must establish that the company desired to prefer a creditor *or* a guarantor of one of the company's debts, that is, intended that person to be treated more favourably than other creditors. It seems not improbable that Gandalf would be regarded as having been preferred and the court could make such order as it saw fit, for example, recover the money paid to the bank and leave it to pursue Gandalf if Reindeer Ltd does not pay. As noted above, Gandalf is probably a shadow director and his conduct in seeking to prefer himself is a factor to be considered in deciding whether to seek his disqualification.

(c) Non-payment of withholding tax

Reindeer Ltd, in collecting income tax from employees (under the PAYE scheme), was acting as a tax collector for the government. Withholding taxes of this type are treated as preferential debts and preferential debts are payable in priority to all other debts (s 175 IA 1986)—thus, the sums collected but not remitted are a first charge on the assets of the company. Failure to account for taxes already deducted has been treated as an important, but not a crucial, factor in determining whether a director should be disqualified. Section 1 of the Company Directors Disqualification Act (CDDA) 1986 permits a court to disqualify a person from being a director, or being directly or indirectly concerned in the management of a company, in a number of prescribed circumstances. The majority of reported cases involve s 6 CDDA 1986, which provides that a person shall be disqualified (for a minimum of two years) from corporate management where he is or has been a director (or shadow director) of a company which has become insolvent *and* his conduct as a director of that, or any other, company makes him unfit to be concerned in company management. Acting as a director, etc, while disqualified is a criminal offence punishable on indictment, by a fine and/or by imprisonment for up to two years.

Judges determining cases on s 6 CDDA 1986 have stressed that the Act, while designed to protect the public and while not a purely penal statute, can result in penal consequences for a disqualified person, in that a person may be precluded from trading through a limited company—Gandalf, for example, if disqualified would, unless exempt, have to give up his directorship of Elk Ltd. Consequently, it is not surprising that judges have recognised these possible practical consequences, while seeking to give effect to Parliament's intention to limit the activities of unfit directors, in interpreting the Act's provisions. Factors taken into account (see also Sched 1 of the Act) include breach of fiduciary duty, misuse of assets, responsibility for breaches of mandatory requirements and, where the company is insolvent (necessary for s 6 of the Act), the extent of the director's responsibility for the insolvency. The leading case on s 6 CDDA 1986 is *Re Sevenoaks Stationery (Retail) Ltd (1990)*, in which the Court of Appeal held that the words 'unfit to be concerned in the management of a company' should be treated as ordinary English words, which should be simple to apply in most cases. Each case turned on its own facts, said the court, but a director need not display total incompetence to be unfit.

The court approved earlier cases which had held that simple commercial misjudgment should not merit disqualification while a lack of commercial probity and an appropriate degree of incompetence could do so (see, for example, *Re Lo-Line Electric Motors Ltd (1988)*). In *Sevenoaks*, five years' disqualification ensued. In *Re Vintage Hallmark plc (2006)*, the maximum period of 15 years' disqualification was imposed on two directors of a public company who had falsely and knowingly misrepresented subscribers of shares in the company the value of the assets of the company to and who had persuaded investors to invest in wines and spirits with promises of impossible high returns. The directors had been 'recklessly indifferent and grossly negligent' in the course of their activities and were 'utterly unfit' to be concerned in the management of a company.

Since each case turns on its own facts, it is impossible to state definitively that any member of the board will be disqualified, but Gandalf's conduct seems to warrant the penalty. The appropriate period for disqualification was discussed in *Sevenoaks*, in which Dillon LJ suggested that a 10–15 year disqualification should be reserved for particularly serious cases (for example, where this was a second disqualification) and 2–5 for not very serious cases, leaving 6–10 years for serious cases which do not merit the top bracket.

▌NOTE

With effect to any new insolvency after 15 September 2003, the Crown loses its status as a preferential creditor. The employees' status remains unchanged. These changes were brought about by the Enterprise Act 2002, amending the IA 1986.

Question 46

The business of Unfairpack Ltd is the supply of Christmas food and drink hampers to consumers who deposit money with the company in advance of receipt of the hampers. To finance the business, the company obtained a loan from Business Bank plc in 2003 which was secured against the company's entire undertaking, with the title deeds of various properties being left in the company's possession. The instrument creating the charge expressly stated that Unfairpack Ltd was not to create any mortgages or charges upon its properties in priority thereto. In 2004, as security for a loan from Commerce Bank plc, Unfairpack Ltd deposited the title deeds of its distribution depot with Commerce Bank plc. Nine months prior to liquidation, Unfairpack Ltd received further finance from Trade Bank plc, the loan being secured against the company's book debts.

In September 2006, Unfairpack Ltd was the subject of a winding up petition and the company went into liquidation. The liquidator seeks your advice as to the nature of the claims of the creditors of the company and the priority of each creditor. In addition to monies owing to Business Bank plc, Commerce Bank plc and Trade Bank plc, claims are being made by other creditors, including employees of the company for arrears of wages and salary, HM Revenue and Customs for unpaid tax and VAT and customers for the failure of the company to deliver hampers.

Advise the liquidator accordingly. Assume that any charge was registered at Companies House.

Answer plan

It will be necessary for the question to consider the nature of each creditor's claim and to provide an order of ranking in terms of the priority of each creditor. A consideration of the changes made by the Enterprise Act (EA) 2002 is likely to be required, as the date of the company's liquidation is after 15 September 2003, the date the amendments to the Insolvency Act (IA) 1986 by the EA 2002 were brought into effect.

Answer

Where a company decides to borrow money to expand its business, any creditor is likely to require security. Companies have two forms of security they can deploy—fixed charges, that is, a charge over a specified asset or property, or floating charges, that is, a charge over a class of asset, and current shareholders are largely unaffected by the type preferred. Both types of charge are subject to registration and, if not registered, are void (s 395(1) of the Companies Act (CA) 1985, although the underlying debt remains valid and becomes immediately repayable (s 395(2) CA 1985). Both types of charge may be set aside if the company goes into insolvent liquidation within a statutory period of the charge being created and the charge was designed to prefer one creditor over another (s 239 IA 1986). Further, floating charges can be declared invalid if caught by s 245 IA 1985.

▌FIXED CHARGES

A fixed charge may be legal or equitable. For example, if the company charges its real property to its bank by means of a mortgage, the bank has a fixed legal charge over that property. The bank will obtain the title deeds to the property, which effectively precludes the company from dealing with the property without the knowledge and consent of the bank. A fixed equitable charge is less formal and can be achieved by the deposit of title deeds, as in the case with Commerce Bank plc. A fixed charge holder does not claim against the general assets of the company on winding up, he simply claims against 'his' asset, provided that he has ensured that it is of adequate value and he is not in competition with other creditors for the same assets of the company. If the same asset has been used as security for a further loan, then a question of priority will arise. A fixed charge, generally, prevents the company from dealing with the charged asset without the consent of the charge holder and is, thus, an inappropriate form of security for assets which are constantly changing such as stock in trade.

FLOATING CHARGES

There is no statutory definition of a 'floating charge' and what the parties call 'the charge' is not conclusive evidence of its status (see *Re New Bullas Ltd (1993)*; *Agnew v Commissioner of Inland Revenue (2001)*; *National Westminster Bank plc v Spectrum Plus Ltd (2005)*, but judicial pronouncements have identified certain factors which are likely to be present if a charge is to be classified as a floating charge. These factors identified in *Government Stock Investment Co v Manila Rly Co Ltd (1897)* and *Illingworth v Houldsworth (1904)* are (a) that the charge is over a class of assets both present and future; (b) that the class is one which, in the ordinary course of business, changes periodically; and (c) that the charge leaves the company free to deal with the charged asset in the ordinary course of conducting the company's business (this freedom need not be absolute). The type of asset frequently subject to a floating charge is goods in the course of production, but it is possible, as in the case of Business Bank plc, for a floating charge to embrace the whole corporate enterprise (*Re Panama, New Zealand and Australian Royal Mail Co (1870)*).

NEGATIVE PLEDGE CLAUSES

Since a floating charge leaves a company free to deal with its assets, and dealing may include the creation of further charges, a company may grant a second fixed or floating charge over charged assets. This raises a question of priorities between such charges. As we have seen, a fixed charge will generally obtain priority even if there is notice (which registration provides) of the existence of the prior floating charge, since one of the features of a floating charge is that the company is free to deal with its charged asset. Logically, the same must be true where the second charge is also a floating charge. It could be argued that, where there is no restriction on the creation of later charges, the company's general freedom to deal with a charged asset allows the creation of a later floating charge with priority. Since there is the risk of a later charge obtaining priority, prudent charge holders (for example, Business Bank plc) commonly insert negative pledge clauses in their agreements with companies, a negative pledge clause being a clause specifically precluding the creation of a second charge with priority. Assuming that such clauses are deemed valid, the question that would need to be addressed is whether such clauses are effective. The first charge will retain priority only if the second charge holder has notice of the first charge (which is provided by registration) and of the restriction on the freedom to deal. There is no constructive notice, it seems, of a restriction (a restriction need not, at present, be registered) and, even if a charge holder has actual knowledge of a floating charge, this seems not to be notice of a restriction or to require the potential charge holder to make inquiries (*English and Scottish Mercantile Investment Co Ltd v Brunton (1892)*. Where, however, a potential (fixed) chargeholder (in this case, Commerce Bank plc) searches the register of charges and obtains actual knowledge of the charge and of any restriction registered with the charge, then Business Bank's claim will take priority over Commerce Bank's claim. In the question, the effectiveness of the negative pledge clause would prove to be as between Business Bank plc and Commerce Bank plc. The negative pledge clause would not be relevant to consider in respect of the relationship between Business Bank plc and Trade Bank, as Trade Bank plc has a floating charge (see book debts, below) and, as floating charges rank on creation, Business Bank plc would rank ahead of Trade Bank plc, irrespective of the negative pledge clause. A proposal in the Companies Act (CA) 1989 enabling the Secretary of State to have the power to require that negative pledge clauses to be part of the registered particulars, with deemed notice of such a clause, has not been implemented. As with the rest of the changes to the system of registration of charges introduced by the CA 1989, but not given effect, it is unlikely to be implemented in the future, given the suggested changes to the registration suggested by the Company Law Review Steering Group (2001) and the Law Commission (*Registration of Security Interests: Company Charges and Property other than Land*) (2002). In fact, the Companies Act 2006 abolishes the provisions of the CA 1989 relating to company charges, although this part of the Companies Act 2006 is not in force.

BOOK DEBTS

Book debts may be the subject matter of either a fixed charge or a floating charge. Whether a book debt is the subject matter of a fixed or floating charge depends on whether there are any restrictions contained in the charge contract on how the company can deal with the debts as they become extinguished. If, for example, the company must place the money in a separate bank account and is prevented from using it in the ordinary course of business, the charge created over the book debts would be described as a fixed charge (*Talby v Official Receiver (1888)*). However, in the absence of such restrictions, charges over book debts are regarded as floating charges (*Re Brightlife (1987)*; *Agnew v Commissioner of Inland Revenue (2001)*; *National Westminster Bank plc v Spectrum Plus Ltd (2005)*). Given that the question indicates that there are no restrictions present, the preferable view is that Business Bank plc's charge is a floating charge. In *National Westminster Bank plc v Spectrum Plus Ltd*, the House of Lords restated the general position that, in the absence of any restrictions, charges on book debts are regarded as floating charges. The

House of Lords also confirmed the view of the Privy Council in *Agnew v Commissioner of Inland Revenue* (2001) that a charge that states that it is a fixed charge over uncollected book debts and a floating charge over collected book debts is a floating charge, not a partly fixed charge and a partly floating charge. The charge placed no restriction on the use that could be made of the balance on the account as monies collected were paid in. The House of Lords held the charge was a floating charge and the fact that the charge was expressed as a fixed charge did not prevent the company drawing on the account. With reference to the question, assuming the instrument creating the charge over book debts contains no restrictions, Trade Bank plc's charge is a floating charge.

VOID CHARGES

Section 245 IA 1986 provides that a floating charge created within 12 months of the onset of insolvency is invalid, except to the extent of any money paid to the company after the creation of the charge and in consideration for the charge. (Where the creditor is a connected person, the relevant period is two years.) As Trade Bank plc provided 'further finance' to Unfairpack Ltd, it seems that the exception applies and that the floating charge over the book debts is a valid floating charge.

PRIORITY OF CLAIMS

Where a company goes into liquidation, the liquidator will need to rank the creditors in accordance with the priority of their claims and, where a company's liabilities are greater than its assets, it becomes important to ascertain which of the creditors will be satisfied and which will remain unsatisfied, in full or in part. The priority of creditors depends on a number of rules, including new or amended rules introduced by the EA 2002, with effect from 15 September 2003.

A fixed charge ranks over any floating charge including any earlier floating charge. This is because it is the nature of a floating charge that a company retains the freedom to grant further security over its assets in the ordinary course of business and this includes the company having the right to grant fixed charges (*Wheatley v Silkstone and Haigh Moor Coal Co (1885)*). As such, fixed charge holders, whether the fixed charge is created before or after a floating charge, take priority over the holder of the floating charge. Where there is more than one floating charge, such holders rank in accordance with creation, and it is immaterial if the second floating charge holder is given priority by the instrument creating the charge (*Re Benjamin Cope & Sons Ltd (1914)*; cf *Re Auto Bottle Makers Ltd (1926)*). Where there is a competing claim, fixed charges also rank on creation. Where the earlier charge prohibits the company from granting priority to any later charges, a subsequent fixed charge holder will take priority over the earlier floating charge, unless the subsequent fixed charge holder has notice of the prohibition (*Re Castell &*

Brown Ltd (1898); *English & Scottish Mercantile Investment Co v Brunton (1892))*. These clauses are known as negative pledge clauses. Mere registration of such a clause (as opposed to the charge) at Companies House as part of the particulars of registration does not constitute effective notice.

Assuming that Business Bank's negative pledge clause is ineffective, Commerce Bank's claim would rank first (the fixed charge over the warehouse). If, on realisation, the value of the warehouse is less than the amount owed, Commerce Bank plc would rank as an unsecured creditor for the balance. After the payment of the costs of liquidation, next in line, ranking equally, would be the creditors having a preferential debt in accordance with s 251 Enterprise Act 2002. (The decision of the House of Lords in *Buchler v Talbot, Re Leyland Daf Ltd (2004)* which allowed a floating charge holder to rank ahead of the costs of liquidation is likely to be reversed on the Companies Act 2006 coming into force.) The preferential creditors would be the company's employees for unpaid wages and salaries up to a maximum per employee of £800. Any amount in excess of £800, the employee would rank as an unsecured creditor. The Crown, however, loses its status as a preferential creditor in respect of any insolvency after 15 September 2003. HM Revenue and Customs therefore will rank as an unsecured creditor. After payment of the preferential creditors, the next in line would be the floating charge holders, namely, Business Bank plc and Trade Bank plc. As there is a competing claim (Unfairpack's entire undertaking includes the company's book debts), Business Bank plc and Trade Bank plc would rank on creation. In this case, as Business Bank plc's floating charge was created before that of Trade Bank plc, Business Bank plc would take priority. Any unsecured creditor, including creditors possessing an unsecured debt, such as Unfairpak's customers, would rank after the payment of floating charge holders. However, as Unfairpack Ltd has gone into liquidation after 15 September 2003, the liquidator has the power to set aside a portion of the asests that would otherwise be realised to meet the claims of the floating charge holders for distribution to the unsecured creditors (s 176A IA 1986). How much can be set aside depends on the value of the company's net property. Where the company's net property (after the payment of the costs of liquidation and the preferential creditors) does not exceed £10,000 in value, the amount to be set aside is 50%. Where the company's net property exceeds £10,000, the amount to be set aside is 50% of the first £10,000 and 20% of the remainder, with a ceiling of £600,000. Where the value of the company's net property is less than £10,000, the liquidator does not have to distribute the funds to the unsecured creditors if he considers that this would be disproportionate to the costs involved.

Deferred creditors, that is, shareholders with unpaid dividend claims, are paid after the claims of the secured and unsecured creditors have been met. In the event of a surplus, the members are entitled to a return of their capital in accordance with the provisions of the articles of association. Thereafter, any surplus is distributed to the members in accordance with the rights stated for example in the articles of association.

CHAPTER 8

ADMINISTERING THE COMPANY

▌INTRODUCTION

The administration of companies is a wide ranging topic, covering such issues as the conduct of meetings, voting rights and resolutions, the maintenance of statutory registers and the role of the company secretary. Administration is 'everyday' company law, going on all the time in the background. It is not one of the most spectacular company law areas, concerning dispute and dissension, and questions on it tend to crop up less frequently. Some aspects of administration have arisen in previous chapters—the qualifications and powers of a company secretary, for example, and some are inherent in most questions—the passing of resolutions nearly always arises. This chapter seeks to consider some basic areas of the administration of companies, ending with a brief outline of administration of a failing company.

It should be noted that you either know the material relating to administration or you do not; waffle is impossible. Even if you do know your stuff, it is impossible to display anything better than competence when answering questions on this area. However, some aspects of administration may also be seen as aspects of corporate governance, ensuring that the company operates properly.

Question 47

Henry and Wendy operate a niche market business which they have recently incorporated as Comp-u-Clean Ltd; they are the sole directors and own between them 51% of the shares. They do not anticipate becoming a public company or the issue of further shares in the near future. They have sought your advice on whether they need to undergo an annual audit and whether they can limit the amount of accounts and reports they need to produce. They would also like to dispense with company meetings and conduct any necessary business between shareholders in writing or informally.

Advise them.

Answer

Wendy (W) and Henry (H), as the promoters of Comp-u-Clean, are concerned about the accounting, reporting and decision making processes applicable to a company as opposed to the unincorporated business they have been operating. They have no doubt heard that the government is pledged further to reduce the administrative burden upon entrepreneurs and hope to benefit from any previous lifting of the burden. Are they to be disappointed?

(a) Reports and accounts

Section 221 of the Companies Act (CA) 1985 requires all companies to keep accounting records, and failure to comply is a criminal offence. The Companies Act 2006 extends the amount of information which must be collected. Since 1908, companies have been required to circulate the annual accounts of the company to members and members are now also entitled to receive a copy of the profit and loss account. The original basis underlying the requirements relating to reports and accounts was that those who have invested in the company should be kept informed of the state of the company and, thus, their investment. These rules on disclosure are immensely detailed but assume that, if the directors have to tell the shareholders certain things, this will, even if shareholder approval is not required, constrain the behaviour of the directors to avoid shareholder disapproval. As explained below, a small company may be able to avoid some of the more onerous reporting requirements. However, the reports and accounts which are required are also designed to provide information for interested third parties, for example employees and creditors, so that their provision can be justified even for a company where there are few shareholders and the directors control the company. Reports and accounts are presented not just to the shareholders but must also be available, via submission to the Registrar of Companies (s 242 CA 1985), to the wider public. Listed companies also have to disclose information in accordance with the Listing Rules, which also include provisions of the Combined Code, while quoted (and unquoted) companies are required to comply with the provisions of the Directors Remuneration Report Regulations 2002 (unless a small unquoted company). For financial years beginning on or after 1 April 2005, quoted companies must also produce an operating and financial review (OFR). Small and medium sized companies can deliver abbreviated accounts to the Registrar. There are strict time limits for the preparation of accounts and their delivery to the Registrar. Late submission renders the company and its directors liable to a fine (ss 242 and 242A CA 1985). Comp-u-Clean has 10 months from the end of the company's accounting reference period to file the accounts, etc.

Since the purpose of these accounts is to inform the shareholders of the state of financial health of the company and provide an account of the directors' stewardship in the previous year, these accounts must present a true and fair view of the company's financial position and must comply with Sched 4 to the Act (s 226 CA 1985). Section 241 CA 1985 requires the directors to lay the accounts before a general meeting of the company. However, a private company, as this is, can elect to dispense with the laying of accounts before a general meeting if such election is in compliance with s 252 CA 1985 (an elective resolution is required: see below). The election to dispense with the laying of accounts lasts indefinitely (it can be revoked by ordinary resolution), but an auditor or shareholder can require the company to hold a general meeting for the purpose of laying accounts (s 253 CA 1985). If no meeting is held, the members must be circulated with the relevant accounts. Whether or not a meeting is held, all reports, etc, must, within a specified time, also be sent to all debenture holders (s 238 CA 1985).

The CA 1985 requires four documents to be presented to the shareholders and the Registrar annually. These are the balance sheet, the profit and loss account, the directors' report and the auditor's report. Generally, the accounts presented to shareholders will need to comply with the CA 1985 and any applicable accounting standard (such as the Financial Reporting Standards issued by the Accounting Standards Board). Directors may also choose to issue other reports, for example a chairman's report, but are not required to do so. Comp-u-Clean must prepare a profit and loss account for each financial year and a balance sheet as at the last day of the year (s 226 CA 1985). The profit and loss account, which shows such things as the company's trading record, other income and expenditure, is a temperature chart of the company's financial health throughout the year. The balance sheet is a snapshot of the company's financial position on a particular date. Both documents must give a 'true and fair view' of the company's profit and loss for the year and the position at the end of the year (s 226 CA 1985). The Act specifies the content, format and valuation rules to apply to the balance sheet and profit and loss account (there are various formats prescribed—Comp-u-Clean is probably a 'small' company—see Sched 8 CA 1985). Compliance with relevant FRSs gives rise to a presumption that the accounts give a 'true and fair view', and deviation therefrom gives rise to a presumption that they do not. The Act also lists various disparate items which must be included as notes to the accounts.

Failure to comply with the statutory requirements relating to accounts has civil and criminal consequences. Section 245 CA 1985 allows, but does not require, the directors to issue revised accounts (or a directors' report) if the original accounts did not comply with the Act—the absence of compulsion is designed to encourage openness and compliance rather than relying on punishment, which may induce concealment.

The whole system is aimed at providing the best possible information to shareholders and others. However, the Secretary of State can require the directors to explain the deviation from the statutory provisions and he can instruct the directors to revise the accounts and, if the directors fail so to do, (or others authorised to act on his behalf) he can seek a court order instructing the directors to issue revised accounts.

In addition, it is a criminal offence for directors to approve annual accounts which they know do not comply with the Act or are reckless as to whether they comply or not (s 233 CA 1985). Failure to produce proper accounts is a matter which would be of concern to a court if the company went into insolvent liquidation and it was considering a disqualification order against H and W. The Court of Appeal has said that failings in this area are 'serious matters'; it has stressed that the privilege of limited liability carries with it responsibilities. Directors must be punctilious in observing the safeguards laid down by Parliament for the benefit of others who have dealings with their companies. They must prepare proper books of account and prepare annual accounts; they must file their returns and accounts promptly; and they must fully and frankly disclose information about deficiencies in accordance with the statutory provisions, although isolated lapses in filing documents may be excusable. However, persistent lapses which show overall a blatant disregard for this important aspect of accountability are serious and cannot be condoned, even if they do not involve any dishonest intent.

The minimum content of the directors' report is set out in the CA 1985 (ss 234, 234ZZA, 234ZZB), 234ZA and 234A and Sched 7). It must include such items, as information about the directors (for example, the size of their shareholding), and information about the company's business (a business review using key performance indicators), for example, the principal activities of the company, any significant changes from the previous year and any likely future developments. The directors' report must also include information about employment and any charitable or political donations (political donations are generally prohibited, unless approved by the company in genereal meeting (Pt XA CA 1985)). The directors' report, unlike the accounts, is not audited although relevant parts of the directors' remuneration report produced by quoted companies in accordance with the Directors Remuneration Report Regulations 2002 are required to be audited. The Listing Rules require directors of listed companies to include, in the Director's Report, a statement that the company is a going concern. This statement must be reviewed by the auditors.

There can be no question of H and W dispensing with the statutory accounting and reporting requirements, even though they are reporting to themselves. Some modification to the reporting and accounting requirements of companies are proposed by the Companies Act.

(b) Audit

Traditionally, all companies are required to appoint auditors (s 384 CA 1985) in accordance with s 385 CA 1985 (or s 385A CA 1985). However, the Companies Act (Audit Exemption) Regulations 1994 amended the CA 1985 to exempt small companies from the requirement to hold an annual audit. Comp-u-Clean will qualify as small if it is not part of a group, has a balance sheet total of less than £1.4 million and a turnover of not more than £90,000. If its turnover is between £90,000 and £350,000, it will be exempt if the directors send a special report to the shareholders (in compliance with s 249C CA 1985). An exempt company must hold an audit if a member or members holding at least 10% of any class of shares demands one (s 249B CA 1985).

If an audit is required, s 385 CA 1985 provides that the members appoint the auditor at each general meeting at which accounts are laid; if the company has elected not to hold such a meeting, the auditors must be appointed at another meeting of the company. However, since the company has up to 10 months before it need hold a meeting at which accounts are laid, the section also provides that the first directors, H and W, can appoint auditors who remain in office until the conclusion of the first relevant general meeting. To appoint auditors at every general meeting may be thought cumbersome, even if the same auditors are just nodded through, and the company may wish to use s 386 CA 1985 to dispense with annual appointment. Section 386 CA 1985 permits a private company to dispense with the annual appointment of an auditor and provides that the auditors, once appointed, continue in office until a resolution is passed to terminate the appointment (s 393 CA 1985) or the company becomes dormant (s 250 CA 1985). To take advantage of this section, the company must pass an elective resolution in accordance with s 379A CA 1985 (see below). The auditor must be a member of a recognised supervisory body (s 25 CA 1989) and be qualified under that body's rules for appointment as an auditor, be independent of the company (s 27 CA 1989) and hold appropriate qualifications (Sched 11 to the CA 1989). To remove an auditor requires an ordinary resolution (s 391 CA 1985) but special notice of any such resolution is required (s 391A CA 1985).

The function of the auditor is to report to the members on the financial statements made by the directors, particularly as to whether they comply with the CA 1985, and give a true and fair view of the state of the company's affairs and results for the period under consideration (s 235 CA 1985). In preparing his report, the auditor must satisfy himself that proper accounting records have been kept and that the annual accounts agree with the underlying accounting record. If the auditor is not satisfied that records, etc, are accurate, he must state this in his report.

In order to prepare his report, the auditor has a right of access at all times to the books and accounts of the company and can require the company, its subsidiaries and its directors to provide any information required for the performance of his duties. Any failure to provide information must be reported in the auditor's report and it is a criminal offence for an officer of the company to make, knowingly or recklessly, a false statement to an auditor. Where information is not provided, the auditor has a duty to try to remedy the omission. As part of the Directors Report, directors are required to state that there is no relevant audit information of which the company's auditors are unaware and that all steps have been taken or ought to have been taken to make themselves aware of any relevant audit information and to establish that the company's auditors are aware of that information (s 234ZA). Small and dormant companies are exempt from this requirement. H and W should be advised that, in addition to the statutory duties, the accountancy bodies have laid down a number of guidelines relating to the auditor's report (FRSs) which should be complied with unless the company can justify departure from them. Additional auditing requirements apply in respect of listed and quoted companies and the powers of auditors are strengthered by s 389A CA 1985 and the audit provisions of the Companies (Audit, Investigations and Community Enterprise) Act 2004.

H and W will seek to avoid the ongoing costs of the audit if possible.

(c) Meetings and resolutions

We have seen that a private company can dispense with the need to hold a meeting for the laying of accounts and can appoint auditors instead. H and W would be well advised to adopt s 379A CA 1985, which would permit other deviations from the usual requirements to have formal resolutions. An elective resolution can be used to confer authority to allot shares on the directors (for an indefinite period in a private company) and to dispense with the holding of an AGM. An elective resolution, which is part of an attempt by government to lighten the administrative load on smaller companies, must be approved by all the shareholders, in person or by proxy, at a meeting (21 days' notice of resolution is required). It can be revoked by ordinary resolution.

Where meetings are apparently required, the CA and Table A try to balance the need for proper democracy with the practicalities of running small companies, where to hold formal meetings of very few shareholders (who may be related) seems unrealistic. To avoid unnecessary meetings, s 381A CA 1985 allows much shareholder business to be conducted by written resolution, although such resolutions must be properly minuted (s 382A CA 1985). Written resolutions must be unanimous, that is, H and W will have to agree, but, while they remain on good terms, use of this procedure effectively dispenses with the need to hold meetings. The only resolution which cannot be made in written format is one to remove a director or auditor.

In October 1999, the Department of Trade and Industry, through the Company Law Review Steering Group, issued a consultation paper, *Modern Company Law for a Competitive Economy: General Meetings and Shareholder Communication*, advancing suggestions in respect of improving the efficiency and conduct of general meetings and the passing of resolutions. Some of the suggestions made their way into the Companies Act 2006, such as the right of private companies to dispense with the need to hold general meetings or to pass written resolutions without the need for unanimity. However, to date, provisions of the Act are not in force.

Question 48

In respect to the management of a company to what extent do you consider that the provisions of the Companies Act 2006 achieve the government aim that company law needs to be modern, flexible and accessible?

Answer plan

An answer requires setting out and analysing the major benefits to companies the Companies Act 2006 is expected to bring. The question does not demand a wholesale look at the Act but to consider those provisions that relate to company management. To that extent, the law relating to company meetings, the interests of shareholders and the position of directors needs to be considered, noting any differences between those provisions of the Act applying to public companies and those provisions applying to private companies. It is important to make the distinction between public and private companies as a main objective of the Act is ensuring, that company law as it applies to public companies does not by default apply to private companies, as is largely the case of current company legislation, such as Table A. It should be noted that, although the Companies Act 2006 has been passed, most of its provisions, including the ones referred to have, are not in force.

Answer

The Government's overall objective was to produce clearer law which responds to modern business needs without unnecessary burdens. To this extent, the White Paper 2005 identified four key objectives: (a) ensuring better regulation and a 'think small first' approach; (b) enhancing shareholder engagement and long term investment; (c) making it easier to form and run a company; and (d) providing flexibility for the future. In the light of these objectives, the Companies Act 2006

249

was seen as providing a number of 'key benefits' for all companies, but for private companies in particular. Overall, the Act proposes to make it easier for small, private companies to transact their business in respect of the procedure relating to meetings and to reform the law relating to meetings for all companies. This is designed as a means of enhancing shareholder protection, by offering companies and shareholders increased flexibility in respect of decision making. The Act also codifies the duties owed by directors to the companies they serve.

ADMINISTRATION AND DECISION MAKING

The law relating to meetings is complicated and contains a number of provisions of the Companies Act (CA) 1985 and Companies Act (CA) 1989 that are more applicable to public companies than private companies. For private companies, several key benefits were identified, as a basis of reform, reflecting the way small companies operate. First, a separate and simpler model articles for private companies would be set out. The White Paper (2005) contains a draft of model articles for a private company. Second, private companies will not be required to appoint a company secretary, unless they choose to do so. Third, private companies will not need to hold an annual general meeting, unless they opt otherwise and it will be easier for companies to take decisions by written resolutions. Private companies will no longer have to pass an elective resolution dispensing with the requirement to hold an annual general meeting. In future, written resolutions of private companies can be passed by a majority of all eligible votes, rather than the unanimous consent of all shareholders as currently is required. Fourth, private companies will no longer be prohibited from providing financial assistance for the purchase of their own shares and there will be simpler rules on share capital. This is designed to remove provisions that are largely irrelevant to the vast majority of private companies, but without compromising creditor protection.

Other changes include the abolition of extraordinary resolutions and elective resolutions and the default majority required to agree a shorter notice period at a private company to be reduced from 95% to 90%.

For shareholders of all companies, the Act is designed to enable members to benefit from (a) higher quality narrative reporting by quoted companies, (b) a statutory procedure for bringing a derivative claim on behalf of the company against a director for breach of duty, (c) enhancing the rights of persons who hold shares through nominee shareholders as well as enhanced proxy rights, (d) shareholders to receive more timely information through the availability of technology and (e) the notice period for any meeting to be 14 days unless the company's constitution states otherwise. In addition, for shareholders of public companies, the Act proposes to enhance shareholder protection on the ground of accountability by requiring public companies to hold their annual general meeting within six months of the financial year end, although a quoted company will be allowed a 15 day holding period after the annual accounts have been published. During this period, members will have the right to requisition a resolution for the meeting at which the accounts are to be laid. There will also be a new right for shareholders of quoted companies to have a resolution proposed for annual general meeting to be circulated at the company's expense if received by the company before the financial year end.

DIRECTORS

The statutory statement of directors' general duties is designed to make the law in this area more accessible and to bring the duties in line with modern business practice. Apart from the fair dealing provisions contained in Part X of the CA 1985 (relating to certain types of transactions between a company and a director, such as loans and 'substantial property transactions'), directors' duties are based on case law and not statute. Law reformers have suggested that better compliance by directors with these duties might be better served if the various case law duties were codified in statute. As part of the Department of Trade and Industry's review of company law, the Law Commissions (*Company Directors: Regulating Conflicts of Interests and Formulating a Statement of Duties*, 1999) and the Company Law Review Steering Group (Final Report, 2001) proposed that there should be a statutory statement of directors' duties and that directors, in promoting the company's success for the benefit of its membership as a whole, should take account of long term as well as short term consequences and to recognise the importance of relations with employees, suppliers, customers and the community. These recommendations were adopted by the White Paper (2005) and later became proposals for reform in the Companies Act. By codifying the duties, it is hoped that directors will become more aware of their responsibilities towards the companies they serve, which, in turn, will aid the interests of shareholders.

The general duties in the Act form a code of conduct, which sets out how directors are expected to behave. The duties are derived from equitable and common law rules. The codification is hoped to provide greater clarity on what is expected of directors and in whose interests companies should be run, as reflecting modern business needs. There are, however, two areas where the code departs from the current law, both based on the recommendations of the Company Law Review Steering Group (2001) and both relating to the regulation of conflicts of interest. First, there are certain transactions or arrangements with the company that do not have to be authorised by the members or the board. Second, board authorisation of most conflicts of interest arising from third party dealings by the director (for example, personal exploitation of corporate resources and opportunities) is allowed, so long as the interested director has not participated in the taking of the decision or if the decision would have been valid even without the participation of the interested director. Board authorisation of conflicts of interest will be the default position for private companies, but public companies will need to make provision in their constitution. Board authorisation, however, will not be permitted in respect of the acceptance of benefits from third parties. The reasoning behind the change of emphasis is that, in practice, most companies permitted a director to have an interest in a proposed transaction or arrangement with the company provided that the interest was disclosed to fellow directors and that the current strictness of the rule in respect of personal exploitation of corporate opportunities fettered entrepreneurial and business start up activity.

The statutory duties are based on, and have effect in place of, certain common law rules and equitable principles, but it is expected that the general duties will be interpreted and applied in the same way as the common law rules and equitable principles. As with the existing law, the general duties are owed by a director to the company and therefore only the company can enforce them. The Act sets out the mechanism for action to be taken to enforce the duties on behalf of the company, by members or derivative claim. The duties forming a code are set out as follows:

- duty to act within the powers of the companies constitution and to exercise the powers for the purposes for which they are conferred;
- duty to promote the success of the company for the benefit of its members;
- duty to exercise independent judgment;
- duty to exercise reasonable care, skill and diligence;
- duty to avoid conflicts of interest;
- duty not to accept benefits from third parties; and
- duty to declare interest in proposed transaction with the company.

COMMUNICATION

An important aspect of company management or administration is communication between a company and its members and the submission of company documentation to Companies House. Under the CA 1985 (Electronic Communications) Order 2000, it is possible for a company to communicate electronically with shareholders and Table A has been amended so as to give a company the option of notifying members via electronic means. The CA 1985 (Electronic Communications) Order 2000 also provides for the registration of a company by delivering some of the particulars of registration in electronic form and it is also possible for the administrative requirements of the CA 1985 to be complied with using electronic communication. The Companies Act 2006 enhances the provisions relating to electronic communication, by allowing, for instance, the electronic transmission of annual reports and the formation of a company by electronic means. Lower fees are paid where a company complies with the administrative requirements of the CA 1985 through the use of electronic communication.

CONCLUSION

The Government recognises that most registered companies are private companies and that most of these are run informally. The provisions of the CA 1985 and associated subordinate legislation, however, does not fit particularly well with the informal nature of the running of a private company. Table A of Tables A–F Regulations (1985) and its forerunner, Table A of Sched 1 CA 1948, were created for all companies to adopt (s 8 CA 1985—if on incorporation a company either fails to have registered articles or fails to disapply Table A, Table A becomes the company's articles by default) but are more appropriate to a public company. New articles will be made under the Act for different types of company and the White Paper (2005) contains a model form of articles for private companies to adopt. Similarly, changes to the law relating to meetings are proposed, reflecting the common way in which many private companies are run. If formality is required however, the Act provides for this. For example, when in force, it will no longer be a requirement for a private company to have a company secretary, although a private company can appoint a company secretary if it wishes to do so. Further, there will be no requirement for a private company to hold an annual general meeting, unless the company so chooses.

It is too early to say whether the proposals of the Act will achieve the desired objectives of the government, but certainly the language and spirit of the proposed legislation suggests that company law for the future will aid the running of companies as they operate within an increasingly competitive environment. In respect of private companies, at least, the Act recognises the informality in which the vast majority of private companies are run. Where changes need to be made to company law in the future, a new power is vested in the Secretary of State by the Act which will prevent the need for primary legislation to be required. The Secretary of State will have the power to pass a 'company law reform order' with the effect of reforming restating or codifying the law relating to companies as and when the situation demands.

NOTE

Some of the proposals for change, such as the nature and scope of the office of director (for example, in respect of eligibility) and the fair dealing provisions could be made here, as could the proposed changes to the rules on auditing, accounting and reporting and the company's constitution, to the extent that they relate to company management. Under the Act, the company memorandum will become a formal document recording the position at the point of registration, with the articles becoming the continuing constitutional document. On auditing, shareholders will be able to agree to limitations on the liability of auditors and, as part of a 'think small first' agenda, new legislation will set out a separate, comprehensive code of accounting and reporting requirements for small companies.

Question 49

Reading plc is a small unlisted public company with an issued share capital of £60,000, divided between Whiteknights and Bulmershe, who each hold 40% of the shares, and Earley, who holds the balance. Whiteknights and Bulmershe, who are also the directors of the company, would like to dispense with the holding of meetings but are uncertain how to achieve this aim and how, if achieved, resolutions could be passed. Earley rarely attends meetings or replies to letters and the directors would like to acquire his shares.

Advise them.

Answer plan

This is a question in which a specific administrative problem is addressed— once the right route is identified, re-registration as a private company. It is simply a straightforward question on how to re-register, dispensing with meetings and non-meeting resolutions. A broader question, acquisition of Earley's shares, also arises.

Answer

(a) Meetings

The management of companies is in the hands of the directors, particularly the executive directors, in this case Whiteknights (W) and Bulmershe (B), who conduct the day to day running of the company. However, certain matters, predominantly constitutional issues such as amendments to the memorandum and articles, can be implemented only with the agreement of the shareholders. The agreement of shareholders can be obtained by obtaining individual assents from *each* of them (*Re Duomatic Ltd (1969)*) but is more usually procured by passing a resolution at a company meeting. A resolution passed at a general meeting binds all shareholders, whether they attended or not and whether they voted for or against the resolution, and the company. A resolution, unlike a decision reached informally by all shareholders, will (subject to registration) bind third parties. A meeting of shareholders, a general meeting, also has a residual power to run the company when the directors are incapable of doing so and it can sack the directors (under s 303 of the Companies Act (CA) 1985. Decisions taken at meetings, that is, resolutions, may require a simple majority of those present and voting, or a simple majority of those voting in person or by proxy (an ordinary resolution), but a three-quarters majority of those voting (in person or in person and by proxy) is required to pass a special or extraordinary resolution. The underlying reason for requiring companies to hold meetings is that members can attend to debate, and perhaps be influenced by others, and vote.

Companies have two types of general meetings—annual general meetings (AGMs) and extraordinary general meetings (EGMs)—and, for both types, the CA 1985 requires adequate notice to be given. Reading plc must hold an AGM in each calendar year (s 366 CA 1985) and not more than 15 months should elapse between meetings. The AGM provides a means for members to receive reports and assessments on the company's performance. However, when a company has only three shareholders, it might be thought, as W and B do, that the holding of an AGM so that the directors (W and B) can report to themselves (and perhaps Earley (E)) is not very sensible and, in practice, many smaller companies fail to comply with the rules on meetings. In response to a proposal by the Institute of Directors, s 366A CA 1985 permits *private* companies to dispense with the holding of an AGM by the passing of an elective resolution. On the issue of general meetings, the Company Law Review Steering Group, in its consultation paper, *Modern Company Law for a Competitive Economy: General Meetings and Shareholder Communication* (DTI, 1999), suggested that private companies should be able to dispense with an AGM without the need for an elective resolution. The Steering Group also proposed amendments to the laying of business at an AGM in an attempt at improving the efficiency and conduct of general meetings. These are provisions in the Companies Act 2006 based on these recommendations.

An elective resolution, which is part of an attempt by government to lighten the administrative load on smaller companies, is a resolution which must be approved by all the shareholders, in person or by proxy, at a meeting (21 days' notice of resolution is required: s 399 CA 1985), and the resolution must be registered within 15 days (s 380 CA 1985). An elective resolution can be revoked by ordinary resolution. However, Reading plc, being a public company, cannot adopt this route. As for EGMs, the directors can call an EGM whenever they see fit (Art 37 of Table A) although the shareholders could remove this power by amending the articles (s 9 CA 1985: special resolution required). Further, s 368 CA 1985 permits the shareholders to require the directors to convene a meeting provided that the requisitionists hold at least one-tenth of the paid up share capital carrying voting rights and they have deposited at the company's registered office a signed requisition stating the objects of the meeting and the resolutions that will be proposed by them. If the directors fail to call an EGM, the requisitionists can call the meeting and recover their expenses. The Companies Act 2006 contains several provisions relating to the calling of meetings by shareholders. The court can, on the application of a director or member, call an EGM, and the directors of a public company must call an EGM if the company's net assets fall to below half of the amount of its called up share capital (s 142 CA 1985) to report that fact to the shareholders. The majority of matters which might be the subject of a resolution at an EGM could be dealt with by a written resolution if Reading plc was a private company. Consequently, it seems that the procedures within Reading plc would be somewhat simplified if the company re-registered as a private company, becoming Reading Ltd.

(b) Re-registration

A public company may re-register as a private company under the procedure laid down in ss 53–55 CA 1985. Reading plc must pass a special resolution (three-quarters majority of those present and voting), alter its name by deleting 'plc' and substituting 'Ltd' and amend its memorandum of association to omit any features which identify it as a public company. W and B can achieve this change without the support of E. The company must then apply to the Registrar for re-registration and, subject to any application by E, the Registrar issues a certificate of re-registration. E, if he did not vote in favour of the change, has the right to petition the court to cancel the re-registration, since he holds in excess of 5% of a class of share capital, provided that he applies within 28 days of the passing of the special resolution. Minority shareholders are given this right because the conversion of a company from public to private may result in diminished marketability of the shares, although this is unlikely in this case given the size of Reading and the fact that it is unlisted. Instead of striking down the re-registration, a court can postpone a hearing to allow the other shareholders in the company, or the company itself, to buy out the dissentient shareholder or holders. As indicated above, once Reading was a private company, it could, by elective resolution (E would have to agree) dispense with an AGM. However, the company cannot contract out of its power to hold an EGM and E holds sufficient shares to requisition a meeting, if he so desires.

(c) Written and informal resolutions

If the company had elected to dispense with an AGM, and neither the directors nor E called an EGM, how would the shareholders in Reading Ltd reach binding decisions? There are two possibilities. First, s 381A CA 1985 provides that anything which could be done by a resolution in general meeting, *except* dismissing a director (s 303 CA 1985) or the company's auditor (s 391 CA 1985), may be done by written resolution. A written resolution must be signed by all members who would have had a right to attend and vote on the matter in hand had a meeting been held. Assuming that all members do sign, a written resolution is effective from the date of the final signature and the signatures need not all be on the same document, that is, several copies of a resolution could be circulated among members. The Companies Act proposes to extend the use of written resolutions by allowing the same majority to operate as on a vote at a meeting. Section 381A CA 1985 permits the written resolution procedure to operate whatever the type of resolution required. Section 381B CA 1985 provides that a company's auditors can require a meeting to be held to discuss and vote on a resolution which concerns them as auditors. Thus, W and B could conduct the business of the company, insofar as shareholder approval was needed, by written resolution, provided that they felt confident that Earley would sign up. Second, if E refused to sign, an EGM could be called by W and B, who could out-vote E. Note that s 381A CA 1985 provides a method for passing resolutions by written agreement and it does not validate a decision agreed by all the members informally, that is, one which is not in compliance with written resolution requirements. However, s 381C CA 1985 states that the written resolution procedure does not affect the common law so, if the common law permits unanimous non-written decisions to bind the company, that remains the law and there are two parallel procedures for passing resolutions without formal meetings. Note that the common law is not limited to private companies.

In a series of cases, the courts have accepted that decisions unanimously approved by the shareholders who are entitled to attend or vote at a meeting, whether they all agreed at the same time or consecutively, bind the shareholders and the company (from *Re George Newman Ltd (1895)* to *Re Halt Garage Ltd (1982)*), even if made informally. Difficulties arise when the shareholders purport to give unanimous informal consent to a matter which the Companies Act provides must be agreed by a special or extraordinary resolution, particularly when the Act says that such a resolution is the only way to achieve a particular end. The general view is that, where the Act provides that a special, etc, resolution is required to do X, such a resolution may be regarded as *a* means of achieving a decision and that a unanimous informal agreement is an equally valid means—although an unregistered informal decision will probably not bind third parties. However, where the Act says that X may be done by special resolution, some writers argue that it can *only* be done by a proper resolution and not informally. Additionally, it is obvious that an informal agreement cannot overcome absolute prohibitions imposed on a company—the shareholders cannot, even unanimously, alter unalterable provisions of the memorandum. In *Re Bailey Hay & Co Ltd (1971)*, the judge even held that informal consent could be assumed from acquiescence, and in this case he treated the company as bound by an informal decision which had been positively approved by only two out of five shareholders (the majority had abstained), although it must be said that the three were happy to go along with the consequences of the decision for five years.

Thus, even if E remains a shareholder, there is scope for W and B to dispense with many company meetings and solicit shareholder approval in writing or informally.

(d) Acquiring E's shares

If W and B feel that E is likely to be too obstructive or absent, even if the company goes private, they may seek to acquire his shares either for themselves or with a view to selling them to some third party. They can approach E and offer to buy him out or, if the appropriate procedures are followed, propose that the company buy his shares. However, while W and B can propose the purchase, the decision whether to sell is for E—though, if the price is right, it would seem foolish to refuse. What W and B cannot do is confiscate or cancel E's shares, even if the articles permit such behaviour, unless it is *bona fide* for the benefit of the company and they are exercising the power for the benefit of the company. Nor could a confiscation clause be inserted, unless W and B, as shareholders, voted to insert the provision in the articles *bona fide* for the benefit of the company, which seems improbable. An attempt to expel E might trigger a petition by E under s 459 CA 1985, which might suit W and B very well (apart from the cost), since the normal remedy for disgruntled shareholders is an order for their shares to be bought by the majority or the company, thereby achieving W and B's aims!

Question 50

In examining the procedures for insolvent companies, discuss the changes introduced by the Enterprise Act 2002 as a means of facilitating a 'rescue culture' for failing companies.

Answer plan

You will need to explain how the main forms of corporate insolvency and the changes introduced to the Insolvency Act (IA) 1986 by the Enterprise Act (EA) 2002 have met the objectives of the Government in reforming the law on corporate insolvency. A consideration of the law relating to 'old' insolvencies and 'new' insolvencies will need to be made, as the regime relating to old insolvencies is likely to continue to have effect in respect of corporate insolvency for a number of years to come.

Answer

A stated objective of the Government was for the Enterprise Act (EA) 2002 to bring about changes that would promote a rescue culture for failed businesses. In a spirit of enterprise, the EA 2002 was designed to promote a reform of personal bankruptcy law and corporate insolvency law so as to enable a swift return to business of failed companies or business people where business failure was caused by commercial factors and not by irresponsible or reckless trading. The amendments to the Insolvency Act (IA) 1986 by the EA 202 on corporate insolvency took effect from 15 September 2003. With the exception of a company voluntary arrangement, the principal procedures dealing with insolvent companies are receivership, administration and liquidation.

RECEIVERSHIP

Where a company is in financial difficulty, it is the right of a secured creditor to appoint a receiver or administrative receiver to manage the company's assets that are the subject mater of the creditor's security. Receivership involves appointing a person to either sell or collect any income arising from the assets subject to the charge in order to satisfy the outstanding debt owed to the creditor. A receiver is a person appointed to manage the assets that are subject to a fixed charge while an administrative receiver acts as a manager of all or substantially all the assets that are subject to a floating charge.

Receivership is a procedure which is not implemented by the company but by a secured lender (or the courts) in accordance with the terms of the loan. While the procedure cannot be implemented by the company, it may be initiated by the company in conjunction with a creditor when the company recognises that it cannot continue to trade in its current format. This is not to say that the company can veto the appointment of a receiver, merely that a more orderly and timely process from the viewpoint of the troubled company may be achieved. Receivers may be appointed by a fixed charge holder or by a floating charge holder and in the latter case the receiver is called an administrative receiver and must be a licensed insolvency practitioner. The function of a receiver is to receive income or realise property to which the charge attaches to pay off the charge holder. Receivership does not preclude a creditors' or members' petition to wind up the company being presented. Where a liquidator is appointed, the receiver remains in office and continues to manage and realise the assets to which the charge attaches but is monitored by the liquidator on behalf of the company's creditors. After the receiver has satisfied his clients (the charge holder), the liquidator disposes of any surplus assets, in compliance with the order of priority for the payment of creditors. Where the charged asset is insufficient to meet the claims of the charge holder, the balance of the debt is unsecured. A receiver appointed by a fixed charge holder is concerned only with the asset to which the client's charge attaches and s/he has no general power to run the company. However, a receiver appointed by a floating charge holder has the enhanced powers of an administrative receiver. An administrative receiver has considerable powers designed to enable them to keep potentially successful companies afloat, perhaps by selling the enterprise to another company or by restructuring the company and jettisoning loss-making portions of the business. The enhanced powers of administrative receivers include some of the powers given to liquidators and administrators, but not the powers to re-open or set aside preferences and certain floating charges or to initiate proceedings for fraudulent or wrongful trading. An administrative receiver becomes the agent of the company unless and until the company goes into liquidation. It must be stressed that a receiver's principal duty is to his client and he is not obliged to consider, other than as a secondary matter, the interests of other creditors.

Receivership does not inevitably lead to liquidation but it is obviously not a very promising sign and the EA 2002 provides several changes to administrative receivership in order to lessen the likelihood of companies going into receivership. With effect from 15 September 2003, the changes introduced by the EA 2002 diminish the right of floating charge holders, typically banks and other lending institutions, to appoint an administrative receiver. This is designed to 'encourage' administration in order to give the company a better chance of recovery than receivership which often leads to the company proceeding into liquidation. Further, under the changes introduced by the EA 2002, it will be possible (under the IA 1986) for an administrator to be appointed out of court, by the company's floating charge holders (who will no longer be able to appoint an administrative receiver), the company or the directors of the company, subject to certain conditions being met. There are some exceptions to these provisions and the provisions do not apply to a floating charge holder whose charge was created before 15 September 2003.

ADMINISTRATION

Prior to the IA 1985, a company becoming insolvent was likely to be wound up. There was no formal system in the UK for rescuing a company in financial difficulty and little protection afforded to unsecured creditors. Administration, as a type of insolvency procedure, was introduced. Administration is a relatively recent innovation, designed to permit restructuring of a debt-ridden business—it is comparable with Chapter XI of the American Federal Bankruptcy Code. Administration was introduced to provide a company with 'breathing space' to enable it to continue as a going concern or at least to result in a better realisation of the company's assets than a forced sale on liquidation. Administration may be preferable for the company and creditors than liquidation—it is likely to be cheaper, it may allow the sale of a going concern better than a 'fire-sale' on liquidation, it allows a company currently trading profitably but burdened by debt from past enterprises to trade on with some form of debt moratorium or restructuring operating, and directors, etc, owed money by the company may have better prospects of payment than in a liquidation. An administration order, which can be sought by the company, a company's directors or a creditor, is a court order to the effect that, for the duration of the order, the company's affairs are to be managed by an administrator who must be a licensed insolvency practitioner. An administrator becomes, in effect, the board and runs the company on behalf of everyone (unlike the administrative receiver, who acts for the charge holder).

Administration, however, is not necessarily a cheap or simple alternative to receivership or liquidation and, as part of the Government's stated intention of rescuing failing businesses, the EA 2002 has simplified the process of administration. The EA 2002 has introduced an out of court mode of appointment of administrator, enabling the appointment of an administration by the holder of a qualifying floating charge, a company in difficulty or the directors of the company (Sch BI 1986). Further, with a few limited exceptions, so as to encourage administration as opposed to receivership, after 15 September 2003, a floating charge holder can no longer appoint a receiver in respect of any floating charge created after this date. Administration therefore is considered by the Government to be the preferred option for ailing companies.

The administrator must perform his/her functions in the interests of the company's creditors as a whole and, following the introduction of amended objectives by the EA 2002, in accordance with three objects in descending order of importance, as follows:

(a) To rescue the company as a going concern (the primary purpose);

(b) To achieve a better result for the company's creditors than would be achieved if the company was wound up; and

(c) To realise property to make a distribution to one or more secured or preferential creditors.

An out of court administrator can be appointed by a qualifying floating charge holder. This is a floating charge holder whose charge or charges relate to the whole or substantially the whole of the company's property. A company or the directors of a company can appoint an administrator, but not where an administrative receiver has been appointed, a petition for winding up has been presented or where a qualifying floating charge holder appoints the administrator.

Where a company is in administration, any petition to wind the company up will either be dismissed or suspended until the period of administration is over. An administrative receiver who has already been appointed is dismissed and no steps can be taken to enforce any security without the consent of the administrator or the permission of the court. An administration order cannot be made, and neither can an administrator be appointed where the company is in liquidation or is already in administration, although in respect of a liquidation, the court can discharge a winding up order where an administration order is made on the application of a floating charge holder or the liquidator. In respect of the out of court procedure, an administrator cannot be appointed where an administrative receiver is in office nor, in the case of an appointment by a company or its directors, where there are any outstanding winding up petitions or applications for administration in respect of the company.

The administrator may do anything necessary or expedient for the management of the affairs, business and property of the company, including removing or appointing directors. The administrator takes control of all the property to which s/he thinks the company is entitled and s/he may pay creditors. S/he can sell property which is subject to a floating charge, but the charge holder gets the same priority in respect of any property acquired, and by court order, s/he can sell property that is subject to a fixed charge.

An important feature of administration is that it applies a moratorium. This means that creditors are prevented from bringing claims against the company during the course of the administration. In the past, the moratorium, however, applied only from the date of the administration order coming into effect. In order to provide further protection to the company from creditor claims, the EA 2002 provides for an interim moratorium which comes into force on the date of either the application to the court or the date of the presentation of the notice to appoint an administrator. During the period of the interim moratorium, however, it is possible for a winding up petition to be presented to the court and a floating charge holder with a charge created before 15 September 2003 can appoint an administrative receiver. It is likely that receivership will continue to exist as a common form of insolvency since many floating charges were created before the changes introduced by the EA 2002 took effect.

PREFERENTIAL AND UNSECURED CREDITORS

The IA 1986 gives preferential status to certain unsecured creditors who rank in priority to all creditors except fixed charge holders and the costs of liquidation. Preferential creditors rank equally. In the past, creditors with preferential debts included the Inland Revenue, Customs and Excise and company employees for unpaid wages up to £800, including any outstanding and accrued holiday entitlement. In respect of any insolvency after 15 September 2003, the Crown loses its preference. Given that leading petitioners for a winding up were the Inland Revenue and Customs and Excise, it is considered that this change of status for the debts of HM Revenue and Customs will reduce the number of winding up petitions being sought against insolvent companies.

Under the Employment Rights Act (ERA) 1996, where, on application by the employee, the Secretary of State pays certain amounts due to the employee, the Secretory of State is subrogated to the employee's position in the employer's insolvency, including the employee's preferential rights. However, the Secretary of

State's right under the ERA 1996 to be paid before employees of the insolvent employer will be lost under Sched B1 IA 1986.

Under s 176A IA 1986, the Secretary of State can, by order, prescribe a part of the property which would otherwise be payable to floating charge holders to be reserved for unsecured creditors. The amount to be set aside depends on the value of the company's net property. Where the company's net property (after the payment of the costs of liquidation and the preferential creditors) does not exceed £10,000 in value, the amount to be set aside is 50%. Where the company's net property exceeds £10,000, the amount to be set aside is 50% of the first £10,000 and 20% of the remainder, with a ceiling of £600,000. Where the value of the company's net property is less than £10,000, the liquidator does not have to distribute the funds to the unsecured creditors if s/he considers that this would be disproportionate to the costs involved.

CONCLUSION

As the law relating to old insolvencies will continue to exist for sometime to come, it is perhaps too early to say how effective the changes introduced by the EA 2002 will be on enabling failing companies to be rescued from oblivion. However, reducing the costs of administration by reducing court involvement is a conclusion that can be drawn from two early cases on corporate restructuring under the new Sched B1 IA 1986. The decisions of *Re Transbus International Ltd (2004)* and *Re Ballast plc (2004)* suggest that administrators are being encouraged by the courts to execute administration in a cost effective and efficient way.

INDEX

Routledge•Cavendish Questions & Answers Series

Company Law
2007–2008

Routledge-Cavendish Q&A series

Each Routledge-Cavendish Q&A contains 50 questions on topics commonly found on exam papers, with comprehensive suggested answers. The titles are written by lecturers who are also examiners, so the student gains an important insight into exactly what examiners are looking for in an answer. This makes them excellent revision and practice guides. With over 500,000 copies of the Routledge-Cavendish Q&As sold to date, accept no substitute.

New editions publishing in 2007:

CIVIL LIBERTIES & HUMAN RIGHTS 4/E

COMMERCIAL LAW 4/E

COMPANY LAW 5/E

CONSTITUTIONAL & ADMINISTRATIVE LAW 5/E

CONTRACT LAW 7/E

CRIMINAL LAW 6/E

EMPLOYMENT LAW 5/E

ENGLISH LEGAL SYSTEM 7/E

EQUITY & TRUSTS 5/E

EUROPEAN UNION LAW 6/E

EVIDENCE 7/E

FAMILY LAW 4/E

INTELLECTUAL PROPERTY LAW

JURISPRUDENCE 4/E

LAND LAW 5/E

TORTS 7/E

For a full listing, visit www.routledgecavendish.com/revisionaids.asp